Last Diaries

LEO TOLSTOY

Last Diaries

Translated by Lydia Weston-Kesich

Edited and with an Introduction by

LEON STILMAN

COLUMBIA UNIVERSITY

CAPRICORN BOOKS

G. P. Putnam's Sons   New York

With this book the translator pays tribute to
Vassar College on the occasion of its centennial.

Library of Congress Catalog
Card Number: 60-6121

MANUFACTURED IN THE UNITED STATES OF AMERICA

Note

Tolstoy's diaries and notebooks were first published in full in the Complete Edition of his works undertaken in the Soviet Union in 1925 and which is now nearly complete with close to one hundred volumes. The diaries for the year 1910 are published in volume 58 of the edition which has been used for this translation.

In 1910, in addition to the diary of the kind he had kept during most of his life, Tolstoy kept another diary, which he began toward the end of July; it opens with the words: "I am beginning a new diary, a real diary for myself alone." In this translation, the entries in the two diaries under the same date are given consecutively; those from the "Diary for Myself Alone" are set in italics. People often mentioned in the Diaries are identified in a "List of Characters"; others in footnotes.

Introduction
by Leon Stilman

Tolstoy continued the daily routine of answering his mail and keeping his diary up to the very last days of his life. On November 3,* 1910, ill with pneumonia in the little house of the station-master of the village of Astapovo, he began dictating in English to his friend Chertkov his reply to a letter from Aylmer Maude, Tolstoy's English translator and biographer. Chertkov took down: "On my way to the place where I wished to be alone I was . . ." Chertkov supplied "taken ill," hoping that the dictation would be resumed, but Tolstoy was overcome by weakness and the letter remained unfinished. November 3 was also the date of the last entry made by Tolstoy in his diary, a few barely legible lines noting the arrival of his elder son and daughter and of some of his close friends; then followed the last lines written in Tolstoy's hand: "And this is my plan. *Fais ce que dois adv.* . . . And all is for the good of others and chiefly my own . . ." The French phrase, *Fais ce que dois, advienne que pourra,* here left incomplete, occurs earlier in Tolstoy's diaries. "Do as you must, happen what may." This disregard for consequences,

---

* All the dates are given in the "old style," used in Russia before the Revolution, thirteen days behind the calendar used in the West.

this *"advienne que pourra,"* was essential for Tolstoy the moralist and the logician; since moral values are absolute, they may not be measured in terms of "consequences," that is, in terms of the relative categories of time and causality. So one must do what is right, and happen what may. Was this the "plan" mentioned in the entry under the date of November 3? If it was, there was very little time left to carry it out, three more days, with only brief, intermittent moments of consciousness. Death came in the early morning of November 7.

In the years 1904 and 1905, Tolstoy compiled a volume of readings for every day; it was made up of bits of wisdom gleaned from the writings of authors of all ages and many nations, including Tolstoy himself, short quotations, maxims, parables, short stories with a moral lesson. Tolstoy had a copy of this volume, *The Cycle of Reading,* with him at Astapovo, and, as one of his friends reports in his reminiscences, Tolstoy drew his attention to the texts for October 28. These texts, selected from the writings of Marcus Aurelius, Thomas à Kempis, Pascal, Kant and other thinkers, dealt with the inevitability and the value of physical pain and moral suffering. October 28 was the day when Tolstoy left his home and his family. The theme for November 7, uncannily appropriate, was death. Tolstoy himself supplied the last of the texts selected for November 7: "We may only conjecture about what will be after death; the future is hidden from us. And not only is it hidden, but it does not exist, since *future* means time, and when we die we remove ourselves from time."

Tolstoy, as he wrote in his last, unfinished letter, was, at the Astapovo station, on his way to the place where he wished to be alone. But where was that place? And if a man can escape the company of others, there is still his own consciousness, the company of his own self. This only death can remove, together with the irksome limitations of time, space and causality.

Tolstoy had more than once considered leaving his family and his home at Iasnaia Poliana before his escape in the night of October 28. He had also been repeatedly urged to do so by others, by some of the zealots of the new faith. Thus, in February, 1910, a letter from a student of the university of Kiev, Boris Mandjos by name, exhorted Tolstoy to offer himself in sacrifice: " . . . Give your life to man and to humanity . . . ," the letter said; "Perform the last act which remains to you in this world and will make you immortal in the minds of humanity. . . . distribute your possessions to your relatives and to the poor and, penniless, begging alms, go from town to town . . ." Tolstoy dutifully answered his young correspondent, and told him that his letter had moved him deeply; his advice, Tolstoy explained, coincided with his own most fervent desire; however, he continued, he must take this step not to impress others, but in response to an inner spiritual urge, at that time when it would become morally impossible for him to continue his present life of shameful luxury amid the surrounding poverty, a situation which is for him a source of ever-increasing torment.

The young enthusiast had to wait eight months for the "last act." His letter, demanding that the eighty-two-year-old Tolstoy take to the road and beg alms is a remarkable instance of the disciple urging the Teacher to perform the purifying sacrifice and to become the hero of a new myth, to die a death befitting a founder of a new religion, to satisfy humanity's craving for a new Socrates, or Christ, or Buddha. And indeed, in the circumstances of Tolstoy's death there was much that fitted the archetype. But the twentieth century, even the early twentieth century, was, perhaps, too late a time for the birth of a myth. The atmosphere was lacking; there were, at Astapovo, too many reporters, cameramen, telegrams; there were the special trains bringing people by the carload, there were the medical bulletins, and the newspaper headlines. These were the early years of mass-communication, but by 1910 it was effective enough.

There is in Tolstoy's diary, under the date of May 11, 1910, this diatribe, in the form of rhetorical questions, one

9

of many diatribes against modern civilization with its faith in technological progress, which provides the "means" but fails to provide "ends":

Machines to make what? Telegraphs, telephones, to transmit what? Schools, universities, academies, to teach what? Books, newspapers, to spread information about what? Railroads, for whom to travel, and where to?

In November, 1910, the telegraph, the telephone and the newspapers were busy spreading news about Tolstoy's escape from Iasnaia Poliana, about his last illness, then about his death and his burial on the grounds of Iasnaia Poliana where his body was brought from Astapovo.

Tolstoy's fame was universal, his prestige was immense, and it is no wonder that the dramatic circumstances of his death drew world-wide attention.

Leo Tolstoy, the author of *War and Peace* and *Anna Karenina,* was undoubtedly one of the greatest masters of the art of the novel not only in Russian literature, but in world literature as well. He completed both these masterpieces before he reached the age of fifty, *War and Peace* in 1869 and *Anna Karenina* in 1877. Tolstoy did not cease to be a creative writer during the remaining thirty-three years of his life, but if in some of the shorter works of the later period he equaled the artistic quality of his two great novels, his third full-length novel, *Resurrection,* finished in 1899, was most certainly inferior to the earlier two.

The last stages of Tolstoy's work on *Anna Karenina* coincided with a moral crisis of great intensity. It would be an exaggeration to describe this crisis as the death of Tolstoy the artist and his rebirth in the guise of a moral teacher. Tolstoy never ceased to be an artist, nor were religious and moral concerns alien to him before the crisis of the late 'seventies. But his anguish over the human condition, over the meaning—or the lack of meaning—of life had never before reached such overwhelming

10

intensity. In his *Confession* (1879-81), Tolstoy tells of how the question of the purpose of life thrust itself upon him more and more often, more and more urgently, until, to use his image, the tiny flickering dots merged into one ever-present black spot, until the obsessive "question" became paralyzing and brought his life to a halt. If his life were to continue, he would somehow have to answer the challenge of this very simple thought: that since death is inevitable, nothing in life can have a purpose or a meaning. He had been, Tolstoy thought, blinded and deceived by the joys of life; but now he was no longer deceived or blinded and saw, with clarity and with horror, the "gaping mouth of the Dragon," the only truth and the only reality. His anguish was not so much a fear of death, as a feeling that the inevitability of death cancelled out all meaning and purpose, leaving a horrible vacuum in which it was impossible to live. Paradoxically and irresistibly, this obsessive presence of death was driving him to self-destruction.

There is an unfinished story of Tolstoy's "The Notes of a Madman," written in 1883 and known to be based on a real experience that the author had many years earlier. The narrator (the story is written in the form of a diary), who is on a business trip, finds himself one night in a small hotel room. Alone in this room, which is clean, whitewashed, and square ("how unbearable, I remember, it was, precisely, that the little room was square"), with a bit of red curtain over the window, the traveller is suddenly overcome with anxiety: he is running away from something, but from what? Why this anguish (which is "like the anguish before nausea, only spiritual"), what is he afraid of? Death reveals itself at this point, in the horror of its inevitability, as the cause of this nauseating anxiety:

> "I tried to shake off this horror. I found a brass candlestick with a candle, half burned down, which I lit. The red flame of the candle and its size, a little smaller than the candlestick, all this said the same

11

thing. There is nothing in life; only death *is,* and it must not be. . . . It's dreadful. It seems that you fear death, but then you begin to remember, you think of life, and then it is this dying life that you fear. Somehow life and death merged into one. . . . Once more. . . . I tried to fall asleep; but it's there, the same horror, red, white, square. . . . It is tormenting, drily, angrily tormenting; not a drop of kindness do I feel in myself, but only even, calm anger against myself and against that which has made me."

This crisis is followed by others, but finally the narrator is delivered from his anguish and despair by a revelation, that of human brotherhood as set forth in the Gospels; and more specifically, of brotherhood understood as social justice. After this revelation, Tolstoy's character renounces the purchase of a highly profitable estate, because his profits would be gained at the cost of the poverty and the misery of others, the peasants, our brothers in Christ. This he tells his wife. "My wife was angry and abused me," he notes in his diary. "But I felt joy. That was the beginning of my madness. But complete madness came later, a month later." One day the "madman," who has attended a church service, sees an even brighter light, with the following consequences: "There, in front of the church, I distributed all I had, thirty-five rubles, to the beggars and went home on foot, talking to the people . . ."

This somewhat unexpected "happy ending," very probably an addition of Tolstoy the moralist to the actual experience powerfully recalled by Tolstoy the artist, is, however, a condensed account of Tolstoy's own journey from the despair of his years of crisis to the faith of his later years. He told this story in much more detail, with more logic and eloquence in several of his non-fictional works. In essence, after his shattering experience of man's loneliness in the face of death, of the loneliness of the reasoning and helpless ego, Tolstoy turned to religious faith. But in doing so he continued to reason; he reasoned

12

that life is finite, limited and constricted by time, space and causality, but that the answer to the question "what for" must needs lie in the infinite; that the problem, therefore, was that of bridging the gap between the finite and infinity; and he finally reasoned that reason could not bridge this gap and that only faith could accomplish this and actually did accomplish it, for millions upon millions of people, of plain people, of working people and peasants, do live without being scared away from life by the sight of the dragon's gaping mouth, and if they do live, it is because they have faith. So Tolstoy first turned to the Christian religion as taught and practiced in Russia by the Orthodox Church. But the convert pursued his analysis, and soon found himself faced with contradictions between the demands of his implacable logic and the dogma of the Church. The full power of Tolstoy's questioning logic was aggressively put to use in his treatise entitled *An Examination of Dogmatic Theology*. After this examination, and repudiation, of dogma and ritual, Tolstoy proceeded to formulate a religion of his own based on a rational, if at times perhaps somewhat arbitrary, interpretation of the Gospel of Christ, in which he gave the most prominent place to the Sermon on the Mount and especially to the verse expressing, according to him, the very core of the teaching of Christ, the key to all truth: "Ye have heard that it has been said, an eye for an eye, a tooth for a tooth: But I say unto you, that ye resist not evil." This principle of non-resistance to evil became the cornerstone of Tolstoy's faith and of his teaching.

Tolstoy's literal acceptance of the simple but infinitely demanding words of the Sermon on the Mount, the discovery of Christian love and of God within oneself, this was Tolstoy's answer to the tormenting questions of his spiritual crisis. He had exorcised the dragon with the Sermon on the Mount.

Tolstoy insisted on the intensity of his spiritual crisis of the late 1870's and on the decisive changes that it brought about in his spiritual life. It is noteworthy however that many of those themes which came to the fore so dramatically in the years of crisis were already present in his fiction written long before. To mention his major works only, the search for meaning and purpose in life is very prominent in the two central characters of *War and Peace*. Prince Andrei discovers on his deathbed that love is life, that love is God, and that death means the return of one's "self", a particle of love, to the universal and eternal source. This discovery is made once more, in similar circumstances, in *The Death of Ivan Ilyich* (completed in 1886), a later and more didactic work in which the futility of man's pursuits is made very deliberately obvious. To return to *War and Peace*, Pierre Bezukhov, in his quest for truth and purpose, moves through different stages, meeting at one point the symbolic and, perhaps, a little synthetic, Russian peasant Platon Karataiev with his unconscious and impersonal wisdom, and his instinctive and resigned optimism; later salvation appears to Pierre in a vision of his ego merging into one all-embracing whole, a union with all men, and with God. But in the end Pierre's search leads him to something that is, perhaps, both more and less than a mystical experience or a new Weltanschauung; it is family happiness, conjugal love and procreation; the soiled diaper is the standard raised in the epilogue of *War and Peace*.

In *Anna Karenina*, the tragedy of Anna's and Vronski's adulterous love is in contrasted balance with the story of Konstantin Liovin and Kitty, a story in which once more the themes of family happiness and childbirth sound triumphantly. Liovin comes the closest of all Tolstoy's characters to self-portrayal and autobiography, and he goes through a severe spiritual crisis closely reminiscent of the one experienced by Tolstoy himself. There are actually several textual coincidences between Tolstoy's *Confession* and the thoughts attributed by him to Liovin. Liovin, it is true, as he frees himself from the grip of those very questions that tormented Tolstoy, is willing to accept established religion; he does not go through the next stage, that of the *Examination of Dogmatic Theology*. At the very end of the second of Tolstoy's two great novels, in an affirmation of love as the principle and the justification of life, there appears the image of the mother and the infant, just as it had appeared earlier, in the epilogue of *War and Peace*:

> Kitty, her sleeves rolled up, stood beside the bathtub, leaning over the baby that was wiggling in it, and, as she heard her husband's footsteps, she turned her head to him calling him with her smile. With one hand under its head, she was supporting the chubby baby, afloat on its back, kicking its little legs, while with her other hand, contracting its muscles at regular intervals, she squeezed the sponge over it. "Look here, look, look!" she said when her husband approached her, "Agafia Mikhailovna [the nanny] is right. He knows us."

There is much autobiographical material in these blissful scenes, as there is generally in Tolstoy's work. The image of a young mother hugging her child in her arms is already present, however, in the concluding scene of *Family Happiness,* Tolstoy's short novel written in 1859, three years before his marriage and, as it were, in anticipation of his own experiences in happy family life.

Tolstoy's *Confession,* an account of spiritual torment and of salvation found in his new faith, was also a confession in the more literal and traditional sense, for in it he accuses himself of many grievous crimes and mortal sins. Tolstoy's feelings of guilt were most certainly genuine; but his self-accusations, manifestly exaggerated and perhaps a little rhetorical, were also accusations directed against the immorality of his fellow-men. All the abject and criminal acts he had committed, driven as he was by pride, ambition and lust: gambling, and fornication, and even murder (he took part in a war), all this, Tolstoy insisted was not condemned by society, quite the contrary; he received society's approval, even its praise. Tolstoy's self-denunciation was quite clearly also an attack against the moral standards of a society which, among other things, tolerated adultery and prostitution, approved dueling and glorified war. Tolstoy's exaggerated self-accusations were thus a prelude to the penitent's crusade for society's moral reform.

Tolstoy made another confession, before his literary one. Soon after his marriage, in 1862 to Sofia Andreevna Bers, who was eighteen, sixteen years his junior, he insisted on her reading his diary in which were recorded certain episodes of his bachelor's life including liaisons, visits to brothels, and an *affaire*, shortly before his marriage, with a peasant woman from Iasnaia Poliana, Aksinia by name. Young Sofia Andreevna could not be expected to share the cynically tolerant views of "society," and her husband's excessive and rather brutal honesty injured her painfully and deeply. Aksinia, the robust and primitive female, appears years later in one of Tolstoy's stories, "The Devil" (1889-90), in which the unconquerable animal passion she inspires to her former lover, now married to a young woman of his own social class, leads him to suicide (or, in a variant ending, to murder). The story was not published in Tolstoy's lifetime. Sofia Andreevna, however, not only read it, but copied it, as she did so many of her husband's manuscripts.

Konstantin Liovin in *Anna Karenina* struggles, just as Tolstoy did, with the question of the meaning of life, and emerges from his crisis with his new faith; this faith, and the radiant image of young motherhood shine over the last pages of the novel. Ten years later, in *The Kreutzer Sonata* (1889), sexual love, marriage, and childbirth become images of horror. To be sure, *The Kreutzer Sonata* is a work of fiction; but in the non-fictional writings of his later years Tolstoy also preached the ideal of chastity, even in the relations between husband and wife. Tolstoy's preaching hardly created any immediate danger of the human race becoming extinct; but in theory Tolstoy readily accepted this consequence.

Thus Tolstoy's personal religion of an increasingly impersonal love lead him finally to the conclusion that since procreation meant sin, there ought not to be procreation, and that humanity may as well perish; and since it will perish some day anyway, it had better do so morally and reasonably. At this point Tolstoy had reached the end of the path upon which he entered years earlier, when he emerged from his crisis with a new awareness of the limitations of reason and the newly acquired knowledge that salvation was in a communion with men, in sharing the simple faith of simple humanity.

Tolstoy's condemnation of sexual love in his late years (an outgrowth, it seems, of his early feelings of guilt about sex) was a condemnation of life itself which he had glorified in his creative writings with the unique powers of his genius. His earlier critical examinations and attacks were directed against accepted beliefs, dogmas and institutions in the name of the essential and the organic, and therefore, according to Tolstoy, the real and the true in man's condition. Now Tolstoy was condemning not the inventions of civilization that impoverish and falsify human life, but the principle of life itself.

But in spite of this, Tolstoy was never indifferent to immediately present injustice and suffering. His intense feeling of sympathy, especially for the lower classes, never weakened. Till the very end he continued to denounce, with daring, vigor and eloquence, the injustice and corruption of Russia's social and political order. He did not approve, however, of the revolutionaries and of their belief that the use of violence was legitimate in the struggle against political tyranny and social exploitation. No "ends," in Tolstoy's thinking, could justify the use of violence. Violence, he believed, would generate more violence; violence was evil no matter by whom or against whom it was used, and evil could beget only more evil. The chain reaction of evil and violence could be arrested only by the opposite chain reaction of love.

It was in the name of these beliefs that Tolstoy sounded

17

his eloquent protests against the death penalty, or called for refusal of military service which he abominated as an act of violence by which thousands of hungry and illiterate peasants were made potential participants in mass murder for purposes alien and unintelligible to them. Most of Tolstoy's propagandistic writings were published illegally, or printed abroad and illegally circulated in Russia. Many of his disciples were persecuted for spreading his teaching. Tolstoy himself, however, was protected by a unique immunity. The enormous moral prestige he enjoyed throughout the world forced the Russian government to refrain from prosecuting him. The spiritual authorities, however, did take action against Tolstoy: early in 1901, an edict of the Holy Synod excommunicated the "false teacher" from the Orthodox Church.

The excommunication, it must be said, was well earned by Tolstoy who in his *Examination of Dogmatic Theology,* and in other writings, had used the powers of his logic and of his eloquence not only to show the discrepancies between dogmatic theology and the teaching of the Gospel, but also to prove that official dogma was a deliberate distortion of Christ's teaching for the purpose of exploiting the people's ignorance and credulity in the interests of the church hierarchy.

If other institutions than the Church could use against heretics the weapon of excommunication, Tolstoy would have been anathematized by most of them. He had spared no accepted belief or established authority, no convention or institution, no power and no dogma. He exposed medicine and Shakespeare, the courts of law and historiographers, the journalists, the symbolist poets and, above all, all those who exercise power over man. Tolstoy's attitude in his critique of conventions and institutions was often reminiscent of the "savage" of the eighteenth-century philosophers, endowed with reason and a moral sense, but neither able nor willing to understand conventions and therefore seeing things "as they are," or at least as they appear to him in the light of his own logic and

18

moral sense. Tolstoy's criticism was often valid, eloquent and convincing, at times even prophetic. And if he spared little, there is perhaps not very much to spare in our civilization if it is to be judged from the vantage point of Voltaire's Huron, and even less if it is judged by the standards of the Sermon on the Mount.

The year 1910, the last year of his life, finds Tolstoy living in the Iasnaia Poliana estate, where he had been born eighty-two years earlier, surrounded by family and friends, enjoying an immense, world-wide prestige, leading, despite his age and his failing health, a very active life, and caught in a tragic and destructive conflict.

At a serious risk of oversimplification, it might be said that this conflict grew out of Tolstoy's efforts to practice what he preached. These efforts were sometimes carried out regardless of consequences, which were often injurious; and sometimes they stopped halfway, resulting in unsatisfactory compromises. Tolstoy's last years were dominated by the conviction that to own property is sinful and that in deriving profit from property, one shares responsibility in a cruelly unjust social system. This condemnation was directed not only against the land owned by the family, but against profit derived from literary property as well. His older writings, Tolstoy believed, were futile and useless, or even harmful; the more recent ones, dedicated to moral purposes, could obviously not be used as a source of profit.

The autobiographical hero of Tolstoy's "The Notes of a Madman," who ironically calls "madness" his newly acquired convictions, mentions his wife's violent disapproval of his views and plans.

Tolstoy's own conflict with his wife, the domestic tragedy of his last years with its often pathetic and often sordid episodes, has been described by many eyewitnesses; there were many inmates of and visitors to Iasnaia Poliana who concerned themselves with leaving to posterity detailed records of all they saw and heard. The facts recorded in these accounts as well as in the diaries of the two main protagonists have been discussed in many biographical studies.

Tolstoy himself examined the consequences of an attempt to live by the precepts of the Sermon on the Mount in a dramatic work, *And the Light Shineth in Darkness,* curious if not especially successful, which he began in 1880, took up again in 1902, but left unfinished.

Tolstoy was a good chess player, and as many chess players do, he liked to re-play games by himself, especially those he had lost, varying the moves, seeing what the outcome would have been if he or his adversary had made a different move. And it seems that he often did something similar in his fiction: starting with a real situation, he would experiment with alternatives, with the possible consequences of different moves. In *And the Light Shineth in Darkness,* the central character, Saryntsev, follows very closely the phases of Tolstoy's own drama after his conversion. Saryntsev's efforts, however, to live by his faith lead to a series of disasters. In the last act, barely outlined, Saryntsev is assassinated by the mother of a young man, his most devoted follower, who refuses military service and is locked up in a lunatic asylum where he perishes.

Aside even from this somewhat melodramatic finale, the pessimism of the play lies in the utter defeat of the man of good, and in the failure of acts of love to produce more acts of love; the attempts to live by the precepts of the Sermon on the Mount generate hatred and violence in Tolstoy's drama, which seems to express his doubt, perhaps only momentary, in his own beliefs.

Early in the play there is a short scene, written with a touch of humor, in which Saryntsev's sister-in-law, Aleksandra, discusses his new faith with a young village priest whose orthodoxy has been shaken by Saryntsev's ideas:

Aleksandra: Well, is it true that according to the Sermon on the Mount one must distribute one's possessions to strangers and send one's family begging?

20

The Priest: The Church blesses, as it were, if I may venture to say, the family, and so did the fathers of the Church who also, so to speak, blessed the family, but highest perfection demands, if I may say so, the repudiation of all earthly possessions.

Aleksandra: Yes, that's what the saints did, but as for us, simple mortals, I think we must act simply, as befits good Christians.

The conflict both in the play and in Tolstoy's own household was indeed one between a man attempting to apply the Gospel literally, and "good Christians" who had no desire of becoming saints. One of them was Tolstoy's wife, Sofia Andreevna. She could probably be described as a "good Christian" in the widely and generally accepted sense, if not in the sense of "absolute perfection." The picture of Sofia Andreevna, however, that emerges from Tolstoy's diary for the year 1910 is a very painful one indeed.

Sofia Andreevna seems to have always been an emotional person, and her own diaries tell of spells of melancholy and depression even during the early and happy years of her married life. In the late years she presented symptoms of what was referred to in her entourage as "hysteria." By 1910 these symptoms became so alarming that a psychiatrist was called to Iasnaia Poliana for consultation. He diagnosed a "degenerative double constitution, paranoiac and hysterical, with predominance of the first." This bit of the particular psychiatric verbiage then in use gives little useful information.

For many years the Tolstoys shared in an active, creative, and, by common standards, a good life. Tolstoy's literary work brought fame and also a very substantial income; children, thirteen in all, were born and raised; the family estate was successfully managed; the peasants, the needy and the sick received benevolent attention. Sofia Andreevna's diaries reflect her great interest in her husband's creative work and intellectual life (with, at times, even in the earlier years, a touch of bewilderment and remoteness), and a constant preoccupation with the household and the children; the diaries record in detail the ever-recurring stories of nursing and weaning, of sore throats and diarrheas, of doctors, poultices, and enemas, and later of pranks and French lessons, of growth, and then of gradual, always unexpected, estrangement. Also recorded in the diaries are moments of withdrawal from all the labors and worries when Sofia Andreevna, her husband being absorbed in his work, would play Chopin, or read the novel serialized in the *Revue des deux mondes,* or simply reminisce.

But even if a shadow did appear at times, Sofia Andreevna's life was a happy and a full one, with strong attachments and well defined purposes. Then came the "crisis" from which Tolstoy emerged with his new faith renouncing all those "worldly concerns" that were the very foundation of Sofia Andreevna's life; the "good" and successful life she was sharing with her husband was condemned as wrong, even sinful. Sofia Andreevna could not follow Tolstoy on his path toward Christian perfection; she could not repudiate her committments to the worldly concerns with the welfare of the family, to that ideal of "family happiness" which she had shared with her husband for many years. Tolstoy's new religion of love meant for his wife above all a loss of his love for her. Sofia Andreevna wrote in her diary, in August, 1882:

Twenty years ago, happy and young, I began to write this book, the story of my love for Liovochka. There is hardly anything in it except love. And now, twenty years later, I am sitting up alone in the night, reading it and weaping over my love. For the first time in our life, Liovochka left me and went to sleep in his study. We quarreled about a trifle. . . . But . . . what does matter is his growing indifference toward me and the children. He shouted today that his most fervent thought was to leave the family. Not on my deathbed will I forget these heated and candid words; it was as if he had cut my heart out of my breast. I pray God for death; it is dreadful to live without his love, and I felt clearly that his love had left me. I cannot show to him how strong my love is now, just like it was in the old days, and in all these twenty years. This would be humiliating for me, and it would irk him. He is penetrated with Christianity and thoughts of perfection. I am jealous of him . . . Iliusha is ill, he is lying in the drawing-room with a fever, he has typhoid; I must give him quinine at regular intervals, which are very short, and I am afraid to miss the hour. I will not go to sleep in the bed which my husband has abandoned. God help me! I want to take my life from me, my thoughts are all confused. The clock just struck four.

Further Sofia Andreevna notes that a day later her quarrel with Liovochka was made up, that they both wept and that she saw with joy that their love had not died yet. Their love was not dead, and that made the struggle all the more painful. In the course of this struggle various accomodations were attempted; Tolstoy resorted to compromises between his desire to practice what he preached and his reluctance to deal the last blow to his wife, that of leaving her. In May, 1883, Tolstoy gave Sofia Andreevna a power of attorney over all his property; nine years later, a legal deed was made transferring the property rights over his estates to his wife and children. As for literary property, Tolstoy authorized Sofia Andreevna to publish his works written before 1881; and a few years later, in 1891, he made a public announcement to the effect that all his works which had not been published before 1881 were free of any copyright protection, and could be published by anyone.

All this "giving away," however, fell short of solving Tolstoy's problems and was tainted with the ambiguity of half-measures. Tolstoy the enemy of property had disposed of Iasnaia Poliana in favor of his wife and children,

23

but he continued to live there; the advocate of non-resistance to evil and the enemy of authority renounced all authority, and so had to look on in helpless dismay when an armed guard, hired by Sofia Andreevna to guard the property, manhandled trespassing peasants; the vegetarian and the enemy of luxury ate simple vegetarian dishes, but they were especially prepared for him by the cook and served by a white-gloved lackey. All this appeared futile to the more benevolent critics, hypocritical to the less benevolent ones who depicted Tolstoy as a bearded Tartuffe in the garb of a Russian peasant, comfortably living in the estate transferred to his wife. Tolstoy was aware of all this, and accepted criticism and mockery with equanimity, as part of his trial.

More important for him was that the disposal of property and the other compromises into which Tolstoy entered did not bring peace, but only widened the chasm between him and his wife and added venom to the family strife. Sofia Andreevna had been rejected and condemned by her husband for doing what she believed to be her duty, and which was the only thing she was able to do: being a good wife and a good mother and caring for the welfare of the family. She was condemned not for violating any norms acceptable and intelligible to her, but for her inability to recognize that the beliefs in which she had been raised and by which she had lived, and all her instincts, and her whole life were wrong and sinful. As a result of the "compromises," she had become the custodian of all those rights and interests that were, in her husband's eyes, sin and corruption. Having lost the most important battle, the one for her husband's love, she continued to fight against him the battle for the family property; she could thus still perform her duties as a mother if she was rejected as a wife.

The voice Sofia Andreevna raised in opposing her husband had been by common standards (those of "good Christians") the voice of reason; gradually, it became irrational, and no wonder. Sofia Andreevna may have become "hysterical"; but her "hysteria," her repeated, easily frustrated suicide attempts, the scenes and the threats, all these were the last weapons of a helpless, rejected and aging woman who was fighting against unintelligible hostile forces.

In the last stage, the bone of contention was the disposition of Tolstoy's authorship rights, and Sofia Andreevna's arch-enemy in the struggle she was carrying on was the man whom Tolstoy called his closest friend, Vladimir Chertkov.

Tolstoy first met Chertkov in 1883. Two years earlier, at the age of twenty-seven, Chertkov, a brilliant young officer of the guards, the son of a wealthy family of the nobility connected with the St. Petersburg court, resigned his commission and retired to his family estate, far from the capital, and devoted himself to the betterment of the conditions of the peasants. Chertkov had embraced ideals very close to Tolstoy's, independently from Tolstoy and possibly under the influence of English Evangelists with whom his mother was connected. Tolstoy's first meeting with Chertkov was the beginning of a very close association and an extremely intimate friendship that lasted until Tolstoy's death.

Chertkov was a man capable of sustained, organized effort, cool, systematic and businesslike, and he very usefully combined these qualities with an apparently sincere dedication to idealistic goals. Soon after his meeting with Tolstoy he devoted his energy to an important publishing business, *The Intermediary*, which was inspired and sponsored by Tolstoy and published various edifying and didactic works, including a number of Tolstoy's writings or selections, in very cheap editions intended for mass circulation.

Chertkov engaged in many other activities as well, and soon became a full-time Tolstoyan, the leading Tolstoyan, spreading the Teacher's word, publishing his writings, taking an active part in various philanthropies and campaigns. One of these campaigns, in favor of the Dukhobor sect whose members refused military service and were mercilessly persecuted by the Tsarist government, resulted in 1897, in the exile of Chertkov and of two other of Tolstoy's disciples. The place of Chertkov's exile was England. The punishment inflicted upon him for his subversive activities, if perhaps rather unusual, was most certainly not especially cruel. Chertkov had means and he had many connections in England, so that he could settle down in his exile to a very comfortable and active life. The main activity among his various pursuits was the publishing of those of Tolstoy's works that were forbidden in Russia by the censorship.

Chertkov was allowed to return to Russia early in 1905, and hastened to visit Tolstoy in Iasnaia Poliana. Soon he settled in the estate of Teliatinki, bought from one of Tolstoy's daughters, whose property it was, situated some two miles from Iasnaia Poliana. In the spring of 1909, Chertkov, who was under police surveillance, was forbidden to reside in the province of Tula where both estates were situated; this measure was lifted in June of the next year, so that during the last months of Tolstoy's life at Iasnaia Poliana, Chertkov was again in the immediate neighborhood, living at Teliatinki with his mother, his wife and his son Dima, a staff of aides and secretaries employed at this headquarters of the Tolstoyans, and many zealots of the new faith.

Chertkov had established himself as the leader of the Tolstoyan movement, and he had acquired considerable ascendancy over the Master himself. This was a strange and perhaps also an ironic situation. Tolstoy's thought was in its very essence heretical and non-conformist; he was above all a demolisher of accepted beliefs, of dogmas, cults and institutions. He was neither a very consistent nor a very original thinker, and if there was anything admirable in him, it was the intensity of his experience, the experience of a man of great spiritual and creative powers. But now this non-conformist, this anarchist, found himself faced with a high priest, stern and demanding, ruling over a new church, the depositary of the message that the aging messiah had delivered, the custodian of the Truth. And Tolstoy was forced to conform, to follow his own teaching. Tolstoy was forced to be a Tolstoyan: his thought, propagated by Chertkov, was returned to him in the form of dogma.

The influence that Chertkov acquired over Tolstoy was bound to result in a protracted and increasingly venomous conflict with Sofia Andreevna. The last months of Tolstoy's life were dominated by the strife between Sofia Andreevna and Chertkov, each of them supported by different members of the family and the entourage.

As mentioned before, the struggle was focused on the testamentary dispositions made, or to be made by Tolstoy of his literary property. Tolstoy's public statement renouncing all copyright privileges on his works published after 1881 had no legal force as far as the rights of his heirs were concerned, since it had not performed a transfer of property to any particular persons; legally the announcement was merely a permission given by the owner to make free use of his property. In 1895, and again on a later date, Tolstoy entered in his diary a request to his heirs that they would not attempt to exercise any property rights over his works after his death. But this was only a request, which was not binding, and it seems that for a long time Tolstoy was reluctant to use in this matter any legal coercion. His wishes were to be executed by free consent or not at all. Later, however, and quite clearly under Chertkov's pressure, Tolstoy decided to execute a will that would be binding for his heirs. This was, it seems, no easy undertaking; beginning in 1909, several drafts were made, then revised because some legal technicalities were omitted. The final draft was written by Tolstoy and signed by him and by two witnesses on July 22, 1910. Since it was legally impossible simply to renounce property rights, Tolstoy instituted his daughter Aleksandra sole legatee of all his literary property, including works published and unpublished, manuscripts and copyrights. A separate document, however, that Chertkov had drafted, expressed Tolstoy's will that all this be made public property. It further expressed his will that all this property be passed on to Chertkov as administrator, editor and publisher of all that constituted Tolstoy's literary heritage, Chertkov to exercise his authority in the public interest.

Tolstoy's earlier testamentary dispositions made a distinction between his writings published before 1881 and the later ones, the former being reserved for Sofia Andreevna during her lifetime. No such distinction was made in the document signed in July, 1910.

All the transactions concerning Tolstoy's will were carried on in secret from Sofia Andreevna. The final act was executed in a wood, a few miles from Iasnaia Poliana; Tolstoy rode to the secret meeting place alone and was joined by the witnesses. Chertkov did not attend.

Sofia Andreevna suspected that Chertkov had finally prevailed on Tolstoy to execute a will; she sensed the conspiracy, and made frantic efforts to find out the truth, spying, eavesdropping, threatening, rummaging through Tolstoy's papers. This searching in his papers was the immediate cause of Tolstoy's escape on the night of October 27, 1910. He describes the scene in his diary.

Sofia Andreevna's prowling and spying could most certainly be exasperating, but the "conspiracy" was not a product of a deranged mind; Tolstoy *did* sign, in the woods, sitting on a stump, the document drafted by Chertkov which dispossessed his family of his literary heritage. And it does not seem that Sofia Andreevna was motivated by greed; she was engaged in a frenzied struggle with enemies who were conspiring to take from her, her children and her grandchildren, everything that she once had shared with her husband, who were dominating him and exploiting him, who had turned him against her.

Some time after the signing of the will, Tolstoy discussed the matter with Biriukov, one of his most devoted followers; Biriukov expressed the opinion that the will was a mistake, for it implied recourse to law and the state, and that it would have been preferable, instead of secretly sign-ing the document, to call the family together and an-nounce his intentions, relying for the rest on their moral sense. Tolstoy agreed with him, and wrote to Chertkov to tell him that he had changed his mind. Chertkov re-plied by a very long letter, carefully drafted, carefully rea-soned, quoting dates and earlier documents, to demon-strate that the will was the only proper course that could be taken. Tolstoy hastened thereupon to withdraw his be-lated objections, with proper apologies and expressions of gratitude to Chertkov.

In his secret diary, however, under the date of July 30, 1910, eight days after the signing of the will, Tolstoy wrote: "Chertkov has drawn me into a struggle, and this struggle is oppressive and repulsive to me."

Three months later Tolstoy left Iasnaia Poliana. Sofia Andreevna sent him frantic letters begging him to return, and once again, attempted to commit suicide. Then, on November 2, she went to Astapovo, but she was allowed to see her husband only five days later, about an hour before his death; Tolstoy was unconscious and did not recognize her.

There is a photograph (photographers were numerous and active at Astapovo) representing Sofia Andreevna during those days when she was waiting to be admitted, a rather stout old lady, wrapped in a fur coat, with a shawl over a fur hat, standing in the snow, behind a low fence, close to the station master's wooden house in which her husband was ill in bed; he had been taken ill, to quote again his unfinished letter to Aylmer Maude, on his way to the place where he wished to be alone.

List of Characters

Note. Russian family names have a masculine and a feminine form; *Mr. Chertkov,* but *Mrs. Chertkova; Mr. Sukhotin,* but *Mrs. Sukhotina;* in translations from the Russian it is customary to use the masculine forms only. Russians use, in addition to the first name, the "patronymic," a form derived from the father's first name and meaning "son of" or "daughter of"; thus, "Sergei Lvovich" means "Sergei, son of Lev (Leo)," "Tatiana Lvovna," "Tatiana, daughter of Leo." The first name alone is used between, or in addressing, very young people, between close friends and relatives; very frequently special (diminutive) forms of the first name are used in such cases, e.g. Seriozha for Sergei, Kolia for Nikolai, Misha for Mikhail, Sonia for Sofia, Tania for Tatiana, etc. The older pronunciation of Tolstoy's given name, especially, it seems, in his social milieu, was "Liov" (more exactly "Liof"); nowadays the prevalent pronunciation is "Lev" ("Lef"); the diminutive, however, is still "Liova." In translations, the Western form is ordinarily substituted for the Russian one: Leo (rather than Lev) Tolstoy.

The Tolstoy Family

a. living at the Iasnaia Poliana ("Clear Glade") estate, Tolstoy's birthplace, in the province of Tula, some 120 miles south of Moscow:

1. LEO NIKOLAEVICH TOLSTOY, 1828-1910.
2. SOFIA ANDREEVNA, "Sonia," *née* Behrs, his wife (1844-1919).

3. ALEKSANDRA LVOVNA, "Sasha," their daughter b. 1884, (now living in the United States).

b. visiting Iasnaia Poliana:
Tolstoy's children and their families:

4. SERGEI LVOVICH, "Seriozha," (1863-1947), married to Maria Nikolaevna *née* Zubov, living in Moscow and at the estate of Nikolskoe-Viazemskoe, some 15 miles from Iasnaia Poliana; not sharing his father's views, but loyal and devoted to him.

5. ILIA LVOVICH, "Iliusha," (1866-1933), married to Sofia Nikolaevna *née* Filosofov, working in a bank in the town of Kaluga, about 60 miles from Iasnaia Poliana.

6. LEO LVOVICH, "Liova" (1869-1945), living in Moscow and often in Paris; in his father's late years hostile to him and his ideas.

7. ANDREI LVOVICH, "Andriusha," (1877-1916), married to Ekaterina Vasilievna *née* Goriainov (after divorcing his first wife, Olga Konstantinova Dieterichs, a sister of the wife of V. G. Chertkov); in the estate of Taptykovo, then moves to St. Petersburg; hostile to Leo Nikolaevich.

8. MIKHAIL LVOVICH, "Misha" (1879-1944), married to Aleksandra Vladimirovna *née* Glebov; two brief visits are mentioned in the diaries for 1910.

9. TATIANA LVOVNA SUKHOTIN, "Tania" (1864-?), married to Mikhail Sergeevich Sukhotin (1850-1914), a member of the first Duma (1906) and an honorary Justice of the Peace; living in the estate of Kochety, some 90 miles from Iasnaia Poliana; in 1910, Tolstoy stayed with the Sukhotins at Kochety from May 2 to May 20 and from August 15 to September 22; Tatiana Lvovna, though not a follower of her father's philosophy, was entirely loyal and devoted to him.

c. living in the convent of Shamardino, a little over 100 miles from Iasnaia Poliana:
10. MARIA NIKOLAEVNA T., "Masha" (1830-1912), Tolstoy's sister, a nun; Leo Nikolaevich visited her at the convent on his last journey; he arrived at the village of Shamardino in the evening of October 29 and left in the early morning of October 31.

(Tolstoy's grandchildren mentioned in the Diaries are identified in footnotes.)

Friends, Associates, Frequent Visitors

a. living at or near Iasnaia Poliana:

1. VLADIMIR GRIGORIEVICH CHERTKOV (1854-1936), in Tolstoy's words, his "closest friend," the head of the Tolstoyan movement, writer, propagandist, organizer, editor and publisher of Tolstoy's works and Tolstoyan literature; was exiled to England for the dissemination of Tolstoy's ideas and, after his return to Russia, was forbidden residence in the province of Tula where Iasnaia Poliana is situated; in May, 1910, he was permitted to meet Tolstoy at Kochety, the estate of the Sukhotins; in June was given permission to reside in the estate of Teliatinki, but only when his mother resided there, and finally, in September, the government lifted the earlier imposed restrictions. Teliatinki, less than two miles from Iasnaia Poliana, became a center of the movement; Chertkov lived there with his family, a secretarial staff and a small colony of Tolstoyans. He was married to Anna Konstantinova *née* Dieterichs, "Galia" (1859-1927); their son, Vladimir, "Dima," "Dimochka," (1889—), also lived in Teliatinki.

2. VALENTIN FIODOROVICH BULGAKOV (b. 1886), student at Moscow University and follower of Tolstoy whom he first met in 1907; in January, 1910, was invited by Chertkov to Teliatinki, then was recommended by him to Tolstoy as secretary and served in this capacity until Tolstoy's death. Author of an important diary recording the last year of Tolstoy's life.

3. DR. DUSHAN PETROVICH MAKOVITSKI (1866-1921), a Slovak, Tolstoy's faithful follower and his personal physician, residing at Iasnaia Poliana since December, 1904; accompanied Tolstoy on his last journey.

4. VARVARA MIKHAILOVNA FEOKRITOVA, "Varia" (1875-1950), a friend of Aleksandra Lvovna, Tolstoy's youngest daughter; worked for Sofia Andreevna as copyist helping her in her work with Tolstoy's manuscripts, then joined the anti-Sofia Andreevna forces.

5. MARIA ALEKSANDROVNA SCHMIDT (1843-1911), an educator by profession; became a zealous follower of Tolstoy's in the 1880's; in 1895 came to live on one of the Sukhotin properties, Ovsiannikovo, some three miles from Iasnaia Poliana, occupying a little hut and cultivating a small plot of land. Tolstoy showed great respect and affection for Maria Aleksandrovna and often visited her.

6. PAVEL ALEKSANDROVICH BOULANGER (1864-1925), a close friend of Tolstoy's and his follower, living in the village of Ovsiannikovo; in 1909 and 1910 was working on a book, *The Life and Teaching of Siddhartha Gautama, called the Buddha, with Selections from Buddhist Texts*; Tolstoy wrote an extensive introduction for this book which was published in 1910 by *The Intermediary*, the non-profit publishing house of the Tolstoyans.

7. SERGEI DMITRIEVICH NIKOLAEV (1861-1920), a friend of Tolstoy's, living in the village of Iasnaia Poliana during the summer; translated the works of the American economist Henry George (1839-1897) for whose views on property and advocacy of a "single tax" Tolstoy professed a great admiration.

b. visiting Iasnaia Poliana:

8. ALEXANDER BORISOVICH GOLDENWEIZER (b. 1875), a distinguished pianist, professor at Moscow Conservatory, a friend of Tolstoy, frequently staying at Iasnaia Poliana and Teliatinki; author of important reminiscences of Tolstoy.

9. PAVEL IVANOVICH BIRIUKOV, "Posha" (1860-1931); close friend of Tolstoy and one of the most important figures in the Tolstoyan movement; author of a well-known biography of Tolstoy in four volumes; one of the founders of *The Intermediary* publishing house and for two years (1886-1888) its manager; in 1910 living in Kostroma, to the north-east of Moscow.

10. IVAN IVANOVICH GORBUNOV-POSADOV (1864-1940), friend and faithful follower of Tolstoy; author of stories from peasant life; managed *The Intermediary*.

Diary for 1910

I skipped two days. Today is *January 2, 1910*.

Yesterday everything as usual. Again revised "Dream." [1] The Landowskis[2] left. I went riding. Called on Maria Aleksandrovna [Schmidt] and Boulanger. I never cease to be ashamed of my life. I am making at least a little progress though, in refraining from ill feelings.

Dimochka [Chertkov] came over to say goodbye. A long business letter from Chertkov. Did not have time to answer. This evening talked about the land with Seriozha. They all will have their own theories. I played chess and cards with my dear Adamych.[3]

The day before yesterday, the 31st, I revised something in the morning, I think. I rode over to the district offices.[4] The people are indignant. The Landowskis are rather difficult, but I liked him. Olsufiev arrived that evening. Seeing the New Year in with extravagant luxury was very annoying, both in itself and because I participated.

January 2, 1910. Went walking in beautiful weather. A woman, miserable, sick after childbirth, was brought over. Children, starvation. Dear, it's sad. I am sitting down to letters and coffee. A Frenchman, Marchand, has arrived.[5] I had a heated discussion with him, answering his questions. Revised "Dream." Went riding with Dushan [Makovitski]. Usual evening, and the Frenchman.

I am well. Good, interesting letters. Revised "The Poverty of the People" [1] and "Dream." Letters. Went riding with Olsufiev. His Orthodoxy comes from a sense of propriety, and therefore he defends it heatedly. Yes, if religion is not of first importance, then it takes last place. People defend heatedly only immovable religion, that is, religion taken on trust.

Nothing special this evening. Boredom.

Sad, dreary, but am in a kindly mood. I feel like crying. I am praying. Revised "Dream" again. I do not know if it is good, but it is necessary. Letters, answered a few. Went riding alone. Very sad. Those around me are very alien to me. I thought about my relations with people of our class, irreligious people. They are like my relations with animals. I can love them and pity them, but cannot enter into spiritual intercourse with them. Such a relationship brings out ill feeling. They do not understand, and by their lack of understanding and self-assurance, by their use of reason to obscure the truth, and their disputing truth and goodness, they draw me into ill feeling.

I cannot express it, but I feel that I must work out within myself a special relationship with these people in order not to destroy my love for them.

I am going to dinner. Lord, help me to be with Thee, unceasingly to know myself to be only Thy workman.

This evening Seriozha talked very well about the resettlement of the Dukhobors. [1] Again mummers and dancing. I read some trifle, played cards. Wrote answers to Solovov's questions. [2]

Woke up early. Walked about the garden. It becomes more and more difficult to see slaves working for our family. I tried to remember my prayer on communicating with people. Dear Nikolaev and Abrikosov arrived, and I was very glad to see them. Talked for a while with Nikolaev. Abrikosov is full of spiritual life. Received many letters. I wrote answers to Smitt[1] and a Mohammedan from Samara.[2] Did nothing else. Sadness.

Am going to dinner. This evening I read "Dream" to all present. Many objections. But I think it is good. Whist, and the same sadness and shame.

Many letters, few interesting ones. A cinematographer[1] came. Revised "Dream" and "Poverty"[2] a little, and I decided to send them to Chertkov as they are. In general I must stop writing and worrying about what I have written. Yesterday a Jew came, demanding a compressed formula for the meaning of life. Whatever I said to him was not what he wanted; it was all subjective. It had to be objective, based on "evolution." Appalling, this stupidity and dull-wittedness of those who have sampled learning.

Wrote nothing. Same as yesterday, only more shameful and sad. Went riding with Dushan Makovitski. Sasha wronged against Sonia. Am going to dinner.

This evening dull cinematograph. Whist.

Feel a bit better in my soul. No more helpless anguish, only unceasing shame before the people. Is it possible that I shall end my life in this shameful condition? Lord, help me, I know what is in me; be in me and help me. Got up late. Went to meet the sleigh from Kozlovka railroad station.[1] The cinematographers took pictures. It does not matter. Beggars and petitioners also came, and that too does not matter. But I met three well-dressed people who begged from us. I forgot God and refused. And when I remembered it was already too late. I had a good talk with a pitiful ragged boy from Pirogovo.[2] I met Sasha and Varia, and again the cinematograph. I had the following thoughts:

1) I felt especially vividly what I have known for a long time, that each person is aware of his "I" as I am aware of mine. This might seem very simple, but for me it was both very new and especially important, unusually so. If only we could always remember this. If we could only remember this, we would stop condemning others, to say nothing of acts which are unpleasant to others.

2) This is important mainly because, even if we are not directly conscious of, but vividly imagine another's "self," just like our own, then we know also that every other "self" is the most fundamental "self"; and that it is not only similar to mine but that they are one and the same.

3) Such an awareness of another's "self" as the same as one's own is important for man's welfare, because by recognizing that another's "self" is the same as one's own, one can do good not only to one's own "self" but to all others.

4) Love is nothing but recognition of other's "selves" as one's own "self."

Read letters. One was unpleasant, as it expressed agreement with my convictions and asked for 500 rubles to spread Christianity. I do not feel like writing anything. Now it is after twelve.

Nothing done. Went riding with Dushan. Yegor Pavlovich from Iasenki[3] was here. About the peasants purchasing land. My good Bulygin came for dinner. Said goodbye to Olsufiev. Again the cinematograph. Boring. And a weakness has come over me, time for bed.

I have recovered, but am very weak. A peasant from
Volyn Province wants to be a book pedlar. Yes, I would
like to go into the desert. A good letter from Gusev,[1] and
to Sasha from Chertkov. How both of them . . . —well,
all's well that ends well.[2] Chertkov's letter is so warm and
serious. And Sasha can understand and feel what he says
about the main problem, apart from my personality. God
grant it. I only answered a few letters. I began to write
about taxes, and put it aside; I did not feel up to it. I
went walking. Now it is after four, and I shall lie down.

This evening I read an interesting almanach, *Coenobium.*[3] It is interesting because one senses how all the
more or less advanced people feel dissatisfied with their
spiritual condition. Whist this evening. Did not write yesterday.

This morning got up very early, wrote some more on my
letter to Smitt on science. Then letters, then I finished
writing about taxes, well enough. Read in the evening.

Got up early this morning, added some more to my letter to Smitt on astronomy. Went walking. I still cannot
remember to recognize the "self" in other people with
whom I come in contact; I forgot about the Demenki
woman.[1] Remembered later. Am sitting down to coffee and
work. After 10.

Read and answered letters. Many unkind ones. Reread
the second and third "Day in the Country" for a little. To
note what is very important:

1) Thought how essential it was to preach to people an equal love for *ALL*, for Negroes, savages, and one's enemies, because if we do not preach this, there will not and cannot be any liberation from evil, there will be only what is most natural: one's fatherland, one's people, its defense, armies, and war. And if there are armies and war, there will be no end to evil.

An ideal is essential for life. And an ideal is only an ideal when it is *PERFECTION*. The direction can only be indicated when it is indicated mathematically, by a *straight line* that is nonexistent in reality.

January 11   I : 10

Got up late. Sleepiness and dissatisfaction with myself. Petitioners. I refused Zharova. Remembered, but I could not fulfill it.[1] Uninteresting letters. Rode over to the lieutenant's[2] to telephone. Read *Coenobium*. Many good things, and the idea is a good one. Religious awakening everywhere. Had a good time playing. Now to bed.

January 12   I : 11

Slept little. Am in good spirits. Nazhivin came. I enjoy him. Maria Aleksandrovna and Boulanger. Uninteresting letters. Revised the second and third Day. Went riding for a bit. I wronged a woman who came from afar; I refused. Dinner and evening pleasant and purposeful with Nazhivin and Boulanger. Boulanger spoke magnificently about Buddha. I have something to note down but shall leave it to tomorrow. Sasha went with Dushan to Tula to a concert.

Usual letters. Reread all of "Three Days." [1] And I'll finish it, I think. Went riding with Philip.[2] Am going to dinner. I must write down a few things. The woman whose husband killed the man who had raped her.[3]

1) It is not anarchism, the teaching by which I live. It is fulfillment of the eternal law, which does not permit violence or participation in it. The consequence will be either anarchism or its contrary, slavery under the yoke of the Japanese or the Germans? This I do not know and do not wish to know.

2) The comet[4] will engulf the earth and annihilate the world. It will destroy all the material traces of any activity, including mine. Let it. This only shows that any material activity, which supposes material consequences, is senseless. Only spiritual effort to fulfill a given impetus, a law, is sensible. What the conquences of this activity will be I do not know, and I could not even imagine them, because they, these conquences, are all temporal, while spiritual activity is timeless, but I know that only this activity makes sense. (I must think more about this.)

Am going to dinner. After dinner went to see Sasha, who is sick. If Sasha were not going to read this, I would write something nice about her. Took some Gorky [stories][5] she had. Read them. Very poor. But the worst about it is that the false appraisal of him is unpleasant to me. I should see only good in him. Felt very weak all evening.

1) Aside from the usual Lord's Prayer, "The Cycle of Reading," [6] and "For Every Day," [7] a prayer is also needed that would correspond to one's spiritual movement. My last four consecutive prayers were:

1) Thou, who art in me, help me.
2) Help me to be with Thee.
3) Help me to know myself *only* as Thy workman.
4) Help me in all intercourse with people to see myself in them.

Got up early, went walking, and had good thoughts, which I note here:

1) Man has one job to do: to grow spiritually. To think of the consequences can only be harmful for the fulfillment of our calling and for the unknown work which we are to do, and even for the consequences which we can perceive. "No man, having put his hand to the plow, and looking back, is fit for the kingdom of God."

Our situation in life may be compared to that of a horse or any harnessed animal. It is natural for the animal to move forward, and so is it for man to move toward spiritual perfectibility. The animal is harnessed, and whether it wishes to or not, if it moves it pulls whatever is hitched to it, even if it does not know what is there or how it does so. Man too in his moral growth pulls after him something else as well. (He perceives something. He sometimes perceives how his movements affect the movements of others). This why the Comet is not frightening. All that is done in the spiritual sphere cannot be destroyed by the destruction of material objects.

2) More and more clearly I envision the meaning of life in the present. Life, that is, my effort, is only in the present. And the present is spiritual and therefore outside of time. The recollection of the past and the notion of the future are only means by which I may guide myself at present. (This is poor, but when I thought of it, it seemed good.)

Now it is after ten. I am sitting down to write letters and work. What work I do not know. I started to make a few corrections in "For Every Day." Went riding with Dushan. Spent the evening with Bulygin. Had a talk with Seriozha.[1] He agreed with me about the presence of God in men. I feel unwell, it's the stomach.

I still feel ill. Letters of little interest. I worked on *For Every Day*. Finished five or six days after a fashion. Did not go riding. Went for a little walk. Notes:

1) I remembered very vividly that I am conscious of myself in exactly the same way now, at eighty-one, as I was conscious of myself, my "I," at five or six years of age. Consciousness is immovable. Due to this alone there is the movement which we call "time." If time *moves on*, then there must be something that stands still. The consciousness of my "I" stands still. I would like to say the same of matter and space: if something exists in space, then there must be something that is non-material, non-spatial. I do not know as yet to what extent the latter may be asserted.

Am going to dinner. Nothing special this evening.

I woke up in good spirits and decided to go to the court in Tula.[1] I read letters and answered some. Then I left. First the peasants were tried: lawyers, judges, guards, witnesses. It was all very new for me. Then came the trial of a political offender. He was accused of reading and disseminating, which he did with utter disregard for himself, certain ideas for the ordering of life that are more just and sane than the accepted ones. I was very sorry for him. People gathered to look at me, but not many of them, thank goodness. The oath upset me. I could hardly restrain myself from saying outright that it was a mockery of Christ. My heart contracted, and for that reason I kept silent. On the way Dushan and I had a good talk about Masaryk.[2] I rested this evening, and I could not help feeling glad about the publication of *The Cycle of Reading* in Odessa. Now it is nine o'clock. There is nothing to note.

I lost the day. I was in a somber mood all day. Bulgakov came with a letter and messages from Chertkov. Could do nothing. Went riding with all the children through the Zaseka. Maria Aleksandrovna and Boulanger.

Still more depressed. Offended a cadger from Tula. Besides letters, I wrote eight or nine "Days" after a fashion and talked with Bulgakov. Only one thing is good, that I feel that I am bad and repulsive, and I know that I deserve this. It is now after four. Nothing special this evening.

Got up in a better mood. As I walked, I thought that it would be good to run a school again, to pass on what I know about faith and to check on myself. Then letters, not very interesting, and I wrote the "Days" up to the twentieth, not badly. Went riding with Tania, Sasha and the children on my circle through the Zaseka. There was a pathetic lady from Sevastopol. What I told her was pretty good; I said what I could. Now it is after four.

The evening passed as usual. I worked for a bit on *For Every Day.*

Slept little. Before dressing, I worked on *For Every Day.* Walked for a bit. Pathetic petitioners. Letters; a stupid, revolting one from Kuzminski.[1] For a long time I could not overcome my unkind feelings, to my shame. Finished *For Every Day.* A pathetic soldier's wife came. I gave her some cotton cloth. Then went riding. B. [Bulgakov?] came. Somehow I do not feel at ease with him. All is not well in my heart—no kindness. I am struggling to overcome it. It is a good thing that I still find myself repulsive. Am going to dinner.

1) The more definite and decisive one's solutions are to questions about the unknown, about the soul, God, the future life, the more indefinite and indecisive is one's attitude to moral questions, to questions about life.

2) There is no more widespread superstition than the notion that man and man's body are something real. Man is only a center of consciousness that receives impressions.

3) Space and matter, time and movement, and also number as well, are concepts which we have no right to extend to phenomena that are beyond time and space, like the soul, God . . . We cannot say of God that He is one or three (number), or of the soul that it *shall exist,* or "in the next world."

All these concepts are spatial or temporal, and are therefore senseless when applied to what is nonspatial or nontemporal.

4) We speak of the life of the soul after death. But if the soul lives "after death," it should have lived also "before life." Onesided eternity is an absurdity.

Woke up with a strange feeling. I did not remember anything, did not recognize the children. Headache and very weak. I could not do anything but thought well about the closeness of death and wrote a bit. Three "Buls" were here: Bulgakov, Bulygin, Boulanger. Slept a lot.

January 22

A bit better, at least my memory has returned. A miserable girl came, also Andriusha. Read letters, interesting ones, and answered many. One especially, despite terrible illiteracy, was remarkable for the depth and the seriousness of thought of a man who has now come to negate all and everything, this being the consequence of manifestly false religious convictions he professed earlier. Am going to dinner.

Felt better this evening. Made some corrections in *For Every Day*.

January 23

Woke up completely recovered, were it not for heartburn and constipation. Walked a little in the garden. Good Seriozha Bulygin wrote me very intelligently and seriously his thoughts about God, inspired by our conversation. Just as I was sitting down to write some letters, the baron[1] arrived. He is a tactful person, and he soon left. Letters. Many interesting ones. One from Totomiants,[2] again about cooperatives. I wrote a bad answer to him and to Golitsyn.[3] Dushan attracts me more and more with his seriousness, intelligence, knowledge, and goodness. I was able to finish the letters only toward two. I took up *For Every Day* and worked a bit on it. But the more I work on it, the more repulsive I find this work. I must be rid of it quickly, recognizing that it is all silly and unnecessary. I feel well in body and soul. Am going to dinner. After dinner worked on wearisome *For Every Day*. Whist.

Slept little. Took some notes in bed. Wrote letters. Then worked a bit on *For Every Day*. Walked in the morning and at noon. Thought well about "the present." Not yet ready. To be noted:

1) If one thinks seriously about one's own life and that of the whole world, then one must admit that there exists SOMETHING which cannot be known at all; but also, that it must be recognized, this Something, because it is the same, both in my soul and within itself. (I thought this was something new, but it has come out completely shopworn.)

2) When dying I may only say that I am at peace, because I know that I go to Him from Whom I came. (Still worse.)

3) I thought what a good, necessary, and highly important work it would be to write a self-teacher for the people, with information arranged according to its importance and necessity.

Iliusha came yesterday.[1] Thank goodness, his visit went well. They are becoming pathetic. I cannot ask for what does not exist. Morning as usual: letters. But I cannot write anything. I would like to, but I lack the persistence and concentration. I thought especially vividly about a timeless life in the present, dedicated only to love. Something of this thought is reflected in life. After three, am going walking. I feel well in my soul, but I am repellent to myself and am glad of it.

Bulgakov and dear Skipetrov[2] came this evening, and we had a good talk. Boulanger read a very good work about Buddha. Seriozha came. Evening as usual. I feel well in my soul.

Got up early. Went walking. To be noted:

1) We are used to imagining, and perhaps we cannot help imagining, God and a future life, but we can come to the same conclusions about God and a future life also without imagining them. Reason, experience, and inner feeling draw us even more definitely to the same conclusion that does *the image of God and a future life.*

This seemed to me very important and requiring a clear exposition.

Worked on *For Every Day.* Went riding. During dinner Sergeenko[1] came with a gramophone. It was unpleasant for me. Yes, I forgot: there were some interesting letters. Later Andriusha came with his wife.[2] I behaved well without special effort, and was affectionate to them. The gramophone all evening.

Slept well. Went walking. Am sitting down to coffee and letters. Revised *For Every Day.* Almost finished. Very dissatisfied. Yesterday, I think, I received a letter from Chertkov with corrections of "Dream." They are fine. Went riding with Dushan. Good letters, as always. Boulanger; a good idea about a self-teacher, but I must think about it. Evening as usual. Sofia Andreevna left for Moscow. All is well, thank goodness.

I do not feel like thinking. Went walking this morning on the highway and talked with Sergei Tsvetkov.[1] At home a pile of letters. A wonderful letter from Smirnov,[2] who is refusing military service. Finished up the last days of *For Every Day*. Answered letters. I do not feel like doing any work. To be noted:

1) In all types of activity it is important to know how to stop before what you do not know and not to think that you know what you do not. But this abstention from false knowledge is most important in matters of religion, of faith. All the madness of religious superstitions comes only from this lack of restraint.

Went riding to the Teliatinki people. Grauberger[3] and Tokarev.[4] Evening as usual.

January 30   I : 28

This morning I met Miss Shanks[1] out walking. Began to rework *For Every Day* in accordance with Ivan Ivanovich's [Gorbunov-Posadov] letter. Worked well. Not very interesting letters. Grauberger and Tokarev. Tokarev is a free Molokan. Had a good talk with him. Went riding with Dushan. This evening Dolgorukov[2] was here with the library [catalogue]. Am going to bed at midnight.

January 31   I : 29

Posha [Biriukov] came this morning. As serious, simple, and good as ever. A correspondent and a photographer came. I began some new work for the *For Every Day* booklets,[1] and prepared the first, "On Faith." Then I had to go to the library.[2] Everything was contrived, unnecessary and false. Dolgorukov's speech, peasants, photography. Went riding with Dushan. It was difficult with Dolgorukov at dinner and this evening. Then Posha and Miss Shanks arrived. Miss Shanks told us very well about a blind deaf-mute;[3] when she was told about love, she said by writing, "Yes, it is so simple, it is what everybody feels toward every . . ." [in English in original]. And about God she said, "I knew it but did not know how to call it." [In English in original.]

All have left.

February 1 I : 30

I am sleeping well. I got up cheerful, but late. Had a thought, but I did not think it out completely. It was very important and good. I shall try to remember it. Letters. Then I began "February" until the 19th. Went walking. I did not treat a murderer's wife at all well. Slept. Am going to dinner. Evening as always. I don't remember.

February 4 I : 31

Strange, I skipped two days.

On the 2nd I wrote and planned the ending of the second booklet, "On the Soul." [1] Went riding. No important letters. Something about superstitions. Spent the evening as usual. S. Mamonova[2] arrived.

On the 3rd Sofia Andreevna came back.[3] I was pleased. I wrote the third booklet, "The Spirit of God in All." [4] Not good. Monotonous, but I shall correct it. I rode over to see the orphans and to Ozerki.[5] To be noted:

1) How important it is to remember that what is required from us is not perfection, but the striving to approach it in everything (including my present work), as much as we can. *Feci quod potui, faciant meliora potentes.*[6] This is very important to remember.

2) If we think of the future, then how can we help thinking of the inevitable future, death? But no one does. But think of it we must; it is good for our souls and even consoling.

I have just come in from a walk and am sitting down to work.

I have done quite a lot of work on the fourth booklet, "God." Went riding. I felt very poorly, and had no dinner. The evening was as usual. Reading, whist.

February 5 I : 32

Slept a lot. I am better, but my bowels are not working. I dropped over to the clinic[1] to see Dushan. Makes one envious. I have finished the fifth booklet, "Love," after a fashion. Went walking. It is very much on my mind to express my pain about life. I am ashamed to admit that I was disturbed by a letter from a girl student about my "transferred property."[2] Am going to dinner.

February 8 I : 33

Skipped two days. Today is *February 8*.

I do not remember the day before yesterday. I know that I wrote the sixth booklet. Yesterday Shmelkov[1] came from the Caucasus. A religious man. Bulygin was here. A touching letter from Felten.[2] I felt ill, but I wrote the seventh booklet; it will be good, I think. I have just written the eighth. My article,[3] it seems, is very stupid. I had an explanation with Sasha, very moving. I have just come from Maria Aleksandrovna's and shall lie down before dinner.

Again skipped two days. Today is *February 11*.

I know only that I was in a bad mood these two days. But still I worked and wrote yesterday and today, and today I even finished two "Days." [1] The day before yesterday Boulanger was here. I must write him a preface for Buddha.[2] And there are many other things I must do. Chiefly the suffering from man's sins, including my own, which divide and torment mankind, are more and more strongly crying for expression. Today this came to me more clearly than ever before, in the form of "The Notes of a Lackey." [3] How good it could be! Was rereading Dostoevsky; no, that's not it.

At home they are all sick, Dorik,[4] little Tanichka, and Sasha. A greeting from d'Estournelles,[5] my mutilated article, and abusive letters. Sofia Andreevna is going to Moscow. To be noted:

1) I forgot, it was something important I was thinking today about God and faith.

2) If time passes, then something stands still. It is the consciousness of one's "I" that stands still. If there is matter in space, then there must be something outside of space. This is again my consciousness.

3) As in the material world everything is attracted to everything else, so it is also in the spiritual world.

I went riding yesterday and the day before yesterday; today I did not go. Now it is after four, and I shall go walking.

I felt very vividly how beneficial for life is the thought that death may occur every instant.

Sofia Andreevna has left. I talked to her yesterday about my wish, and how unpleasant it is that the *Readers*[6] are being sold at a high price. She started to say that nothing will be left for her, and refused outright.

The doctor came; they are all sick. Sofia Andreevna left.

Last night I felt very ill. Had a pain in my side, heartburn, and a cough. Slept little. Bad weather, a wind. I walked a little, wrote a poor letter to Boulanger about Buddha. I corrected one booklet after a fashion, and wrote: I composed the 13th. Many letters, and very interesting ones. Answered several of them. Did not go out before my sleep, dozed off, and now I am going to dinner. I feel well in my soul. There was a very pathetic vagrant boy from a printing house, exiled. In the evening I wrote six more letters. My throat hurt, but all is well. Sasha is better.

Slept well and thought well, and this is what:

1) As I fall asleep I lose consciousness of my waking self; as I die, I lose consciousness of the self which has lived this life; but as what is conscious is not destroyed when we fall asleep, so it is in death. What this thing is which is conscious I do not know and cannot know.

It comes to my mind: well, all right, my soul is what is conscious, what does not die, but somewhere, sometime again (all temporal and spatial concepts) will reappear. But as it does not remember what my former "I" was, it is no longer "I." My consciousness was destroyed by death. Whatever may happen after the death of the "I," the source which comprises my "I," I no longer exist, shall not exist, and cannot exist. But if this is so, then the question arises, what is this "I" of mine which suddenly appeared at my birth? What is this "I"? Why is this "I" I? And how can this "I," which appeared so incomprehensibly outside of time, not disappear as incomprehensibly outside of time?

All right, I shall die. But why shall all life after my death not be my life?

There is something here, but I cannot analyze it clearly and express it.

2) Thought also about my loss of memory. I forgot and go on forgetting what constitutes *myself, Leo Niko-laevich.* What remains? There remains something very important, most important. That which appeared at my birth in this world, and which was, and will not be, but is. And this life of mine is mine alone, and mine for sure, but then why is not every life mine? I am aware of this already through love. Again not clear, but *je m'entends.*

3) People have elevated their malice and vengeance into a legitimate feeling, into justice, and have ascribed it, their own vileness, to God. What absurdity!

I jotted this down this morning. Went for a walk, then letters, and I composed one "Day," poorly. It wouldn't come off. Sasha worries me. Tanichka also has the measles.

February 14   I : 37

Got up weak. Sasha and Tanichka are still sick. Bad weather, and I am restraining myself from a bad mood. A nice letter from Sonia, a good one. Again I composed a "Day" after a fashion, but am dissatisfied with the chapter divisions themselves. Now it is ten o'clock in the evening. I feel weak.

February 15, i.I l.[1]

February 15   I : 38

Got up rather late. Wrote a letter to Khiriakov.[1] A worker came who wishes to settle on the land. He wants to influence people.[2] Yesterday we had a good talk with

Bulgakov about the call to military service which he expects. I read over some uninteresting letters, and am sitting down to work. To be noted:

1) I live badly because life is bad. Life is bad because people, we, live badly. If we, the people, lived well, life would be good and I should not live badly. I am included in the people. And if I cannot make all people live well, I can at least do so myself, and thus can improve, however little, the life of other people and my own. What confirms this reasoning is that if everyone adopted it, and this reasoning is irrefutably just, then life would be good for everyone.

I composed another "Day," the seventeenth, without simplifying it. Sasha moves me and alarms me. I am glad that I love her, and I rebuke myself for loving her too exclusively. I write and am frightened myself. Yes, may His will be done.

I also worked this evening: self-renunciation in the face of sin, meekness in the face of temptation; faith in reason in the face of superstitions, faith in the truth in the face of false teachings.[3]

I am going to bed.

February 16, i.I l.

February 16

Alive, but not well. Sasha seems a bit better. Sofia Andreevna returned. I composed a "Day," badly. Letters, but I did not answer. Weakness. Chertkov's article is very good. Ivan Ivanovich [Gorbunov-Posadov] on bad terms with Chertkov, according to Sofia Andreevna. Boulanger came. He was dissatisfied with my article.[1] It is a little difficult, when one has no practical interests, to deal with people dominated primarily by these interests.

Am going to bed.

February 17, i.I l.

Alive. Received a touching telegram from a Kiev student, urging me to leave home in poverty. My health is better. All morning I revised the letter about Buddha and answered letters. Sasha is no better. Am holding up. It is now after five. I walked a bit and took a nap. Also worked this evening. The chapter divisions are still not clear.

I could not go to sleep until after two. Today since morning I have been writing the booklets "On Life." Still confused on the chapter divisions. Uninteresting letters. Yes, I revised the article on Buddha a little. Walked a bit. Sasha is better, but I have not stopped being afraid. I thought of something very important and shall try to remember it. Now it is after eleven, and I am going to bed.

As I write I feel weak, before going to sleep. I worked hard composing the booklets. Went riding. Mitasha.[1] I cannot overcome an unkind feeling. I was at Maria Aleksandrovna's. Did some good thinking about the madness of personal life, and of dedication to one's own life and even to life in general. The temporal one, in which we do not know and cannot know what is good. One can serve only Him, or rather do what one must for purposes which are good but beyond my comprehension, purposes which always coincide with my true welfare.

February 20, i.I l.

Sasha is dear and good and it is all the more frightening at bad times, not for her but for me. Am alive. I keep working hard on the booklets. I have finished twenty-eight. I like "On the Present." A letter from Chertkov. A Danish Jew,[1] very interesting. Went riding with Dushan. Goldenblat[2] came later. I revised the letter to Posse[3] a little. I am going to bed. Sasha is much better and feels well.

February 21, i.I l.

Alive. Now it is after eleven, am going to bed. Good letters. I finished all the booklets. Went riding. Sasha still feels ill. I thought about deliverance. I spent the evening with the Molostvovs.[1]

February 22, 23, 24. Skipped two days. My overall physical condition is not good. Nor am I in a good, easy frame of mind. Sasha is better. I do not remember well what happened these two days.

22nd. In the morning I met a "political" sailor.[1] I sent him to Teliatinki and wrote Chertkov. I believe I revised the letter to Posse. Dinner and the evening with the Molostvovs. I still cannot forget about people's opinions. Rode over to Teliatinki with Pavlych.[2]

23rd. Walked a long way to meet Filia.[3] I believe I revised a letter to Posse and other letters. Rode over to Ovsiannikovo.[4] In the evening I finished the letter to Posse. We read the article about "The Barricade." [5]

Wrote letters to Lehr[6] and about Masaryk.[7] My leg began to hurt.

Today, the 24th, I checked over all the letters and finally revised the one to Posse. Wrote letters. I feel ill, but I am holding up. Now it is four o'clock. In the evening I read about Bourget[8] and wrote a letter to Galperin.[9]

February 25 I : 46

Slept very badly. A strange state—something like being young in a dream. Got up early. Went walking. Had a good talk with a drunkard who admitted that he was deceiving the women—he was cleansing them of malignancy and drinking up all the money. All day I was *d'une humeur de chien*.[1] I wrote a whole story, "Khodynka," very poor.[2] I wrote an answer to Melnikov[3] in bed. I did not go out in the afternoon. In the evening I read philosophy and on Dushan's advice wrote a letter to the Czechs.[4] Now it is twelve o'clock, and I am going to bed.

February 26 I : 47

Felt very weak. I did not eat anything. I am preparing for death, but badly. I am not indifferent. I corrected "On God." I did not correct it well, but the booklet is good. I went walking this morning. A Jew asked me to recommend him to some men of letters. It annoyed me quite a bit. Also I did not control myself at dinner. I noted down in my booklet, but did not copy, two thoughts and one allegory which had appeared to me in a dream. I did not see Sasha. I am going to bed, feeling a little better. Enough writing. I've done my bathing.[1]

Got up feeling better. Went walking. Two Cossacks
arrived; one wants to set up the Heavenly Kingdom on
earth.[1] They confuse the religious with the worldly. Both
human glory and arranging things constructively. But
they are moving. They came on purpose. I worked on the
booklets, "On God" and "Sin, Temptations, and Superstitions." Not good. Letters from Chertkov and other
interesting ones.

I answered Lapshin[2] and the editor of *New Russia*.[3]
I did not go out, slept before dinner, and now I am going
to dinner. To be noted:

1) To fall asleep actually means to die, it means to
lose consciousness of one's self. What is the "self"? Why
the "self"? (This is the way I noted it down, but now I
cannot remember the significance.)

2) There is no "I"; there is only what is in me.

Got up fairly cheerful. I walked a good deal, and
wrote letters. I saw off the Cossacks and the sailor, and
also an alcoholic Ukrainian and his wife. Sasha was up.
I shall go riding in the sleigh as soon as I have had
lunch.

Went riding with Lena. I spent the evening pleasantly
in Sasha's room. Read *Super Tramp*.[1] Poor English jokes,
in Shaw's introduction too.

Woke up feeling fine, and made some notes. I have no
time to copy them in now. Walked a while. I received

interesting letters and answered them honestly. Thank God, I remember more and more often that I must live only for God, and I remember about death. I revised "On Pleasing the Body,"[1] poorly. Drove with Dushan over to Podivankovo.[2] I am afraid I caught cold. Sonia is ill. I came back late and did not have time for a nap. Going to dinner. I remember one thing to note down:

1) It is time to go to sleep, i.e., to die. I already feel occasionally an awakening and another, more real, reality.

After dinner read and did nothing.

March 2   I : 51

Got up early. I feel very weak. I wrote some letters, and revised one booklet, as well as I could. I went to sleep at three out of weakness. I rode over to Kozlovka. Had dinner. Shestov[1] came. Not particularly interesting; he is a "man of letters" and not at all a philosopher.

Thank God I am remembering fairly well that I live only in His sight. This makes my life very much easier. I think and hope that it will become a habit.

Now it is ten o'clock. Sasha is well and is afraid of Bulgakov.[2]

March 3   I : 52

Still the same: the same weakness, although I am a little better, but I still cannot get to work. I revised one booklet badly, and wrote one insignificant letter. I rode a long way on horseback with Bulgakov. To be noted:

1) Some people think for themselves, and then, when they think that their thoughts are new and important, they communicate them to others. Others think in order to communicate their thoughts to people, and when they

have done so they think these thoughts are true, especially if people praise them.

Am going to dinner. I acted badly toward a young man who had come from Tula. Ivanova couldn't find a job for him.[1] Instead of talking to him and thinking of some solution, I was so tired when I got home that I did nothing.

March 5   I : 53

Yesterday was the worst day of all. I worked a bit and wrote some letters. I rode over to Maria Aleksandrovna's. Quite remarkable is Andrei Tarasov, from Tambov, a peasant.[1] Intelligent and firm. Another letter from Dosev.[2] Goldenweizer came this evening. I am ashamed to admit it, but his playing stirs me deeply.

Today I feel better. I wrote letters and the tenth booklet. I rode to Teliatinki with Andrei Tarasov and had an enjoyable conversation with him and Seriozha Popov.[3] In the evening I read an interesting novel, *Ecce Sacerdos*.[4] Now I am going to bed.

March 6   I : 54

Got up feeling better than yesterday. I went for a long walk, then letters. One, the confession of an ex-revolutionary, was a great source of joy to me and moved me. At times one sees the glad fruits, and they give me great joy. Then I corrected two booklets, the twelfth and thirteenth. I rode horseback for a short while, and enjoyed it. Now I am lying down to sleep before dinner. Stakhovich[1] has come. His politics and his luxury and his quasi-aristocracy are very alien to me. Am lying down. The Sukhotins and Bulgakov left. How much better Andrei Tarasov and Seriozha Popov are than Stakhovich.

Yesterday I wrote two letters, I think. Went riding with Dushan. I have been reading Aleksandra Andreevna's notes,[1] and experienced a very strong feeling; first, I was moved by pleasant memories, and secondly, I felt sad and was clearly aware of how she, poor woman, could not help believing in redemption and *tout le tremblement*. Not believing she would have had to condemn her whole way of life and change it, if she wanted to be a Christian and have communion with God. Irreligious people can live without faith, and therefore have no use for an absurd one; she needed a faith, however; but a rational faith would have convicted her. So she believed in an absurd faith, and how she believed! Thirdly, I also felt how flimsy and unconvincing a bald affirmation of one's own faith and condemnation of others is. She insists with such assurance on her own faith and condemns so resolutely. Fourthly, I also felt that I was often wrong and not careful enough when I touched on the faith of others (were it even only a faith in science).

I spent the evening with Stakhovich. I spoke to him about his luxury. But you can never get through to him either, with his faith somehow compounded from aristocracy, art, and Orthodoxy. But he's a nice fellow.

Today I got up feeling fresher than I had for some days. Letters. One very good one from a peasant. Afterward I worked on a booklet, "The Superstition of Punishment."

Ivan Ivanovich [Gorbunov-Posadov] and dear Nikolaev arrived. Seriozha Popov and Andrei Tarasov came over. My nerves feel weak. I felt like bursting into tears when they were reading the Buddha article and when I said goodbye to Tarasov. A good long letter from Chertkov. I went riding with Dushan. I slept very little, and am going to dinner.

In the evening I read over with emotion my letters to Alexandra Andreevna. One says that life is made up of labor, struggle and error, a letter which I could not change now in any way. We have decided with Ivan Ivanovich about the publishing.

March 9   I : 56

Got up very early. I thought over the letter to the Japanese.[1] Letters. What use to make of the 15,000 rubles?[2] Went riding. Finished the fifteenth booklet. The awareness of what life should be is very much on my mind. I do not know how to express it: my awareness of truth and service to it are very strong. To be noted:

1) About immorality in dreams . . .

Not a very interesting evening with Zosia Stakhovich[3] and Boulanger, but I had a very good conversation with Ivan Ivanovich. I gave five booklets for printing.

March 10   I : 57

Today I also got up early. I met Tania and her husband. Letters: one horrible one from a young man preparing to kill an old man to obtain his certificate of maturity.[1] I worked a bit on the sixteenth booklet. A letter from Chertkov. Wrote an answer to the Japanese, and a letter about the horrors of Christian civilization,[2] and an answer about the 15,000 rubles. Went riding with Dushan. Am going to bed. Dinner, chess, gossip, cards, the gramophone, and I felt painfully ashamed. I shall not participate any more. I shall read.

Got up feeling fine, very early, and took a stroll in wonderful weather. Five petitioners. One was pathetic, but I found him so because I talked with him. All of them would be pathetic if I treated them all as I do Sasha. To be noted:

1) About sleep. I understand more and more clearly that sleep and awakening, which seemed to me to be images of life and death, are more than images. As on awakening I come to a clearer, more real consciousness than I had when I was asleep, so it is at birth. And as I barely remember anything that *was* (?) before birth, so when I am awake I only occasionally remember what I dreamed. As I go to sleep every day, I lose consciousness; so it is in death. (This image is not true only in one respect, that in my sleep I have a lower level of consciousness; this cannot be true in death.) I lose consciousness, and in this loss there is not only nothing bad, but it is even desirable. It is always a rest and preparation for a better life. (This was not successful.) I am tired.

2) The revolution has made our Russian people suddenly see the injustice of their position. This is the talk of the Emperor's new clothes. The child who spoke the truth, and said that the Emperor was naked, was the revolution. The people have become conscious of the injustice they have suffered, and they react to this injustice in various ways (for the most part with anger, unfortunately). But the people already understand it. This awareness cannot be exterminated. And what is our government doing? By trying to crush the inextinguishable awareness of injustices suffered, it is increasing this sense of injustice and stimulating a more and more angry attitude toward injustice.

I am sitting down to write letters and do some work.

My cheerfulness was deceptive. I have done almost nothing, only wrote letters. Went riding. I don't remember the evening. Oh yes, I read over my letters to Aleksandra Andreevna.

March 12

I : 59

I felt quite unwell. Slept until ten. Letters. I worked some on my letter to the Japanese and did not even finish it. Then I slept again. In the evening I read over the letters, which I find very moving. The book about Brahmanism[1] is superb and has stimulated many thoughts.

1) How important the concept of God is, and how instead of valuing what has been given us, we with light hearts spurn it because of absurdities that have been attached to it.

2) How the process of evolution takes place in reverse in religion: from Brahmanism to Zoroastrianism, Judaism, Buddhism, Christianity, Mohammedanism, and why is this? Because religious consciousness is the reverse of the practical improvement of life. In our time they have ended up with the absurdities of evolution in the material world, without beginning or end, in time and space.

Again read my letters to Aleksandra Andreevna.

March 13

I : 60

My health is better. I worked on the letter to the Japanese again. My error was that I dictated it without thinking. I revised it, but can hardly say that I have finished it. I revised one booklet, "Effort." I rode over to Maria Aleksandrovna's, and I took a nap. I still am not well. Am going to dinner.

Skipped three days. Today is the fourth, four o'clock on
March 17. I was sick all these three days. I worked poorly
on the letter to the Japanese, on the preface to *For Every
Day*,[1] and on March 14 on the sixteenth booklet. Alexander Stakhovich[2] was here. I was in a very gloomy mood
all the time. Thank God, yesterday, I regained my senses
in my attitude to what is the most important thing. This
is the material for the work that lies before me, and I am
finding it hard. Molochnikov was arrested.[3] Dear Perevoznikov[4] was here. I wrote Chertkov. I have just rewritten the
preface again. Molochnikov writes me. I think the preface
is better. But all this work on *For Every Day* in general
is becoming tedious. There is a kind of pedantry or dog-
matism in it. Everything is vile. I received two strong
impressions, and identical in character, from reading the
letters of Aleksandra Andreevna and the thoughts of
Leskov.[5]

There is a lot to be noted, I think:

1) If a man knew nothing about the lives of people in
our Christian world and he were told, "There is a certain
people who have set up such a way of life, that the
greater part of them, ninety-nine per cent, or thereabouts,
live in ceaseless physical labor and oppressive need, and
the rest, one per cent, live in idleness and luxury; now,
if that one-hundredth has its own religion, science, and
art, what would that religion, science and art be like?"
I think that there can be only one answer: "A perverted,
a bad, religion, and science, and art."

2) How difficult it is to love, even not to dislike, a
repellent, self-assured, and stupid person. It is difficult,
but what can be done? This is the chief task which has
been assigned to you.

3) They gave a man something which was better than
anything he could imagine. And he said, it is no good,
it is too little. They gave the old woman a nice piece
o' linen. "Too thick," says she. So they give her a thinner

piece, and she says, "Give me more o' this." Yes, if you had not been awakened, you fool, you would have kept on sleeping and would have known nothing and never seen what you now know and see. Your business is to make the best use you can of what has been given you, and you say, "It's no good."

4) (March 15) In order to understand any material object at all, you must know its origin, the reason for its appearance, and its relation to other objects. The origin and cause for the appearance of every material object is concealed in infinite time. Similarly, the relationship of an object to other objects is indefinable, since all objects break down into infinitely small ones and grow to infinitely large ones. So neither the origin nor the cause of the appearance of objects nor their relation to other objects can either be known or comprehended.

The life-span, not only of my body, which has existed eighty years, but of our planet, the earth, even if it were to exist billions of years, is only an infinitely short moment in infinite time. And therefore the reasons for my origin and that of the earth and of everything in the world can be neither comprehensible nor known to us. The same is true of the relations to matter and space of my body, of the earth, or of whatever you will; they are not even a grain of sand amid the world of the infinite, they are nothing. What is amazing is not this infinity of time and matter in space, but the infinite stupidity of people who think that material phenomena are comprehensible and that they suffice to explain life, feeling no need of admitting anything spiritual at all.

5) Life for the peasant is first of all labor, which enables him to continue living, not only he himself but his family and others. Life for the intellectual is to acquire those branches of knowledge or art which are considered important in his circles, and through this knowledge to exploit the peasant's labor. How can the peasant's understanding of life and its problems help but be sensible, and the intellectual's understanding help but be crazy.

6) God is the creator, God is Brahma, Vishnu and Siva, God is Jupiter, God is Christ, etc. All this is so absurd that we boldly reject it, and we cannot help rejecting these absurd concepts. And we do not realize that the concept of God, the spiritual source of all, is such a great and essential concept, that we ourselves would never have conceived of it if it had not been revealed to men gradually through the mental efforts of the greatest sages of the world. This is an immense forward step for humanity, but we imagine that since we have radium, airplanes, and electricity we can get along without it. Yes, we can, but only living like animals and not like human beings, as we do live now in our New Yorks, Parises, and Londons, with their thirty-story buildings.

March 19

Today is *March 19*. I skipped yesterday. My health is getting worse, but I am living well, thank goodness. I don't remember anything in particular happening yesterday. I keep on rewriting the preface and letters. I sent off the letter to the Japanese, a bad one. I read Bodianski's letter;[1] it is hard to write a refusal. I rode over to see Prokofi,[2] and I might have acted more gently. I keep thinking of men and their judgment and not of Him and His judgment. Read in the evening.

Today I got up early, slept little, wonderful weather. Went for a walk. I had a cold, a cough and a chill, and my bowels were not working. I revised the introduction again. I reread my letter to the Indian[3] and it received my approval. On the other hand, the one to the Japanese is terrible. But it is good that this is not important to me. Wrote to Gusev. He was searched. I don't think there is anything to note.

I was very weak yesterday, a cold and a cough, a fever, and my bowels won't work. It was pleasant to think that the idea that this might mean death was not in the least oppressive to me. I did not go out. I wrote letters and revised the booklets. My health was worse in the evening.

Today is the same. It was bad in the morning, then became better. I wrote letters again, interesting ones. Then Iärnefelt[1] was here. His drama is not a very interesting one to me.

It is now after nine and I am a little better. Sasha is ailing again, but she is good. I feel very well in my soul. The clarity of my thought is good. I want to express it but can't, and this is good too. Tania is very sweet and a pleasure to me.

March 22, i.I l.

Alive, and even my cough is much better, but my stomach is still bad. Worthless letters. I corrected one or two galley-proofs of my booklets. And I do not like that work. Ivan Ivanovich arrived. I have just had a nap and am going to dinner. I have some things to be noted.

My health is good. Letters. The work on the booklets is very tedious. I wrote a letter on suicide.[1] I don't like it either, I would like to write a play for Teliatinki.[2] Am going to dinner. A man with a cembalom has come here, a very likeable person.[3]

The cembalist's music is nothing much. I got up well today. But I am still not much satisfied with what I'm doing. I find it too systematic. I shall try to get out of this. There were some interesting letters, and I answered them. I worked a bit on the preface. I want to write a play for Dimochka, but there is no need for this. And if there is no play, it will be just as well. I received a moving letter from Molochnikov with horrifying details about the prison. I still have not had time to write down what I have been thinking.

Went for a long walk. Met Dunaev.[1] I feel sad. My thoughts disturb me. Either I do not have the strength or I cannot find the form to express them. There was a powerful article by Korolenko[2] on the death penalty. Went riding. I spent a depressing evening playing cards. I must stop. Am going to bed.

For a long time I have had a lot to be noted. Today two more thoughts, very important ones. Today's:

1) That the salvation of mankind is possible only through not participating in violence. Not to pay taxes is impossible. They will come and get them, but one can always refuse to be an oppressor. This is not my thought but Bulygin's.

2) My thought. As in youth one is pained by one's own evil and hankers after one's own welfare, the welfare of one's own organism, so in old age, as I painfully feel

now, one is pained by the general evil and hankers after the general welfare, the whole organism in general.

Went walking for more than an hour. Felt fine. I wrote the preface, and am going to lunch. There was a moving letter from a priest about Christ.[1] In the evening I read Korolenko's article. It is magnificent. I could not keep from sobbing. Wrote Korolenko a letter.

I woke up early, revised the letter to Korolenko, and two places in the preface. Went walking.

I read and wrote letters. Could do nothing else. I feel weak. I could not do anything, but I feel very well in my soul. I slept. Now it is five o'clock. I want to note what has not been copied into the diary. There are two thoughts written in the notebook, and I remember that they both seemed important to me, so I jotted them down briefly, sure that I would remember them. They are written down this way: 1) What is the world? 2) Consciousness unites separate organisms. I remember the second, but I cannot read the first or remember it.

1) Why are my tongue, my heel, and my lungs joined in one body?

Not because of proximity; my excrement is closer than my skin, but it is not mine, while the skin, the ear, every cell of my body are mine. All this is joined in my consciousness alone. The worlds cannot be united in this way, through my consciousness; perhaps a consciousness of The Earth, Mars, the Sun, and even many others that I cannot perceive with my temporal and spatial conceptions do not seem to me to be united in one.

There was something more about this, but I have forgotten.

2) What was . . . ? I have forgotten.

3) I have forgotten everything unimportant. How could

71

this help being true, when the inner work of judging myself goes on continuously and this effort takes all my spiritual strength?

4) Faith? What is faith? Faith is the spiritual structure on which the whole life of man stands. This is what gives him support and therefore enables him to move. It is the same for him as a place to stand on for a corporal being. All an insect needs is a filament, a bee needs a blossom or a leaf, a bird needs a branch, a squirrel needs a twig, a bear needs a log. So it is with man's faith. Some need only an ikon, another needs the sacraments, a third needs a prophet, a fourth a personal God, a fifth . . . Everything depends on the weight of his requirements and his reason.

5) In the spiritual world there is still more complexity than in the material.

6) The significance of life is measured by its depth, not by time.

7) You think about people, but God thinks about you.

8) Satisfaction for the body, but blessing for the soul. Satisfaction and blessing rarely coincide.

March 28   I : 70

I read yesterday evening. I ate nothing. Today I got up at eight, walked a bit, and when I returned I felt very weak. I answered some letters listlessly and again scribbled on the preface. I also began to write about suicide. It seems important. I rode horseback and have just returned. I am lying down. I feel weak, but less so than I did. Can what is maturing in me and even begging for expression remain unexpressed? Probably so, almost certainly—and this is good.

Skipped two days. Yesterday was the 29th. In the morning on my walk I met Strakhov[1] and later Masaryk.[2] I like them both, especially Masaryk. The Stakhovichs[3] came the 28th. It was quite tedious. He is just too alien to me. I had two good talks with Masaryk yesterday. I rode over to Ovsiannikovo. I jotted down a comedy. It may come out well. All the same, Masaryk is a professor, and believes in a personal God and in personal immortality.

Today is *March 30*. I am still weaker. Went walking. I met dear Posha. Could not do a thing except write letters, and few of them. Rode horseback to Teliatinki. Did nothing in the evening. Am going to bed. Midnight.

Same physical weakness, but do not feel bored or badly, just sad, but well. By experience I see how great is the joy—not the joy, rather the blessing of inner work. Today I experienced for the first time and completely clearly my success in freeing myself from human glory. There were just little matters: not to be embarrassed at being condemned for drinking wine, playing cards, or living in luxury—and see, I feel an unexpected freedom. I think that I am not mistaken.

Today I slept well. I spilled and broke the pot and got very tired picking and mopping it up, was quite out of breath, choking. It is near and it is good that it is near. Chertkov would not condemn me. I am just at the point of indifference: I do not wish and do not fear either life or death. It is good to serve. It is especially good because I feel clearly that I shall not see the consequences of my service outside of myself, but I know that there will be consequences if I am conscious of them within myself.

Went walking in the morning. A peasant revolutionary

from Panino came to see me, and his father, who is the same as he. They both served terms and they both know me, but they need me only to the extent that they see a revolutionary element in me. I gave him books. I behaved badly when I explained my position to him. Still I do not think that I did it for human glory. He asked for money. That was difficult. Then I began to write the play. It did not come right. A journalist from Finland.[1] I received him and talked long and heatedly with him, and it was good. Then Belinkii brought a letter from Molochnikov.[2] I blubbered as I asked Rydzevskaia[3] to do something about him. Then I read some and slept. Sonia left for Moscow. Sasha has gone to Tula to a concert. Am going to dinner.

Help me to turn so that I no longer be, but only God move through me.

I have two things to be noted, but no time now.

April 1

Yesterday Dimochka came over and retold me a story by Semionov,[1] did it very well. Took Semionov's story and read it all evening. It is very good. Yesterday evening I felt weak, and even more so since this morning. I am burdened by my inability to do anything. But then it is good that I am disgusting and repulsive to myself. To be noted:

1) Matter and space, time and movement separate me and every living creature from the Wholeness of God. How then can one conceive of a personal God, i.e. limited, i.e. in time and space?

2) There are two "I's" in each of us, a corporeal one, which is a union of our bodies with our consciousness, or corporeal life, and a purely conscious one, or spiritual life. In children, when spiritual life manifests itself, it does so in all its purity, without the participation of the mind and its fruits, the temptations, and that is why it is so delightful.

Now it is nine o'clock, and I am sitting down to drink coffee and write letters.

April 3 I : 74

Skipped two days. I do not remember what I did April 1. I only know that I was very weak and did not work. Yesterday was the same. I answered some insignificant letters and nothing more. Today is the same. I sleep a lot, but I am getting increasingly weaker. It is now after five and I have just waked up. There were a lot of letters, and I answered a few. Since this morning I have been wanting to write instructions about my funeral and what should be read at it. I am sorry that I have not written it down. I feel death approaching nearer and nearer. There is no doubt that my life, and probably that of all people, becomes more spiritual with the years. The same is true in the life of mankind as a whole. This is the essence and meaning of all life, and therefore the meaning of my life lies only in this spiritualization of it. In being aware of this and acting accordingly, a man knows that he is doing the task assigned him: he is spiritualizing himself, and by his life, if only in some small measure, he contributes to the general spiritualization, toward perfection.

Somehow I felt this much better and more clearly while I was out walking. Now I feel an irresistible weakness; I can hardly keep my eyes open, and it is hard to move.

April 4 I : 75

I got up feeling stronger and went walking. Did some good thinking this morning and while out walking.

In the morning I thought this way:

1) It is one or the other: either to live in time and space, guided in one's actions by notions of what will come next and by external material conditions, and to fear, and hope, and always be mistaken, and suffer; or one may live only on the basis of the present and the spiritual, which is the soul, and be guided in one's actions, knowing no fear, or disillusionment, or error, or suffering —by the law of the spiritual source of the soul—by love.

Life does not permit us to live entirely in one way or the other. Life is only then life when the spiritual principle conquers over the material, and life lies only in this conquest (Got mixed up, but it was good when I thought about it).

2) Love of God and awareness of Him is like the pull of gravity toward the earth and of the earth toward a greater center, and of that center toward a still greater one, and so on endlessly. Love for one's neighbor and for animals is like the force of gravity between objects, and is dependent on the general force of gravity. We know God just as we know the force of gravity. As we know gravity in the law of gravity, so we know God by His law of love. The law of love for God is the same as the law of gravity for the general, fundamental center of gravity, and the law of gravity between separate objects is the same as the law of love between separate living beings. And as we do not know and cannot even imagine a general center of gravity, we cannot know or even imagine God. But just as it is certain that this inscrutable center exists, so it is certain that God too exists.

A rough conception of gravity is a sense of up and down; a higher conception: the earth attracts; a still higher one: the sun attracts the earth and the sun itself is drawn toward . . . , etc. So it was with the concept of God. The roughest conception of God is an idol, a higher one: Christ, Buddha, etc., and a higher one still is of a personal God. But neither concept is accessible to man, although both are inevitable and necessary as a concept and as a fact.

I woke up feeling cheerful and went to meet Sofia
Andreevna. I jotted down something in bed that was not
bad. Later I wrote letters, corrected the proof sheets for
"October" in *For Every Day*, and looked over the nineteenth and twentieth booklets, but did not get around to
write the comedy. Worked in the evening too. Sasha is
still sick. Am going to bed.

1) How good it is to remember one's insignificance:
that of a man among billions of men, of an animal amid
billions of animals; and one's abode, the earth, a little
grain of sand in comparison with Sirius and others, and
one's life span in comparison with billions on billions of
ages. There is only one significance, you are a worker.
The assignment is inscribed in your reason and heart and
expressed clearly and comprehensibly by the best among
the beings similar to you. The reward for doing the
assignment is immediately within you. But what the
significance of the assignment is or of its completion, that
you are not given to know, nor do you need to know it.
It is good enough as it is. What else could you desire?

I skipped yesterday again. Got up early. A few letters,
answered them. I did not feel like writing anything new.
Et je m'en trouve bien.[1] I rode a long way with Dushan,
and enjoyed it. The spring is insanely lovely. Each time
I cannot believe myself. Can this beauty possibly return
out of nothing? Seriozha came in the evening. I have come
to understand him. And I am glad. Dimochka came with
Bulgakov and the Sergeenko boy.[2] I wrote an answer to
Gradovski.[3] *Today*:

I went to meet the droshky which was to take Mikhail
Sergeevich [Sukhotin] and Seriozha. Then I wrote a

little. Sasha is in bed. I rode with Dushan through the woods. I corrected the booklets; I still do not know what they should be called. Then Filosofov[4] came. He is dead, like almost all of them. A good letter from a peasant.[5] There was a half-crazy girl here. Yes, I forgot, yesterday two peasants came, one from Nizhni-Novgorod Province, the other from Ekaterinoslav. Both came expressly hoping for help.

To live only in order to fulfill not my own but His will: what freedom! And I am beginning to experience it. How can I help being grateful for birth and for life and for death?

Now it is ten o'clock. I want to prepare more booklets for copying. This is already the twenty-fifth.

April 9   I : 78

April 8 and 9. I do not remember anything yesterday. I corrected "Thoughts About Life," and wrote some letters, poorly. I do not feel like doing anything. Went riding with Dushan. Listless and even unkind.

Today is the same. Sasha is worse. She is being sent to the Crimea. To be noted:

1) "You are the Tsar's workmen, and I am God's."

2) One of the most depressing conditions of my life is that I live in luxury. Everyone wastes money on my luxury, giving me things I don't need, and are offended if I give them back. And people beg from me from all sides, and I must refuse them, arousing ill-feeling. I lie when I say that it is depressing. If it is, it's because I am bad. So it must be. That is good. Very good. All day *d'une humeur de chien,* especially when I should be kind. But do remember that the only approval I need is His.

Still in the worst possible mood. And I cannot even think of any original work. I corrected "Thoughts About Life." [1] I met Nikolaev, and received proofs from Ivan Ivanovich. Sasha is leaving.[2] She is sad. I had a good talk with her. We both blubbered. I have only copied in:

1) If you are angry with people, stop and think whether the reason is not that you yourself are wrong. If you are angry with animals, then in all probability the wrongness is in you. If you are angry with objects, then know that it's entirely within you and you must take yourself in hand.

2) I am used to praying when I am alone, thank God. But when I come together with other people, when I need more than ever to pray, I still cannot get used to it. I shall try with all my strength to teach myself when I meet or deal with anyone always to say to myself: "Help me, Lord, to treat him or her with brotherly love."

3) What a great sin I committed when I gave the children the property. I harmed them all, even my daughters. I see this clearly now.

April 11   I : 80

The same condition. I did not work except for letters, and those were poor. But I feel very much like writing them. Had a good talk with Sasha. Bulgakov lost a letter; it was a very good one. I am glad that I needed no effort not to regret it. I was bad with some old woman beggars. I forgot the prayer.[1] To be noted:

1) The devil of vanity is so clever and crafty that when you begin to judge yourself absolutely sincerely and see all your vileness, there he is, suggesting, "Now see how good you are, not like all the others; you are meek and condemn yourself, you are good."

2) We were taught to understand by religion a precise, definite conception of God and His law and for that reason it seems to us that acknowledging an incomprehensible but indubitable God and His requirements, which are written not in books but in our hearts, does not satisfy us. Yet only in this incomprehensible God and in His requirements, which are written in our hearts, is religion indeed, the only true religion.

3) When you meet a man, you should feel only joy and gratitude that there is a possibility for unity.

4) Patriotism is impossible for a man who believes in anything rational.

5) Life is so full of contradictions to all that we think and feel that the daze of tobacco and wine are necessary for us.

April 12   I : 81

Two o'clock in the morning. Still not capable of work. A letter about the death of Petrazhitski.[1] One thing is good, that I sense some progress in feeling indifferent to the judgment of others and great respect for man, a gratitude, as I put it, for the joy in the possibility of communicating with another. I wrote letters in the morning, and I corrected yesterday's letter. Am going horseback riding.

Had no dinner. I felt a tormenting anguish from my awareness of the abomination of my life, surrounded as I am by those who are working so that they can just barely keep themselves and their families from a cold and hungry death. Yesterday fifteen people were gorging themselves on pancakes[2] and five or six people with families of their own barely managed to prepare and distribute the fodder. Tormentingly shameful, terrible. Yesterday I passed by some stone-breakers, and it was as if I had been forced to run the gauntlet. Yes, need and envy and hatred of the rich are difficult and tormenting, but I do not know if the shame of my life is not more so.

April 13 I : 82

Today is April 13. I woke up at five and kept thinking how to get out of this, what to do? and I do not know. I thought of writing. But it is awful to write while I remain in this kind of life. Speak to her? Go away? Change things gradually. . . . It seems that the last is all I can and will do. But it is oppressive all the same. Perhaps, even very likely, this is good. Help me, help me, He who is in me and in everything, and who is, and whom I pray to and love. Yes, love. Now I weep, as I love. Very much.

April 14 I : 83

Yesterday was very depressing. Walked yesterday over to Kurnosenkova's,[1] to Shintiakov's,[2] I forget their names. I did nothing except write a worthless letter. Rode horseback. It is oppressive, but I do not know what to do. Sasha has left. I love her, and I miss her, not for work but for her soul. The Goldenweizers came to see her off. He played. From weakness I got slobbery.

Last night was bad physically, and this has some influence on the spiritual. Got up late. Bodianskaia was here about her husband, who was sentenced in the "Novorossiisk Republic" case. I wrote Olsufiev.[3] I behaved well with some beggars and a petitioner. Rode over to Ovsiannikovo. I was reading over my books. I shouldn't write any more. I think that in this respect I have done what I could. But I do want to, terribly.

In the evening I corrected "Thoughts About Life." Now

it is twelve o'clock. Am going to bed. Am still in a bad
state of mind. Look out, control yourself, Leo Nikolaevich.
April 15, i.I l.

April 15 I : 84

Am alive, but not much so. I got up feeling more cheerful. Again a fuss. Petitioners; I treated them all well,
remembering to be grateful for the joy of meeting them,
except for a drunken woman, whom I answered badly.
Letters. Shaw[1] and about a Peace Society.[2] Not good.
Proofs. And I have still written nothing. Solomakhin[3] is
very nice, and in the evening a railway man came from
Samara.[4] Now I feel a little feverish. Wrote Sasha.
April 16, i.I l.

April 16 I : 85

It is time. Am alive. I got up late. Drank waters. Went
to see Suvorov[1]; there were many people there. I had a
very good time with the old man. I caught sight of him
and had an unpleasant feeling of annoyance. Then I remembered about the possibility of unity, which we should
be grateful for. I chatted with him, satisfied his wish, and
I felt so wonderful and so glad. Then there was a teacher
from the south. A person very congenial to me.[2]

I corrected "Thoughts about Life," and am very much
dissatisfied with it. Not very interesting letters. Menshikov's[3] disquisition about me upset me, I am ashamed
to say.

I rode over to Teliatinki with Bulgakov and had a pleasant conversation with him. In the evening I read maxims
from the Talmud. The same bad mood. Also the cursing
of a peasant to whom I did not give five copecks was

even more unpleasant than Menshikov's unkindness. To be noted:

1) I do not remember who it was, Dosev or the Kiev student, who urged me to abandon my life as a land owner, which I lead, they think, because I cannot be without fine food, riding on horseback, etc. That is good for me; "holy foolishness."

2) How can there help being suicides when faith is so distorted and science is so absurd? From faith to science— from the frying pan into the fire.

3) Faith is mad because people want to believe in the old way but live in the new.

Not clear, but too boring to clarify. What's the use. I am tired—tired of living.

Something else is noted here, but I cannot decipher it and it is not necessary.

April 17   I : 86

It seemed that it couldn't be worse. And today my mood is the worst it has ever been. I am struggling with it with difficulty. There was a good letter from Chertkov, and a journal of the Chinese progressive party.[1] It interests me very much. I did not drive anywhere. After dinner I was looking over the booklets. It must all be changed. Nothing to write down.

April 18, i.I l.

April 19   I : 87

Alive, and I did not write yesterday. Today is April 19. Yesterday was somewhat better. I revised "Thoughts About Life" in the morning, and it was not bad. I was in Ovsiannikovo. In the evening I corrected proofs. Today I am a good deal better.

A visitor yesterday, a spy who had served in the police and shot revolutionaries, came expecting sympathy from me. In addition, he apparently wanted to ingratiate himself by slandering priests. It is very hard that it is impossible, rather that I do not know how, to deal with everyone humanely, or in God's way, lovingly and reasonably. Two youths were just here today to teach and expose me: one demanded that I "fight" with bombs, the other questioned my transferring property rights to my works up to 1880.[1] And I was unable to deal with them meekly, without irony.

Yesterday I had an interesting talk about love.

Most people put nothing higher than exclusive love, and openly call true love hypocrisy. And I must mention in "Thoughts About Life" the depraving influence of novels and the praise of exclusive love in general.

This morning two Japanese came.[2] Primitives moved to ecstasy by European civilization. But I received a book and a letter from an Indian[3] expressing understanding of the defects of European civilization, even of all its worthlessness.

I went riding with Dushan. Now it is after four. I shall lie down before dinner.

1) You judge others without knowing them. And how much filth you know about yourself, but you forget it.

2) Yes, the movement that changes the pattern of life is slow. Steps in this stairway are generations. Now, for example, there can be no movement until they die off, the landlords, the rich in general, who know no shame for their position, and the revolutionary liberals, who are satisfied with themselves, like the two who were here today.

In the evening we went to play the gramophone. There was dancing and a crowd. Saw off the Japanese. Everything is better. I am going to bed. I said goodbye to dear Tania.

April 20, i.I l.

Still alive. Got up rather late. I walked through the little fir trees; watched the ants. Noted down a few things. The colonel again; with, apparently, hostile feelings toward me.[1] I corrected the proofs of two booklets: "Sins, Temptations, and Superstitions" and "Vanity." Not bad. Rode with Bulgakov.[2] Few interesting letters. In the evening I read Gandhi on civilization. Very good. To be noted:

1) Forward movement is slow over the stepping stones of the generations. In order to move one step, a whole generation must die out. Now those who must die are the landlords and the rich in general, those who are not ashamed of their wealth, and the revolutionaries, who are motivated only by the vanity of the revolution as a profession, not by suffering from the discrepancy between life and conscience. How important the education of children of the next generations is.

2) The Japanese accept Christianity as one of the attributes of civilization. Can they also like our Europeans, make Christianity so innocuous, that it will not destroy what they take from civilization?

3) An immense number live only an animal existence. Human matters they blindly submit to public opinion.

4) An effort at thought is like a seed out of which a huge tree will grow; it is invisible. But out of it will grow visible changes in the lives of men.

Got up late in a very bad mood. A peasant was here about the land; I treated him badly. Then a lady with her daughters; I talked with her as well as I could.[1] I read a book about Gandhi, a very important one;[2] I must write him. Then Misha came, and afterward Andreev[3] arrived. Not very interesting, but he has a pleasant, kindly manner. Not very serious. Bad news about Sasha; I want to write to her now. Yesterday I read about suicides; the article made a very strong impression.[4] It is after eleven, and I am going to bed. Nothing to note. A letter from Chertkov.

April 22, i.I l.

April 22 I : 90

Alive. I went for a walk alone, refusing to take Andreev or the man from Archangel.[1] Later talked with Andreev. He does not have a serious attitude toward life, but superficially he touches on all these problems. Letters. I corrected two months in *For Every Day*; I liked them very much. Went walking. The Goldenweizers came. I am still struggling. I wrote Sasha a letter. Am going to bed before dinner. A letter from Sasha which moved me very much. The music stirred me strongly; he played magnificently.

April 23 I : 91

Worked little. I walked with Goldenweizer to the lieutenant's. He played wonderfully after dinner. The music stirred me very much.

April 24 I : 92

Since morning I have had a sense of weakness and a headache. I did almost nothing and did not go out. Sleepiness and stagnation. A letter from Chertkov; he says my play at Teliatinki was successful.[1] I did not write anything.

A little better. Went walking. Letters. Drank coffee and had lunch. I felt a little fresher, but toward evening again weakness and stagnation. But my spirits are good, even very good.

Much better, but I did not work. That is the way it must be, it seems. That is good, too. I jotted down some things and went walking with Olia[1] and the children. I felt gloomy, but I did not sin. Read in the evening. Dimochka [Chertkov] and Alesha Sergeenko[2] came over, and they brought with them the atmosphere of the Chertkovs, very pleasant. Am going to bed. A good letter from Sasha.

I got up feeling very cheerful. I worked quite well on the preface and finished the rough draft. Walked over to Kozlovka and am not tired. Wonderful weather. I was delighted with Semenov's[1] story this evening; took leave of Sergeenko.[2] I wrote Sasha; there was a good letter about her. Am going to bed. I shall not note anything today.

My health is worse. I did nothing in the morning and I still do not feel up to anything. I walked as far as Kozlovka, was caught in the rain, and rode home on horseback with Bulgakov. After dinner corrected the preface. Weinberg[1] from Tashkent was here. I wrote letters. I feel joyless at heart. I want solitude; it is hard to be with people.

April 29, i.I l.

April 29

Alive, but not well. The night was bad. Am drowsy and weak. Good letters. Pliusnin[1] is very pleasant. Am going to bed. To be noted:

1) We pray with words, but we can only communicate with Him, with God, through love, not words.

2) Consciousness wakes us up from sleep. So only consciousness—"Who am I?"—arouses us from the delusion of corporeal life. The soul is consciousness. Consciousness seems to be so small; life is so complex, so palpable, and consciousness is something so small, so imperceptible. Small and imperceptible, but it is *Everything.*

What is consciousness? It is my asking myself, "Who or what am I?" and answering, "I am I." But then I ask, "Who is this second 'I'?" And there is only one answer, "also I," and however many times you ask, all "I's" are I. It is obvious that "I" is something nonspatial, nontemporal; it is the only thing that really is. Everything corporeal might develop under conditions of space and time, except for consciousness. And consciousness is everything. (This is good.)

April 30

I got up feeling fresher. Mr. Durnovo[1] and his wife came. He has been arranging the teachings of Christ by *concepts.* Terrible nonsense. But *cela n'est pas une raison pour se mal conduire.*[2] I was unkind to him. Spiro[3] came later. Then I worked on a letter to the children.[4] Not too bad, I think. Walked to Teliatinki. In the evening came Aleksander Petrovich[5] and Kochedykov[6] who is half crazy: the force of inertia, electricity, and magnetism. Then eight people came from Teliatinki. Everything went off all right.

I said goodbye to Pliusnin and his companion. Wrote Sasha, from whom we did not receive a letter. It is midnight.

May 1, i.I l.

May 1

Alive. To be noted:

1) One of the main causes of suicides in the European world is the false teaching of the Christian Church about heaven and hell. Although people do not believe in heaven or hell, the belief that life should be either heaven or hell is so engraved on their minds that it does not permit a rational understanding of life as it is. It is neither heaven nor hell, but struggle, unceasing struggle, unceasing because life only exists in struggle. This is not the Darwinian struggle of beings and individuals against other beings and individuals, but a struggle of spiritual forces against their corporal limitations. Life is the struggle of the soul against the body. If life is understood in this way, then it is impossible, unnecessary, and senseless to commit suicide. Goodness lies only in life. I seek the good; then how can I depart from this life to attain it? I go to pick mushrooms. Mushrooms are only in the forest. How then can I go away from the forest in order to find mushrooms?

It is now after seven in the morning. I slept very little last night, barely four hours; I feel weak. Sonia is coming. I am getting dressed and shall go walking.

Now it is evening. Sonia has arrived. I packed, then

went for a walk and to look at the automobiles.[1] Some nice boys, young, students, about twenty of them, were here.[2] I had a good talk with them. Then dear Dimochka talked very well. Am going to bed. I did nothing, but I scribbled on the preface. Gave up the letter to the children. It was really no good.

May 2   Kochety

Got ready to leave and left at seven.[1] It was a hard trip. People were curious. The dear Tanias[2] and Mikhail Sergeevich. I lost my way this evening in the park. I do not feel well.

May 3

Got up feeling listless, and did no work. I walked about the park, reading Masaryk.[1] It's weak. Revised the preface, thought about suicide, and read over what I had begun. It is good, and it would be good to finish writing it. I wrote Masaryk, Sasha and Sonia. Am going to bed; it is midnight.

May 4

Before dinner I walked in the woods and rejoiced in life and its "hidden forces." Had some dreams which were amazing in their psychological truth. I thought I would write about suicide, but when I sat down at the desk I felt that my thoughts were weak and I did not feel like it. Again I am tormented by the burden of the luxury and idleness of a landowner's life. Everyone works except me.

It is tormenting, tormenting. Help me to find a way out, if the chief and true way out has not yet come. By the way I must be grateful even for this, and I am. To be noted:

1) All that could rejoice a man who lives for his soul is that I have become a little less repulsive than I used to be. And this is not something that I am saying for the beauty of the thought or of expression, but it is my sincere, most sincere spiritual state, which has recently been tested in fact. And this joy of being conscious of my own least movement is a great joy.

2) It is good to live in such a way as to undertake something which you know you will probably not finish and the consequences of which you will probably not see.

Six o'clock. Am going to dinner. In the evening I read and took a walk.

May 5 I : 103

Again sleepiness and weakness of my brain. I did not write anything and did not try. I read the old Frenchmen, La Boétie, Montaigne, Larochefoucauld. Went walking. I cannot say that I feel well in my soul—I am asleep. Above all, what is necessary is conscious non-doing. All's done. If only I do not spoil it if I keep on living. Mainly I must live only in God's sight, with God, through God. Am going to bed.

May 6 I : 104

Telegrams last night from Sasha and Chertkov. Chertkov is arriving tomorrow, the seventh.[1]

Rain, cold. I am not at all well; weakness, heartburn, headache. I walked for a while. Letters, few of them, but a good and moving one from Chertkov, another from Siksne's brother,[2] and other good ones. Help me, help me, O *Thou*, before my death to live only in Thy sight, always with Thee and through Thee. I had a good talk with Tania. I wrote nothing. To be noted:

Habit, mechanical, unconscious acts, is the foundation of true life, of moral perfectability. Life lies in the effort to attain perfection. What man has attained is relegated to the area of past experience, of habit, and new efforts are made to attain other things and store them in turn in the area of the unconscious, of habit. It is always a negative effort. It cannot be otherwise, because life consists in liberation. Liberation is being accomplished. The task of life is not to do what hinders liberation. And that is why the whole task of life lies in being aware of what life is and in opposing what hinders it.

The effort to transform what has been accomplished into habit is the chief and only task in life. Without effort there can be no human life, only animal life.

And the materialists are completely right when they speak of animal life and reduce it to a struggle for existence and habit. But when we speak of human life we must explain its chief characteristic, effort. What is effort, from a materialistic viewpoint?

May 7   I : 105

Somewhat better today. A great joy: Chertkov has come. I went walking twice. I worked quite well on the preface. I still have something to note down later. It is after ten, am going to bed.

A little better today too. Wrote a little about suicide.[1] Perhaps it will come out well. But the preface still does not come right. I must cut it. I have something to note down, but it is too late, and I shall not begin. A good letter from Sasha.

It is late again, and I shall write only a few words. There are some things to note. I walked a lot. I reworked and abridged the preface. The article on the insanity of life is coming much clearer. Sonia and Andrei arrived. I was not good with Andrei, too abrupt. I told Sonia for the first time in part what was troubling me. And then, in order to soften what I had said, I kissed her silently— This is the language she understands completely.

Nine in the evening. Got up feeling much better, although I had slept little. My thoughts kept me awake, and I made notes early in the morning. Then went walking. I walked with difficulty from bodily weakness, but had thoughts that were vital, important, necessary, for myself, of course. I clearly conceived of how to compose the work, "There Are No Guilty in the World," [1] and a couple of other things. General conversation, then a talk with Chertkov about Gradovski's letter,[2] which was bad and unpleasant for him.

The insanity, the pathetic insanity of people in our world is becoming more and more clear to me. I had a good ride with Egor to Izvekovo.[3] Said goodbye to Andriusha, admitting that we do not understand each other, and that this is too bad. Yes, I forgot, I revised the preface again, I think for the last time. I feel good in my soul now, but this morning it was extraordinary. To be noted:

1) The more I live, the less I understand the material world and on the other hand the more I am aware of what one cannot understand but must only be aware of.

2) There is one and only one salvation from the misery of our life: to admit the *complete* insanity of our life and repudiate it completely.

3) The Christian ideal of our time is complete chastity. To recognize marriage as something sacred, even good, is a repudiation of the ideal. Christian consecration, if one recognizes the act of consecration, can be only the consecration of oneself to complete celibacy, and certainly not to permissible sexual intercourse, and the vow cannot be to be true to one's consort but for both to vow only chastity, which includes faithfulness to one another. "But what about the human race?" I do not know. I know only that just as the animal law of struggle, far from being binding for man, is on the contrary, opposed by the ideal of love, so I know in the same way that the law of copulation, which is the proper attitude of animals, is not binding for man, but that the contrary ideal of chastity is binding. And what will come of this? I do not know. But I know for certain that if I follow the highest strivings of my being, for love and chastity, only good can come of it.

4) Suicides cannot be helped when people have nothing to rely on, when they do not know who they are and why they live, and are moreover sure that this cannot be known.

5) I must put in a long excerpt from a notebook, which relates to suicide.

6) Very important: The concept of creation was engraved on the minds of men, requiring answers to the question: how did the world appear in time? the creation of the world (Darwin), and also another similar ques-

tion, about the origin of evil (the sin of Adam, heredity). Both are blatant superstitions. The world did not originate, but I am, and there is no evil, but again I am.

Of course people couldn't have spoiled human life and have made of essentially good human life, a life which is bad. They could only do what they have done: temporarily spoil the life of the present generations, but they have involuntarily introduced into life something which will force it swiftly forward. They have done and are doing great evil by their irreligious corruption of the people; but by their inventions, which are harmful to them and their generation, they involuntarily bring something that will unite all people. They corrupt the people, but they are corrupting everyone, the Indians, the Chinese, the Negroes, everyone. Mediaeval theology or Roman corruption corrupted only their own people, the minority of mankind, but now electricity, railroads, the telegraph, the press corrupt everyone. Everyone absorbs and can not help absorbing all this, and all suffer identically and are identically obliged to change their ways of life. All are obliged to change in their lives the main thing, their understanding of life, their religion.

Machines, to do what? Telegraphs, telephones, to transmit what? Schools, universities, academies, to teach what? Meetings, to discuss what? Books and newspapers, to spread information about what? Railroads, for whom to travel and where?

Millions of people are gathered together and subjected to one authority, to do what? Hospitals, physicians, pharmacists, to prolong lives but to prolong lives for what?

Millions suffer physically and spiritually only so that those who have seized power may live in corruption without interference. That is what it's all for, the deceit of religion, the deceit of science, the stupor from intoxication and from education; and when this is not enough, then there's brute force, prisons and executions.

For the sake of God, or not even for Him, for your own sake, come to your senses. *Understand all the folly of your lives*. Renounce, if only for a little while the trifles which fill your time and seem so important to you: all your millions, your looting, your preparations for murder, your parliaments, sciences, churches. Break with all this, if only for a little while, and look at your lives, above all at yourselves, at your souls, which live such an uncertain and brief term in this body. Come to your senses, look at yourself and at the life around you, and understand all your folly, and be horrified by it. Be horrified and seek salvation from it. But you do not have to seek it. It is in the soul of each of you. Only come to your senses, understand who you are, and ask yourselves just what it is that you need. And the answer, the same for everyone, will appear to you of itself. The answer lies only in that faith alone which is applicable to us and to our time, faith in God and in His revealed law—not revealed, but put into the soul of each of us—His law of love, of real love, of love for one's enemies, the one that was recognized and could not help being recognized by all the great teachers of the world, and which is so definitely and clearly expressed in the faith to which we profess to adhere and think that we do adhere. Only come to your senses for a little while, and it will be clear to you that the important, the only important thing in life is not what is outside you but only what is in you, what you need. Just understand that you need nothing, nothing at all except to *save your soul*, that only in this way can we save the world. *Amen*.

And it all comes from that most dreadful, most fatal, and most widespread false belief, the one held by all those who live without faith, that men are able to arrange life, and if it were only their own, but they are all arranging the lives of other people, of families, classes, and nations. This false belief is so pernicious because the force of the Soul which is given to man to perfect himself is all expended to *arrange* his life, and not only that, but the lives of others.

96

Sleepiness and weakness again. I can barely move and do not feel like writing anything. But as I walked I jotted down something which seems important to me, and thank goodness I feel no anger and it is easy not to sin. Chertkov copied the preface and looked it over for me; I do not feel like working on that. If God wills me to write, I shall write both "Insanity" and "There Are No Guilty in the World." I went riding on Mongol. A letter from Sasha. The Abrikosovs were here, dear Khrisanf. Must make notes. Now I have to get up and go over to the bed for the note-book, and it is hard to stand up. To be noted:

1) *The false notion of evil. There is no evil.* Life is Good. Evil, the absence of good, is only a sign of confusion, of error. Time exists only so that we may see our errors and correct them, and have joy (the highest good) in correcting our errors. If we do not correct them, then they will be corrected despite our will by death.

But life is Good, and there is no evil. There are only our errors: the general ones and our personal ones. And we are given the joy not only to correct them through time but to make use of all the experience which humanity has accumulated.

May 12, i.I l., a reservation which is becoming more and more necessary.

Alive. This morning went walking and thought well. Then felt weak and did nothing. I only read "On Religion," and found out something new about Chinese religion; it stimulates my ideas. Went riding with Bulgakov. It is depressing at home for several reasons. A little note from Sasha. I talked with a shopkeeper and a village policeman.[1] To be noted:

1) How easy it is for individuals and whole peoples to acquire what is called civilization, real civilization! To pass through the university, clean one's nails, make use of the services of a tailor and a hairdresser, travel abroad, and there you have your most civilized man. And for whole peoples, more railroads, academies, factories, dreadnaughts, fortresses, newspapers, books, parties, parliaments —and you have your civilized nation. That is why they are after civilization, both individuals and nations, for civilization, but not for real enlightenment. The first is easy, requires no effort, and wins approval, while the second, on the other hand, requires concentrated effort and not only does not win approval but is always despised and hated by the majority because it reveals the lie in civilization.

2) We call evil what displeases our body: a vicious dog or horse, a bad pen (which does not write), a wicked table for a child (into which it bumped) an evil man or an evil God.

3) The danger of invasion destroys the religious rigidity of the East. Hence obvious gains for militarism.

May 13

To be noted:
1) I only need to say that the majority wait for work as if it were charity, and this will make clear how horrible our life is, in its immorality, its stupidity, its danger, and its misery.

2) The situation in medicine is the same as in all the sciences: It has gone a long way without examining itself; a few know unnecessary subtleties; and the people ignore elementary hygiene.

3) However much I have tried to live only in God's sight, I cannot. I do not say that I am concerned about the judgment of others, I do not say that I love them, but there is no doubt that I feel them, in an arbitrary and

irresistable way, just as I feel my body, although more weakly and in another way. (This is true.)

I slept a lot and, as is always the case when I do, I got up feeling very weak. I went walking and was in the hospital during consultation. It was interesting. Again wrote nothing. I had a good talk with some teachers.[1] Tania's stepsons came[2]—rather nice. The evening was pleasant; I talked with Dushan and Bulgakov.

To be noted:

4) The clearest evidence that evil is a false notion is that death is regarded as an evil. As for me, I know that it is not an evil.

May 14 I : 112

My side hurt. I got up feeling cheerful, and walked a lot. I did not take any notes. At home I read Veresaev[1] and Semionov,[2] and after lunch I walked to Zheliabukha. The walk was nice. Chertkov came along, and Tania drove over. I had a good talk with the peasants, mostly jokingly affectionate. At home I slept. Gorbov[3] is a civilized merchant, very boring.

1) How wonderful it would be to be in a position to answer the question "How do you feel?" sincerely. I do not know, it does not concern me.

A good letter from Sasha. I am lying down as soon as I write an answer to Leonid Semionov.[4]

May 15 I : 113

Weak all day. I did no work; I did not even open a book. I talked a lot with the people. There was a dull gentleman here. All the household is very nice. There was something unimportant that I wanted to note down, but

I have forgotten it. Chertkov and Tania are demanding that I give them the comedy,[1] but I cannot do it, it is so bad.

May 16

Sick all day, heartburn and weakness. I did nothing, did not eat or go out.

May 17

A bit better today. A good letter from Sasha. I walked a little this morning and read Reville.[1] Interesting; stimulates my thinking. I had dinner in the dining hall. This evening there were guests, and I played cards. It was boring. Not very interesting letters, but they call for answers and attention. Am going to bed at eleven.

May 18

Today I feel completely well, both in body and soul. I walked a while. I revised the play, but it is still bad. I got a sweet letter, very moving, from Ugriumova,[1] and I wrote her a long one. I slept before dinner. And the evening was as usual.

I am still reading Reville and there is a lot that is interesting. Among the Hottentots, if the chief judge pronounces a death sentence, his hand must be the first to strike the prisoner. They say very well that a man must live like the moon, one month; *vivre en mourant et mourir en vivant*.[2] Reville is a very naïve writer; he considers people completely uncivilized if they live without recognizing property or the state. This reading has suggested many thoughts to me:

1) Religious truth is the awareness within oneself of an invisible principle, giving life to all, and the drive to satisfy the demands of this principle, which all may know as well as those who are expecially perceptive. And everywhere it is the same: people unite to express this higher principle; these united peoples under the influence of lust and passions pervert their conception of this principle and its requirements; and the union of some people serves as the basis and cause for their withdrawal from the requirements that they were aware of.

Then again there emerges a clearer expression of the religious principle and its requirements, and some larger groups submit to it, are again perverted, and again the situation becomes worse. And then a still higher, more general, and clearer expression of the demands of religious consciousness is required. Again a greater number of people submit to this higher consciousness, and are again perverted. But each time a greater number, living a common life, improves its life materially more and more. So that constantly, as this understanding of religious truth grows, and as the number of people who accept this truth increases, the truth is uniformly perverted and the material gains of life are increased. The number of people united together increases, and so does communication between them.

So it has been up until our time, to the utmost extent. Half, if not more, of the population of the earth is in close communication, their material achievements are immense, while the last highest truth, Christian or Mohammedan, is perverted to the utmost. (I thought all this out better, and if God permits I shall express it more understandably; this is not the way it should be).

The second point that occurred to me from reading Reville:

2) I feel how beneficial it is for the soul to study or survey the life, especially the spiritual life, of all the

peoples of the earth. Among how many billions who have lived, now live or shall live, I am living, an insignificant, pitiful, worthless being, scarcely conscious of myself. What insanity to think that I, my material "I," has any significance among these billions on billions who have lived or are living, most of whom are superior to me in mind and soul. If I am anything, it is only to the extent that I am divine, in God's sight and in my own.

3) How difficult, but how good and joyous it is to live completely independently of the judgments of others, but only in the sight of one's own consciousness of God. Sometimes I experience this, and how good it is!

4) Memory? How often memory is mistaken for intelligence. People do not see that memory excludes intelligence and is incompatible with that kind of intelligence which solves problems independently. One is a substitute for the other.

May 19

Last day in Kochety. It was very pleasant, except for living the life of seigneurs, well organized as it is, alleviated by just and kind treatment, but still a horrible, crying contrast which never ceases to torment me.

I corrected the play and did nothing else. My health is good. Some photographs were taken.[1] Something is noted down, but I shall not copy it in as it is late and I am tired. I slept barely three hours last night, but all day I felt very well.

May 20, i.I l.

Alive. I slept about three hours again even less, but my head feels fresh and I am cheerful. I went for a long walk. I thought a lot last night and jotted down a few things. I looked over the comedy; it is completely bad. Last night I prayed with the prayer that has recently become my favorite: "Lord, help me to live independently of people's judgments, only in Thy sight, with Thee and through Thee." To be noted:

1) "Help me, Lord, to live, fulfilling only Thy will." What does this mean? First, that I, an individual capable of thinking only within the limits of space and time, involuntarily conceive of an invisible Source, which gives life to all, also as a personality, and I cannot help conceiving of it. Secondly, that I want nothing, or want more than anything to be united with this Source, and I wish to remove anything which would hinder this unity. (It did not turn out right, and I thought it was so strong and so new!)

2) The peasants think that they must lie, and they prefer, everything being equal, to lie rather than to tell the truth. This is because they have been taught to do this, since people always lie when they talk to them or about them.

3) The source of all life is within me. I know this, not because I have studied the world but because I feel the whole world, live through the whole world and I feel it, even when I am conscious of my limitations in time and space.

I am aware of myself completely clearly within the limits of my body; of others, who live simultaneously and in the same place with me, less clearly; and less clearly still of those who are separated from me by time and space, but I still not only know about them, but I feel them. Still less clearly I feel animals, and even less than that inanimate objects. Yet I not only know all these, but I feel them through that sole source which gives life to all the world.

4) The professor very seriously describes the "Taboo," and is horrified by the lack of civilization among the "savages," but he himself acknowledges the Taboo of property, sacred property, property of land.

5) You must climb up to the point from which you can view yourself. Everything lies in this.

6) What we call reality is a dream which continues all our lives and from which we awaken only slightly in old age (we are roused to an understanding of the more real reality), and we awaken completely at death.

7) What a high moral way of life we find in all peasant families, when the adult gives all his earnings to support the old and the children.

May 22

Went walking, and thought.

1) In your relations with someone, do not be concerned with his recognizing that there is love in your attitude toward him, but rather with whether you feel true love for him (very important).

II) The whole matter is really very simple. Conquerors, murderers, and looters have subjugated the workers. As they have the power to dispose of their labor, they make their assistants in looting out of some of those they have subjugated and give them a share of the loot for helping them to spread, maintain, and strengthen their power. What was done simply and openly in ancient times is done deceitfully and secretly now. Among the subjugated there can always be found those who do not shun participating in looting; often, especially now, not aware what they do, they help to enslave their brothers for gain. This happens today, from the executioner, the soldier, the gendarme, the jailer, to the senator, the minister, the banker, the member of parliament, the professor, the arch-priest. And obviously it can only end, first, by an understanding of this deceit and, secondly, by such a high moral development that they will reject their gains so as not to participate in enslaving and causing suffering to their neighbors.

III, 1) One man seeks the truth and finds it himself. Subdivision: a) He who seeks the truth and is satisfied with what he has found, and b) He who is not satisfied and never stops seeking.

2) He who seeks the truth, but not through his own mind and effort but through the searchings of others, and boldly follows what others have found. Subdivision: a) adheres to one faith for all time, b) changes his faith.

3) He who does not seek the truth, but takes whatever comes into his head or happens by, and sticks to it, so long as it does not interfere with his life.

4) He who does not seek but adheres to whatever he happens on out of a sense of propriety. Subdivision: a) religious, b) scientific.

5) He who does not admit any truth. Subdivision: a) admits that he does not, b) does not admit it.

Skipped May 21. I felt just as well. Did little work. Went riding. The village women were complaining; I told Sonia.[1] Andrei and Seriozha were here that evening. I left them early.

Today is May 22. I woke up early and noted down what Bulgakov had copied. I walked along the Zaseka, got lost, and came out at the lieutenant's. I feel very tired. I corrected the play; it is a little better, but still poor. There were a mass of peitioners. Apparently I did not do very badly applying the rule of being concerned about my own spiritual condition, not their opinions. Ivan Ivanovich came for dinner, bringing some proofs, and then a wonderful objector who had suffered for eight and a half years came from Tula District. I asked Bulgakov to write down his story, and I gave him (his name is Fokin) ten rubles.

I had an unpleasant talk with Sonia. I did not behave well. She did everything I asked. It is eleven o'clock; am going to bed.

May 24

Yesterday, May 23, I did not write, but the day was an interesting one. I worked on the booklets, and rode over to Ivan Ivanovich. Andrei and Mitasha[1] were at dinner. A serious, intelligent young man, ready to become an objector, came this evening,[2] then Bulygin, Goldenweizer, Alesha Sergeenko,[3] Skipetrov,[4] Nikolaev. I felt depressed. It is tormenting to talk and talk—because one is obliged to.

Today is the 24th. I got up early, and now it is seven o'clock. To be noted:

1) People come to see a man who has gained a reputation for the contents and the clarity of expression of his thought, and they do not let him utter a word, but talk and tell him either what is much clearer to them or things he has long ago proven to be absurd.

I walked a long way, thought, looked, smelled, and picked flowers. I feel very well in my soul, as if I were alone with God. At home I growled at Ilia Vasilievich.[5] I revised the booklets about "God," "Renunciation," and "Humility." The play is still bad, but I gave it to be read. I rode with Dushan through the woods. This evening Maksimchuk, Skipetrov, Alesha Sergeenko, and Goldenweizer came, and I had a good talk on the balcony. It is after eleven, am going to bed.

Am well. I walked a little. My mind works slowly. I carefully revised and looked over the *booklets*, and they are not bad. I brought them over to Ivan Ivanovich. I wrote one letter, and I received a letter from Gusev[1] and a book, *Christenthum und Monistische Religion*.[2] It is all the same: I do not want to think. I feel that I am very bad, thank God. A letter from Sasha. Seriozha arrived. I have nothing to note, a sign of the weakness of the brain. Yes, a young teacher was here this morning threatening to commit suicide. I did not behave well with him.

I skipped May 26. Today is May 27.

I got up early yesterday. I remember that I behaved badly with the petitioners. I worked quite a lot on the books, and finished five and made progress on two others. I rode a little with Dushan. Sasha is coming. Last evening I read a good article by Vipper about Rome.[1] I would like to write about the soldier who killed a man.[2] Early in the morning, no, last night, I woke up and made notes about a very strong new feeling:

1) For the first time I felt vividly the arbitrariness of this whole world. Why should I, so clear, simple, rational, and good, live in this confused, complex, insane, evil world? Why?

2) (On the courts) If only these miserable, stupid, coarse, self-satisfied evil-doers understood what they were doing when they sit in their uniforms at tables covered with green cloth and repeat and analyze with an air of importance senseless words, printed in vile books which are a shame to humanity! If only they could understand that what they call law is crass mockery of those eternal laws which are engraved in the hearts of all people. A

man who without any evil design shot at a bird in a place which is called a church is sent to forced labor for sacrilege but those who send them commit sacrilege without cease, live off sacrilege against what is most sacred in the world, human life. The Tsar teaches an innocent boy to kill, and they are Christians, those who do this. The soldier who ran away not wanting to serve because he does not need to. Oh, how I need and want to write about this.

27. Sasha arrived today. We both cried for joy. She is too cheerful; I am afraid. I am not in a good mood. But I *worked as well as I could.* Am going to lunch. I went riding with Bulgakov, then slept. A letter from Chertkov about Orlenev.[3] I must try to finish the play. Kolichka Gay[4] was here; he is nice. I listened to him in the evening. Sasha is good. Am going to sleep at eleven.

May 28, i.I l.

May 29

Alive, and skipped a whole day. Today is the 29th. I slept little yesterday. Went walking, took some notes, and worked on the booklets. Not very well pleased. Few letters. Bulgakov left. The evening was spent as usual. I must overcome my ill feelings toward Seriozha.

Today I got up early again, at six. I was very weak. I talked with Sonia; she was upset.[1] I was afraid, but, thank God, it was all right. Trubetskoi[2] arrived; he is very nice. I also did some work which was not bad. I finished all the booklets and gave them to Ivan Ivanovich. I talked a while in the evening. Restrained myself. I left at eleven. Now it is after eleven and I am going to bed. A little note from Tania. There are some things to be written down, but I shall not begin now.

The preface is no good at all. Been revising the play a little yesterday and today.

After my walk I revised the play and the preface. Both
are very poor. Went riding with Trubetskoi. A very independently intelligent person. I don't think there is anything to note. Yesterday evening I had an interesting
talk with Nikolaeva.[1]

Am going to bed; it is after eleven.

Skipped a day again. Today is June 1.

Yesterday I was not in a good mood. I don't think anything bad happened, although there were a lot of petitioners. Few letters, and I am ashamed to say that this
displeased me. I went on revising the play and the preface,
and I rode over to Teliatinki with Trubetskoi again. There
was a crowd of people, Gay, Zosia Stakhovich. They left
in the evening. Dimochka . . .

Today I slept a lot, and I made some pretty good revi-
sions, I think. Trubetskoi went riding with me, and I find
his flattery a bit suspicious and unpleasant. I have just
returned and am lying down to sleep. There was something good to be written down this morning, but I have
forgotten. It is eleven, and I am going to bed. Sasha makes
me happy. I have been reading Chernyshevski.[1] His pert-
ness in rendering coarse judgments against those who do
not think as he does is very instructive. I have a very
pleasant, kindly feeling toward Sonia, a very good one,
spiritually loving. I feel well in my soul, despite my in-
activity.

June 2. Slept a lot, and felt weak. I worked a while
again on two contrasting literary works: the preface, which
sets forth the faith by which I live, and the stupid, empty
comedy. Both are making some progress. I went riding
with Trubetskoi; the ride was very pleasant, but I am
bored by him and his flattery. Dinner. Unkindly feeling
toward Seriozha, which I do not fight sufficiently (not
Seriozha, but the feeling). But I have a very good feeling
toward Sonia. God help me. In the evening arrived a completely crazy lady who owns a gasoline engine and a
turnout *à l'anglaise* and *tout le tremblement*.[1]

Today, the 3rd, I got up early and immediately began
to revise both the play and the preface before getting
dressed. I went walking and am very tired. Then I worked
a bit more on both. To be noted:

1) I still cannot learn to live only for myself, only in His
sight, and to disregard the opinions of others. I cannot
learn, because what my soul demands in His sight is so
intertwined with my desire for the approval of others,
and in some cases they are so completely identical, that
they cannot be separated from the other. But how terribly
important it is: what weakness, anxiety, and uncertainty
you feel when you think of people's opinions, and what
freedom, tranquility and omnipotence when you live only
for yourself in His sight!

Went riding with Dushan. This evening I had a good
conversation with Nikolaev. I have the same feeling toward Seriozha, but I am struggling against it.

I got up early. I dealt with the petitioners very well
and went walking. Afterwards I wrote some letters, one
serious one as an answer about the epidemic of writing.[1]

I began working on the comedy, and put it aside in disgust. Revised the preface pretty well. I went out tired after working, and there were a dozen village women and I behaved badly, not to them, but I rebuked dear, self-effacing Dushan. Everything seemed disgusting.

I went riding with Dushan, and we had a good ride. On the way back I found the Cherkess bringing in Prokofi.[2] I felt terribly depressed, and I really thought of leaving.

June 5   I : 128

And now, today, on the morning of the 5th, I do not regard this impossible.

Dear, dear Tanichka has come. Couldn't repress a sob, when I talked with her. This was quite disgusting. Always myself, my pleasure, not my work. Then I went to Sonia and told her that everything was fine, and I did not have the least unkindly feeling against her. Lord, help me, and I thank Thee, Lord, not because Thou has helped me, but because by Thy will I am able to forgive, and love, and rejoice in this. Dinner. Olga Klodt, a "Tolstoyan," [1] and Bulgakov were here. All as usual, and the same feeling toward Seriozha, but I restrained myself. He is intolerably self-assured. This is instructive: how through this self-assurance, people deprive themselves of the highest good of all, love. To be noted:

1) You tell a man he should work, and he says, "I do not want to." And if you say that everyone should work, "Then let all those rich men, who don't do anything, set me an example. If they go to work, then I will too, but without them I don't want to."

2) To be put in *The Wisdom of Children*, the story of how a child ate a cake by mistake and did not know what to do, and how he was taught to repent.[2]

3) Yes, we must learn how to love as people learn to play the violin. But can we do this when someone is repel-

lent in all his being and with that so self-assured? You want to despise him, which is the opposite of love. Avoid him? Yes, but you must be ready to love him. And for this, 1) you must search well in order to find out if there is not something personal in your dislike, whether your vanity was offended, etc. 2) you must not permit yourself to remember and dwell on unkind thoughts about him.

4) How precious the story of Parasha the fool is.[3]

Today is the fifth. In the morning I got up early, feeling weak, and wrote in the diary. Lord help me, help me.

I behaved badly all day. I did nothing, and all day I pitied myself and wanted others to pity me. I wanted to cry, and blamed everybody else, like a spoiled child. But I tried to restrain myself. Only at dinner I said that I wanted to die. I do want to very much, and I cannot help wishing for it. Goldenweizer played in the evening, very well, but I remained unmoved. I rode horseback and sat for Trubetskoi.

June 6   I : 129

And again the same state of sadness and self-pity. I walked to the "Zakaz" woods[1] and I met a boy who asked me if he could pass through, as the Cherkess beats people. And I became so depressed! I had some very good thoughts, but all disconnected and confused. I worked some on the preface; I couldn't on the comedy. A good letter from Chertkov. Some workers from the Prechistenski worker's school [2] came after lunch, and I had a very good talk with them. Then Dima came over with people from Teliatinki. There was dancing and another good talk with some peasants.[3] Goldenweizer came in the evening. I am on better terms with Seriozha. I went to bed late, very depressed. A strange state, as if I had something in my brain. The same weakness. I keep wanting to pity myself, which is not good.

I slept badly, very little. I revised the preface. Then I spoke to Sofia Andreevna about the Cherkess, and again she is upset and irritated. Very depressing; I keep wanting to cry. I rode over to the lieutenant's. There was this woman, the mother of a murderer.[1] I wrote a letter to the papers.[2] Nikolaev came in the evening; he argued rather incoherently. Nikitin.[3]

Skipped two days. Was ill and extraordinarily weak, especially on the eighth.[1] It's so simple, close to death. The eighth, did nothing except for some trifling letters. A girl came on crutches, to make some vague demands of me, as always. The doctors annoyed me, especially Nikitin, with his belief in his superstition and his desire to convince others of it.[2] I wrote very badly to the newspapers about my inability to give financial help, but I shall not send it. There is no need. Orlenev was here; he is awful. Nothing but vanity, and of the basest physical kind.[3] Simply dreadful. Chertkov compares him rightly with Sytin.[4] It is very possible that there is a spark in both of them, it is even certain that there is, but I have not the power to see it.

On the tenth I was a little better and could work again on the preface. I read a lot about Babism,[5] and I kept feeling badly about myself. This devil is holding on to me, I just cannot drive him away. But even if I cannot, still I know that it is a devil, not myself, and that is good. I did not go out; it is cold too. Today, the tenth, I woke up early, but I did not sleep badly. I feel much fresher. I would even say completely well, except for my headache. Now it is after seven in the morning.

The day before yesterday I revised the preface. Nothing happened that's worth remembering. I went riding with Bulgakov, yesterday too. I had a depressing time with the two girls; they were pathetic, but could not be helped in any way, and they took up my time.

I have decided to go to the Chertkovs.[1] Sasha was planning to come, but changed her mind.

(Otradnoe) Today, the 12th, Sasha came too. I am afraid for her. We had an easy trip. Now it is midnight; I am writing at the Chertkovs, and Sasha is by my side. I did nothing at all. There is a lot to be noted. Yes: in the morning I walked over to see the girls but it was of no avail. I also went to Nikolaev's, to smooth over our dispute.

Slept well. The preface again in the morning. I walked in the morning and midday to Meshcherskoe;[1] enjoyed it. Sasha is not well and is having a dull time, poor girl. What is striking around here is the wealth of Zemstvo institutions, orphanages, hospitals, but still the same poverty. I revised the preface again in the evening. I feel well in my soul; I am particularly affected by the prayer of gratitude, only gratitude for life at present. Yes, I thank Him who has given me life and all its blessings, the spiritual ones, of course, which I do not know how to make use of, but even for physical ones, for all this beauty, and for love, for affections, for joy in communicating with others. Just remember that you have been given the blessing of being a man, which you have not in any way deserved, and immediately you will feel well and happy. Now it is midnight.

I am writing in another book. I asked Chertkov to copy from the notebook:

1) [1]

2) The heart shows us what to love and therefore what we should think of, what we should study.

3) Evil is only retreat from the law, and so is death.

4) We are not permitted to know what will happen after death; but what goodness is, we can and do know.

5) How natural that enlightened people conceal their whole bodies, especially women, leaving exposed only what bears the impress of spirituality, the face. Nakedness of the body is now a sign of decay. The same should be true of men.

6) I am in a very strong, inspired prayerful mood, I want to pray. And I am trying to pray in this way: Help me to be with Thee, to do Thy work, and to overcome all that is evil in myself. Whatever I may think of is not what is right or necessary, and I am aware that I have nothing to ask for, that whatever I might ask for has been given me and is in me. I can only do one thing, be thankful.

7) What can unite people is the understanding that one religion, one understanding of life, can unite us. But there is no such religion among the churches and the Babists, but only a striving for such a united religion. What hinders unity is, first, that people do not understand that this unity is their goal, and secondly, and chiefly, they may understand it, but hold that the unifying religion is found, and that it is Catholicism, Babism, etc.

True religion is first of all the search for religion.

8) I met an Estonian salesclerk, an efficient, sober, handsome man, and for the first time I really understood the meaning of "Russia": the Horde, which has grabbed nations, good ones, superior to the Horde morally and intellectually, and which now takes pride in this and uses all her strength to hold the conquered. However repulsive

the action itself, even more repulsive is the justification celebrated as "patriotism."

June 14, 1910. I am beginning a new copybook at the Chertkovs. I walked through the meadows and worked on the preface. I looked through the old diary. For seven months now I have been working only on this; can it be only a trifle?[1] Letters, not very interesting ones. I walked to Liubuchany to see the madmen.[2] One was very interesting: "I did not steal, I took." I said something about the other world, and he answered, "The world is one." This madman is on a much higher level than many people who are considered sane. Slept and then had dinner. Worked some this evening. Then a Czech[3] came with questions about pedagogy; we had a good talk, only it was inconvenient having it taken down. Am going to bed.

June 15   I : 135

I went walking and then I felt weak and did almost nothing all day. I corrected "December," scribbled on the preface, and read "The Notes of a Lackey." More and more I recognize the futility of writing, of all writing and especially of my own, but I cannot help speaking out.

To be noted:

1) Education has its foundation in religious training by transmitting to children in the most accessible and simple form the main concepts of life and the rules of conduct resulting from these concepts, and which have been worked out identically by all of mankind. But instead of this they instil, actually *instil,* into children a religious doctrine which is outworn, distorted, and not in accordance with other doctrines, and which those who are teaching it do not believe in themselves. This is true of all the major religious doctrines: Brahmanism, Judaism, Buddhism, Taoism, Christianity, Mohammedanism. What a dreadful crime!

2) Terrible to say, but what can be done if it is true, that however much you wish to live only for the soul, for God, you are in doubt and undecided about many, many questions. The only salvation is to do at the present moment what seems best for God and your soul, without answering the questions.

It is a great and harmful delusion to think that you can live without mistakes or without sin.

June 16 I : 136

I got up rather late, and felt the same weakness. I went walking; everyone is affectionate. I am depressed because Sasha is depressed. As I was walking a young man came up and said that I tell fortunes and he asked me to tell his. And a woman with the same thing; also that her husband drinks. I was in a very bad mood yesterday; I saw everything *en noir*. And that is a good thing. You can feel for yourself what you see in others when they are in bad spirits, and you understand them and not only forgive them but do not even condemn them. I do not feel like writing anything. All that I have written seems not only worthless but bad, and I have no desire to write. That is good too. How imperceptibly and easily I am approaching death, and again I feel only gratitude. At three o'clock I walked to Meshcherskoe to see the madmen,[1] and Chertkov drove me the rest of the way. I walked through all the wards. I have not yet analysed my impressions, and therefore I am not writing anything, but I am less impressed than I expected to be. I worked a little correcting the booklet, "On Sins, Temptations, and Superstitions"; I very much want to get rid of this work. Sasha is better. Uninteresting letters. I read Kuprin;[2] he is very talented. "Measles" is not sustained, but the imagery is vivid, true to life, and simple.

June 17, i.I l.

Alive. My head felt a little fresher this morning. I worked on the preface and the booklet "Sins," then rode to Troitskoe[1] with Chertkov. I had a pleasant dream that dogs were licking me affectionately. The evening was empty. I am going to bed, it is after 11. I had a very good talk with dear Sasha. I received a letter from Sonia; I must write her. I want to write a great deal, and am also indifferent as to whether I shall be able to.

I slept little but worked a little better, nevertheless. I revised three booklets. Dictated a bad letter to Belgrade[1] and looked over the preface again, I hope for the last time. I rode to Meshcherskoe and Ivino with Chertkov;[2] sick women. A peasant writer, nice.[3] And some cheerful women; one especially was exactly like everyone else. There was an invitation from Troitskoe to go to a moving picture show. I slept, dined, and in the evening there was chess. I wrote Sonia. There is nothing to note. There was one good letter.

I slept for a long time and am excited. I thought of an important change in the preface, and finished my letter to the Slavic Congress. Now it is after one. To be noted:

1) It is not solitary, disconnected, personal, stupid insanity that is terrible, but the general, organized, social, intelligent insanity of our world.

2) Pascal said that if dreams were as sequential as events in waking life, we would not know what is sleep

and what wakefulness. But I say that if the insanity of the most insane man were the insanity of all in general, and if the insanity in the life of us all were the insanity of only one man, then we would not know which one is living the insane life and which the rational one.

3) Almost every action before us, if we think of it seriously, gives rise to indecisiveness. The matter is solved because at the actual moment one cannot help acting. And therefore thought is precious; it prepares the way for a decision one way or the other.

I rode with Chertkov to Troitskoe. It is extraordinarily clean, spacious, and full of conveniences. We visited 1) men under observation. There was an expropriator who had defended the use of force, an Old Believer sentenced to death, and later to twenty years' forced labor for murder, and then a parricide; 2) the disturbed patients, 3) the semi-calm patients, and 4) the weak ones, also the women's section. The women under observation and the disturbed women were particularly depressing.

We found out at home that Chertkov would be "permitted" to be at Teliatinki during his mother's stay.[1] I had a bath. There were songs, Sasha accompanying them.

June 20   I : 140

I got up feeling cheerful. I revised the letter to the Slavs and the preface, and I wrote "The Wisdom of Children." I want to try consciously to contend with Sonia, using goodness and love. From a distance it seems possible; I shall try to do it when she is close by as well. My spirits are in very good shape. The prayer of gratitude is no longer so effective; now I am using the prayer of universal love, love not only toward those with whom I come close, but with everyone in the whole world, and it works. Other prayers: not to be concerned with other people's condemnation, and to be grateful, have left palpable, joyous traces. Now it is after twelve, and I want to try to write Parasha.

I rode over to Meshcherskoe to the cinematograph. Dull and very silly and purposeless. There were many people here in the evening, including dear Buturlin.[1]

June 21

I have just come in from a walk. I feel like dictating to Sasha, but to be noted:

1) We are given one blessing: love, which cannot be taken away from us. Only love, and all joys will be yours, the sky, the trees, people, and even yourself. But we look for happiness everywhere except in love, in riches, power, glory, exclusive love. This search, far from bringing happiness, is certain to deprive us of it.

I dictated my meeting with Aleksander and how he immediately promised not to drink.[1] Then I worked a lot on the proofs and corrected three booklets, not badly. Strakhov[2] and also a Skopets[3] were here. I talked a lot with the Skopets, or rather listened to him. Berkenheim[4] came too. I did not go walking. I read aloud "On Suicide," [5] and corrected it, then had a short nap. Orlenev read Nikitin;[6] it was alien to me. We went to Troitskoe;[7] there is a wealth of luxury there, the cinema. Sasha had a headache, and I was depressed and bored. The cinema is trashy and false.

June 22

I got up early, having slept rather little. Let us see what will happen, within me, not outside me. God help me. Yes, yesterday dear Aleksander came over for books. He said, "I told my mother. She is glad and thanks you."

I did almost no work; I finished the booklets and went to sleep. Rode with Chertkov over to Liubuchany. There we visited a factory, a product of madness.[1] A crazy Old Believer, and the doctors from Troitskoe. Molochnikov came. In the evening Strakhov read an article about the ideal of Christianity; it's good. Am going to bed. A telegram from Iasnaia, distressing.[2]

June 23, i.I l.

June 23   I : 143

Alive. Now it is seven in the morning. Last night I had only just lain down and had not yet gone to sleep when a telegram arrived saying, "I beg you to come the 23rd."[1] I shall go and am glad of a chance to do my duty. God help me.

(Iasnaia Poliana) I found things worse than I had expected: hysterics and excitability.[2] It cannot be described. I did not behave too badly but was not gentle enough.

June 24   I : 144

Iasnaia Poliana. There is a lot to be noted.

I got up, having slept little. Went walking. Sonia had come in during the night; she could not sleep. She came to me in the morning, still upset, but she is calming down.

1) I went out walking after a tormenting conversation with Sonia. In front of the house there were flowers and barefoot healthy girls cleaning. Later they would turn to the hay, or to picking berries. Gay, calm, healthy. I would like to write two scenes.

I reread the letters and wrote an answer about drinking bouts. Nothing special happened in the evening. Calm.

I got up early and wrote about insanity, also some letters. And suddenly Sonia was in an excited, hysterical condition again. It was very painful. I drove with her to Ovsiannikovo, and she quieted down.[1] I was silent, but I could not be kind and affectionate, I was not able to. In the evening Goldenweizer and Nikolaeva[2] were here, and Maria Aleksandrovna. I do not feel well in my soul somehow. Ashamed of something. Am going to bed, it is after eleven.

Got up early, and went walking and lost my cap. At home wrote letters and only read over "On Insanity," and started to write, but I did not finish. Went riding. It began to rain, so I returned home. Sonia again was upset,[1] and again the same suffering for both of us.

Lord, help me. This is an occasion to pray. 1) Only in the sight of God. 2) Action entirely in the present. And I do not act. 3) I thank Thee for this trial.

Yesterday she talked about moving somewhere. I did not sleep last night, and am very tired. I went walking and thought about only one thing. There is an obligation to God and men which I must fulfill these last days or hours of my life, and therefore I must be firm. *Fais ce que doit, advienne que pourra.*

I am reading *Psychiatry.*[1] How obtuse, often just stupid.

In order to explain consciousness, it speaks of the subjective and the objective, as if the word "subjective" were something other than a bad name for consciousness. And so it all goes. To be noted:

1) How ridiculous to think that matter could be the most comprehensible concept and the basis of everything, while it is only a means of communication for the spiritual source, which is divided within itself. (So I wrote it at first.) I should add that matter, along with movement, is only a means of communication for the spiritual source, which is divided within itself.

2) As there is no sharp division between sleep and waking, so there is no such division between rational life and insanity. Being further from sleep and closer to waking, or further from insanity and closer to a rational life, depends on consciousness' being more or less aroused and thus on capability of moral effort.

3) A man who lives not for himself but to fulfill the law of God, in addition to those consequences of his good deeds which he may perceive, creates infinitely more important consequences which he cannot see. So a bee, that gathers honey for its family, impregnates the plants, and these plants are necessary not only for its own species but for thousands of others.

4) As I walk I pick wonderful flowers and throw them away, there are so many of them. The same is true of the wonderful spiritual flowers of life. We do not value them because there are so many of them.

5) Three hourly prayers: 1) I want to live only for Thee and in Thy sight, and 2) live now, in the present, by love, and 3) I thank Thee for all that I do not deserve and am not worthy of. I was thinking about these prayers as I walked through the woods, and I lost my way and was frightened. And then I remembered the prayers. Yes, with Thee, and now I think only of being with Thee, and I rejoice and am thankful that I lost the way, and immediately I felt well.

6) The insane man kept saying to me, "I did not steal,

123

I took." And he is right. "Stolen" can be said only when someone takes something that belongs to everyone: the land, and the labor of another.

7) Insanity is always the consequence of an irrational and therefore immoral life.

This seems true, but I must think it over and verify it.

8) Insane people always attain their ends better than sane people. This is because they have no moral barriers: neither shame, nor truthfulness, nor conscience, nor even fear.

9) Individual beings feel that they are separated by what seems to us to be our bodies, matter, which would be inconceivable outside of space and movement, inconceivable outside of time. (I have not completely clarified this.)

June 28

I slept little. Sonia has been in a wonderful mood since this morning. She asked me not to go.[1] But then she had a letter from Chertkov, a very good letter, but she is still upset about him.[2] I talked with him and started to Iasenki instead of to Kozlovka. I just gasped and rushed home. We had a good trip. There were no horses; the telegram had not been sent on.[3] We waited three hours, then we came to Seriozha's. The woman journalist told an unpleasant story; good talks with some workers. At Seriozha's there was a crowd of people and it was dull and depressing. I went to the sexton's and talked with the village women. How can we live amid this terrible, intense need?

1) How strange that people are ashamed of their untidiness, cowardice, or lowly condition, but anger—no question of being ashamed of it: people rejoice in it, urge themselves on, whip it up, imagining that there is something good in it.

Iasnaia Poliana. We came back to Iasnaia on the 29th. Nothing special happened on the way. I parted pleasantly with Tania. My general impression is very good, on the whole. Sofia Andreevna is better. I am not completely well, although I cannot complain of being in a bad mood. Weakness and my head aches. This morning I received a copy of my *The Law of Love and the Law of Violence* in French, and some good letters. I read it with great interest, and I confess that I approved of it. It is useful to reread in order to avoid repetitions in what you write. I hope there will be no repetitions in "On Insanity" and I see it is worth writing, but I do not know if this is to be done. I speak of my strength. I slept a lot in the afternoon, and I still want to sleep. Had three visitors, all three very interesting and important. The first was Repin,[1] who is pathetic and has obviously lost his mental life, but I cannot regard him as a madman, and I see him as a man and a brother all the same, and I am glad that this comes naturally to me.

Then came dear Sutkovoi,[2] who was obviously embarrassed at disturbing me, and he and I had a good talk, or rather I did, as he expressed himself very little. Then Chertkov came too. Sofia Andreevna was extremely upset, but I see it will settle down. To be noted:

Beside the book *The Law of Love and the Law of Violence*, I received a brochure by a Frenchman, Polak, *La Politique de l'avenir prochain*. It is interesting to read because he is obviously a scholar abreast of the latest philosophic thought, and he is strikingly unclear and wrong in his understanding. It is enough to cite him that the three main activities of human life are: satisfaction of the feeling for beauty—art; satisfaction of the demands of reason—science, and at the end, in passing, morality. The more I read it, the more I felt the need of finishing "On Insanity."

To be noted. End of June 1910.

The fallacy of the church is in the belief that, supposedly, there were and there are such men who having gathered together and called themselves the Church, can decide once and for all, and for all men, how God and His Law are to be understood.

The fallacy of science, similar to the fallacy of the church, is in the belief that the knowledge acquired by a few men who have liberated themselves from the essential labors of life, is supposedly that knowledge—they call it "science"—which is necessary for all people!

The people feel a growing hatred for their persecutors, for the authorities, but they themselves serve their persecutors. Why is this? Because they are tempted and deceived by religious and scientific frauds.

The fallacy of evil. There is no evil. Life is a blessing. If it is not, then know that you are at fault. And you have been given time to correct your error, to have the joy (the highest blessing) of correcting your fault. That is the only reason for time. If you do not correct your fault, it will be corrected against your will—by death. Yes, life is a blessing. There is no evil! There are only our faults, faults in general and our personal ones, and we have been given the joy through time of correcting them. And there is the greatest joy in correcting them.

We have not progressed in religious understanding. We have the same animism, the same fetishism. In order to understand this, a man must only understand what demands and habits he has and what the demands of his human nature are. Reason and love define the demands of human nature. Then he must ascertain what have become the habitual demands of his nature. And the demands of reason and love must not be subordinated to the demands of habit, as is done now, but on the contrary he must ascertain on the basis of the demands of reason and love what is to be habitual. And then . . . Only imagine a man free of habit in any of the situations which a man of our society finds himself, whether he is a propertyless worker or belongs to the so-called rich upper classes. What would this man see in the world inhabited by us, who do not see or feel or understand all the horror and insanity of our lives?

Iasnaia Poliana. 1) The spiritual principle, which is divided within itself, recognizes that it is divided by what we call the body. It recognizes that it is also divided by what we call movement. The body is inseparable from space, and movement from time.

2) I dreamed that I was talking with Seriozha and told him:

Our life is a quest for gratification. There is physical gratification in health, in satisfying the lusts of the body, in wealth, sexual love, fame, honor, power. All these gratifications 1) are outside our control, 2) may be taken away from us at any moment by death, and 3) are not accessible to everyone. But there is another kind of gratification, the spiritual, the love for others, which 1) is always in our control, 2) is not taken from us by death, as we can die loving, and 3) not only is accessible to all, but the more people live for it, the more joy there will be.

I did not dream it in just this way; it was shorter and better. And in my dream, when I finished, I said, try to prove that this is not true . . . you couldn't. Seriozha and all the rest became silent.

4) Isn't it a strange thing that we understand least of all what we know best of all, or rather: we know best of all what we do not understand at all, our soul, and, one may say, God.

It's terrible, for three days, if not four, I haven't been writing. Yesterday and today I corrected proofs of the booklets. I do not remember the day before yesterday; I don't think I did anything except for some unimportant letters. Sofia Andreevna has calmed down completely.[1] Liova has come. His numerator is small, and his denominator is ∞.[2] I saw Lizaveta Ivanovna Chertkov,[3] and she visited us. She is very nice. Maria Aleksandrovna's house burned down; I am afraid that poor Repin[4] set fire to it. I talked with him; he is quite ill. Manifestations absurd, but I can sense the human being in him. Sutkovoi[5] and Kartushin[6] were here; as always with them, I felt a kind of incompleteness, not reaching the ultimate. Now it is the night of the fourth. I shall try not to skip days as I did this time. I feel weak and sick, and that is good.

I am writing after eleven. In the morning I went walking and did no work. Still weak. I was at Chertkov's. Bulygin and Kolichka Gay[1] came in the evening. A little easier with Leva. Sonia was again very much upset for no reason. God help me, and he does help. A few things to note:

1) That which gives us life, what we know in ourselves as limited by our body and therefore imperfect, we call the soul. That which is not limited by anything and therefore perfect we call God.

Life is striving to be united with that from which it has been separated, with other souls and with God and His perfection.

Got up early, still not feeling well. I said goodbye to Maria Aleksandrovna.[1] Sonia went bathing. I spoke with her, rather well. I could not work, I was too weak. Sonia drove over to see Zvegintseva;[2] too bad. Sutkovoi came in the evening, and I had a good talk with him. Lev is more than alien, but I am restraining myself. There is nothing to note. Am going to bed at midnight.

July 7, i.I l.

Alive, but a bad day. Bad because I have no energy and cannot work. Did not even correct proofs. I rode over to Chertkov's, and when I came home I found Sofia Andreevna in a nervous state and I could not quiet her. I read in the evening. Later Goldenweizer and Chertkov came over. Sonia had an explanation with him and still did not calm down. But late in the evening I had a very good talk with her. I hardly slept all night.

Today is July 8. A little more cheerful, and I thought well about the need for silence and for steadfastly pursuing my task. Went riding with Bulgakov to Maria Aleksandrovna's. I feel well in my soul. Sasha is ill and gloomy. Now it is five o'clock, and I am lying down. Dinner was quiet. I read in the evening and everything was better and better. In the evening Goldenweizer and Chertkov. All was well. I talked with Sutkovoi; he wants to "believe" in something which need not be believed. It is after eleven, and I am going to bed. I read a nice story by Mille, *"Repos hebdomadaire."* [1]

I slept a long time, and afterward I wrote with a feeling of satisfaction and worked on the proofs of the first five booklets. I went riding with Lev. Controlled myself. Came back wet through, which caused worry. After dinner Nikolaev, Goldenweizer and Chertkov. Feel depressed. Am bearing it up.

I woke up at five. Got up, but felt weak and lay down again. At nine walked to the village, to Kopylov's.[1] Gave them some money, quite simply and well. As I walked by Nikolaev's house, he came out and began to talk about justice. I told him that the concept of justice is an artificial one and unnecessary for a Christian. This line cannot be drawn in reality, it is fantastic and completely unnecessary for a Christian.

At home I wrote a long letter to a worker in response to his objection to "The Only Means." Went riding with Chertkov. He spoke about non-resistance in a strange way. I lay down, then woke up, and Davydov,[2] Kolichka Gay,[3] and Salomon[4] were there. I read an empty, pompous article by Salomon, *"Retour de l'enfant prodigue,"* and a marvellous story by Mille. Then Sutkovoi and Kartushin came to say goodbye. I am fond of them. To be noted:

1) One can lose faith in faith. Moreover, two faiths may contradict each other. Truth may be more outwardly manifest in faith than in consciousness, but on the other hand faiths are precarious and contradictory, whereas consciousness is one and unchanging.

I just had another talk about Chertkov, and I declined calmly.

July 11, i.I l.

1) For the first time I clearly understood all the significance of humility for one's life, one's freedom, and one's joy in life.

2) I am no good, and have lived badly, and failed in trying to arrange my life well. But if I have clearly understood, as others apparently do not, not even evil, but the errors of life, then how can I refrain from saying so, if only to redeem my bad life? Perhaps it will prove useful to someone.

3) When someone strikes you on one cheek and you turn the other to him, do not expect him who strikes you to recover his senses, stop hitting you and understand the significance of your act. No, quite on the contrary, he will say, "What a good thing I struck him! Now his patience shows that he feels his guilt and my superiority over him."

But this notwithstanding I know that the best thing you can do, when you are struck on one cheek, best for yourself and for all, is to turn the other. There is "complete joy" in this. Do so, and then you will feel only gratitude for what previously seemed a misfortune.

July 11. Am barely alive. A terrible night, until four in the morning.

And worst of all was Lev Lvovich; he scolded me as if I were a bad boy and ordered me to go into the garden after Sofia Andreevna.[1] Sergei arrived this morning. I did no work, except for one booklet: "Idleness." [2] I went walking and riding. I cannot look at Lev calmly, I am still in a bad state. Poor Sonia has calmed down. It is a cruel and distressing illness. Help me, Lord, to bear all this with love. So far I have borne it somehow. I saw Ivan Ivanovich on business matters. Now it is eleven; I am going to bed.

Still the same. A strange incident with Chertkov; through a mistake of Filia's[1] he was called over, and Sofia Andreevna was upset again. But it has passed by all right. She suffers very much, poor woman, and I do not need to make any effort to pity her lovingly. I went riding with Dushan. I saw Salomon[2] off in the evening and then went to bed, without waiting for the Sukhotins. Chertkov came over and I gave him a letter.

Today is the 13th. The Sukhotins are here. I wrote a booklet and went riding with Mikhail Sergeevich [Sukhotin] and Goldenweizer. Sonia is still very weak and does not eat, but she is controlling herself. God help her and me. I noted some things in the book.

A very painful night. I began writing her a letter in the morning; finished it, then came to her room. She demands the very things I promised and am giving her.[1] I do not know if it was a good thing, whether I wasn't too weak and conciliatory, but I could not act otherwise. They have gone for the diaries. She is in the same upset condition and does not eat or drink. I worked on the booklets and finished three, then rode over to Rudakovo.[2] I cannot be kind and affectionate to Lev; he understands and feels nothing. Sasha brought the diaries; she made two trips. And Sonia has calmed down and thanked me. Everything seems all right. I had a moving letter from

Batia [Chertkov]. I am going to bed, still not quite well and feeling weak. I feel well in my soul.

July 15, i.I l.

July 15   I : 162

I am alive, but it's hard. This morning there was disturbance, over the notion that I will run away, and that I should give her the keys to the diaries. I said that I would not alter what I had agreed to. It was very, very painful.[1] Before this I finished the proofs of the booklets. Only a part of one is left. I went riding with Dushan. In the evening an American[2], and Chertkov, and Goldenweizer, and Nikolaev were here. Sonia was calm, but her calmness seems to be hanging by a hair. Am going to bed; there are some things to be noted—later.

July 16   I : 163

Alive, but am physically in a bad way. I feel confident in my soul. Dear Misha Sukhotin and Tania left. Afterward Sonia left too. She slept, but the situation is threatening. I went walking and prayed well. I understood my sin against Lev; I should not take offence, but should love him. What an absurdity: to put on the same scale, as if one could outweigh the other, insult and love, not love for Ivan or love for Peter, but love as life in God, with God, and through God. I want to have a talk with him. The American writes and composes, but something quite empty, it seems.[1] As I returned from my walk, I came on him, and later met a teacher from Viatka and his wife.[2] He writes too, but he is very nice. I had a talk with him. I finished the last proof, and I wanted to start again on "Insanity," but was not up to it. Now I must copy out of the notebook:

1) We live an insane life and know in the depths of our hearts that we live insanely, but we keep on by habit and inertia, and we either do not want, or cannot change it, or both.

2) This I had noted: Today, July 13th, I rid myself of the feeling of insult and hostility toward Lev, and, secondly and most important, of my own self-pity. I must only be thankful to God for the mildness of His punishment, which I am bearing for all the sins of my youth, and the main sin, my sexual depravity when I married a pure girl. It serves you right, you dirty debauchee. I can only be grateful for the mildness of the punishment. And how much easier it is to bear the punishment when one knows this; one does not feel the burden. I went riding with Bulgakov a long way, and am tired. I slept, and then had dinner. Goldenweizer and Chertkov were here. The atmosphere was a depressing one. Sofia Andreevna behaved quite well. Goldenweizer played magnificently. There was a thunderstorm.

July 17

Slept little. I saw dear Tania off and went walking. When I returned, I could not do anything, so I read some letters and Pascal. I talked with Lev yesterday, and today he explained to me that I am in the wrong. I must be silent and try not to feel unkindly. Sasha left for Tula. Now it is midnight. I feel very, very weak, and have done no work at all. I read Pascal, who is wonderful, then rode over to see Chertkov. It went quite well.[1] Dinner and the evening were dull. Goldenweizer. A while, pleasantly, in Sasha's room.

July 18, i.I l.

Alive, but in a bad shape, as weak as ever. I have
done no work except for some trifling letters and reading
Pascal. Sofia Andreevna is upset again. "I have been
unfaithful to her, and that is why I am hiding the diaries."
And then she is sorry that she is tormenting me. She has
an ungovernable hatred for Chertkov.[1] I feel that there
is an unbridgeable gulf between Lev and me. And I shall
tell him *son fait;*[2] I shall try to do it affectionately. There
was a difficult writing gentleman here. I rode over to
Tikhvinskoe and am very tired. Goldenweizer and Chertkov were here this evening, and Sofia Andreevna was near
losing control. Am going to bed.

I slept fairly well, but I am very weak, pulse irregular.
I wrote a venomous article to the Peace Conference,[1] and
other letters. Sofia Andreevna was better this morning, but
was worse toward evening when the doctors arrived.[2]
Sasha is in poor shape physically; she is coughing and has
a cold. There is no use writing more. It is after eleven,
and I am going to bed. There is something important to
write about young girls. Yes, I rode over to see the nice
people in Ovsiannikovo.

I feel very badly. I sat on the bench under the little
fir trees and wrote Chertkov a letter. The doctors came;
Rossolimo is amazingly stupid in a learned way, just
hopeless. Then I revised the postscript to the Congress.
I feel very gloomy. I did not show it in any way, but it

is bad that I feel dissatisfied. I rode along the Zaseka with Filia. I slept a while, and now I am noting down:

1) An unceasing struggle is going on in my soul over Lev. Should I forgive him, or pay him back with harsh, venomous words? I am beginning to hear the voice of kindness more clearly. Like St. Francis, I must test whether my joy is complete by admitting that the abuses of the gatekeeper are just.[1] Yes, I must.

2) How easy it is to vent one's anger in word and deed, and how hard it is to forgive, but still what a pleasure it is if you master it. I must achieve it.

3) Faith, what people believe in, is nothing but superstition. People prefer faith to consciousness, because faith is firmer and easier, as firm and easy as following a custom, and it easily passes into habit, but faith itself is never firm, it is shaky and it does not stimulate the progress of spiritual life. It is always motionless and aggressive, it stimulates a desire to convert others, and this cannot be otherwise, as it is based on public opinion, and the more people share the faith the firmer it is. Faith is a worldly matter, a convenient condition for our physical lives. An awareness of God is a matter for the soul, a necessary condition for a good and rational life. Faith is always *stationnaire*, awareness is always in motion. For "believers" the movement of life takes place in the physical sphere, but for those who are conscious it takes place in the sphere of the soul.

4) I cannot forgive Vera[2] in my soul for her downfall. And I have just clearly understood all the cruelty and injustice of this. I need only remember my own male sexual past. Yes, nothing shows so clearly that public opinion was established by men and not by women. And a woman should be less liable to condemnation than a man, because she bears all the great weight of the consequences of her sin: childbirth and shame, while the man bears nothing. "If he is not caught, he is not a thief." A fallen woman or an unmarried mother, V. is shamed in the eyes of the whole world, or is directly relegated to the category of

despised creatures (whores), while a man is pure and right, unless he has caught a disease. It would be good to clarify this.

1) You ask how we should understand this or that line in the Gospels, the Revelation, or the Bible, having found in them things that are contradictory or unclear or just plain absurd. This is my answer to your perplexity. We must read the Gospels and all the books that are acknowledged to be Holy Scriptures, and must examine their contents just as we discuss the contents of all the books which we read, and therefore, if we meet something contradictory, unclear, or absurd, we should not hunt for explanations, but should reject outright all of these things, recognizing the importance and significance only of what accords with common sense, and especially our conscience. Only if we have this attitude to the so-called Holy Scriptures will reading them, especially the Gospels, be useful.

2) Science is an almshouse, or rather a path to what is success in the eyes of the crowd, open to the most obtuse intellectually and morally. Having made science his business, a man need not be aware of what he is doing while he counts little insects or makes lists of books, and copies from them whatever is related to the theme of his choice. He may either think of nothing, or through some correlations, unreal and unjustified, he may invent some theory or other, and be completely sure that he is doing the most important business on earth.

3) 1) The scholarly type, 2) the ambitious type, 3) the self-interested type, 4) the conservative believer, 5) the debauchee, 6) the bandit, within accepted limits, 7) outside accepted limits, 8) the truthful man, but deceived, 9) the glory-seeking writer, 10) the socialist revolutionary, 11) the dashing gay type, 12) the complete Christian, and

13) the one who is struggling, 14) . . . . . There is no
end to these types which I perceive.

July 21

I am still just as weak and have the same unkindly
feeling toward Lev. Made notes about different characters;
I must give it a try. I have done no work; had a good
ride with Bulgakov. Dinner, then read *The Herald of
Europe*. Goldenweizer and Chertkov. Sofia Andreevna had
another fit. It is distressing, but I do not complain or pity
myself. Am going to bed. Nice letter from Tania about
St. Francis.

July 22

Slept very little, and did no work. Dozed off before
lunch. Went riding with Goldenweizer, and wrote in the
woods.[1] It was good. At home again agitation and irritation, at dinner even worse. Took it upon myself and invited her to walk, and calmed her down. Chertkov was
here. It was strained, painful, and depressing. Have patience, Cossack![2] I am reading La Bruyère.

July 23

It is very bad, I am in very poor health, but poor
health is nothing compared to my spiritual state. Well,
what's the use. *Je m'entends*. Something wrong with my
stomach and I could not hold out against their demands
that it be tended to. I took a laxative, but it did not work.
I corrected some letters and was in bed all day. Misha

was here with his wife and children, Olga with her children, and Lev. Lord, help me to act as Thou hast decreed. But I seem to be hurting both myself and her by making concessions. I want to try another means.[1]

July 24   I : 172

Again the same, in health and in my relations with Sofia Andreevna. My health is a little better, but with Sofia Andreevna it's worse. Yesterday evening she did not leave Chertkov and me alone, so that we could not talk. Today it was the same again, but I got up and asked him if he agreed to what I have written him? She overheard me and asked me what I had said. I told her that I did not choose to answer, and she left, upset and agitated. I can do nothing; the burden is unbearable. I am doing nothing. A few trifling letters. Am reading all sorts of trash. Going to bed, ill and restless.

July 25   I : 173

Sonia did not sleep all night. She decided to leave, and went to Tula where she met Andrei, and returned completely well, but terribly exhausted.[1] I am still unwell, but a bit better. No work done, didn't even try. Had a talk with Lev; no use. I am going to bed, peacefully because, thank God, I feel love. My good Goldenweizer is spending the night here.

July 26, i.I l.

Alive, but I feel sad, although my health is a bit better, and I worked on "On Insanity." Wrote some letters. I cannot become accustomed to the need for constantly being on guard; I even write this with apprehension. I rode horseback. My sons, Andrei and Lev, were here, both burdensome, though differently, each in his own way. Am going to bed; to be noted:

1) There is one eternal human law of love, and the cultists of science, investigating the beasts, discovered the law of the struggle [for existence] and have applied it to human life. What insanity!

I wrote a short letter to Chertkov and received a good one from him. I agree with him.[1]

The same again, but it seems to be a calm before a storm. Andrei came to ask whether there was the "paper." I said that I did not wish to answer. It is very hard. I do not believe that they want only money; that would be terrible. But it is only good for me. Am going to bed. Seriozha has arrived.

I had a letter from Tania; she and Mikhail Sergeevich Sukhotin have invited me. Tomorrow I shall see.

1) The history of punishment is its continuous abolition. Ihering.[1]

2) Seeking safety from occasional robbers, those who are recognized as robbers, we fall into the hands of permanent robbers, the organized ones, those who are recognized as benefactors, we fall into the hands of the governments.

3) Man feels himself to be a God, and he is right, because God is in him. He feels himself to be a swine,

and he is also right in this, because there is a swinish quality in him. But he errs grievously when he thinks that the swine in him is God.

4) The old woman says that the world and man have been created by our Father, the King of Heaven, and the learned professor, that man's origin is the result of the struggle of species for existence, and that the world is also the product of evolution.

The difference between these two views, and it is greatly to the advantage of the old woman, is that the old woman's words about the creation by our Father, the King of Heaven, clearly recognize the presence of the unintelligible, of something that is inaccessible to the human mind, both in the origin of man and his soul and in the origin of the world. The learned professor on the other hand, wants to use his flimsy observations and his conclusions drawn from them, to cover up that which is basic, incomprehensible, and inaccessible, and which must be recognized as such and separated from the accessible and understandable if the accessible and understandable is to be really accessible and understandable.

5) We do not recognize the law of love, which is the property of man and has been revealed to us by all the greatest sages in the world, and of which we are aware in our own souls, we do not recognize it because we do not see it in the phenomena of the material world. But we do see in it, in the material world, the law of the struggle [for existence], which is the property of animals, and therefore seeing it we recognize this law, and ascribe it to man. What a terrible and gross delusion! And that is an outlook on the world which is held by the most enlightened people.

6) It would be good to ask oneself this question: if you are doing what you believe to be God's work, the one you were called to do, would you agree to leaving aside personal happiness—would you agree to be condemned and despised by all? It is good to ask oneself this

141

and be able to answer, "Yes," but fortunately such a situation, in which a man who does God's work would not find any sympathy, has never existed and never can exist.

July 28 I : 176

The same ill health, my liver, and no mental activity. It is quiet at home. Zosia[1] came over. I went riding with Dushan. Seriozha was here. They have exaggerated everything, thank goodness.[2] Yes, I no longer have a diary, a frank, simple diary. I must start one.

July 29 I : 177

Posha is coming, and I am glad. Still doing no work. I do not feel badly in my soul. A good lad, Borisov, was here. I went riding with Dushan. My sons were here, and it was painful. I wrote Chertkov a note. Zosia gives me pleasure by her artistic, literary sensitivity. Not very interesting letters. Whist in the evening, and I had a good talk with Nikolaev. I thought well about how to break the habit of thinking about the future, and also about—but I don't remember.

July 29, 1910[1] II : 1

I am starting a new diary, a real diary for myself alone. Today there is one thing I must record: that if the suspicions of some of my friends are justified, an attempt has now begun to gain her ends by a display of affection.[2] For several days now she has been kissing my hand, which she never did before, and there are no scenes and no despair. May God and good people forgive me if I am mistaken. And I can easily be misled in the direction of kindness and love. I am capable of completely sincere love for her which I am not as regards Lev. Andrei is just one [of those people of whom it is difficult to believe that they have a divine soul (but he has, one, remember this). I] will try not to be upset and to hold my ground, chiefly by silence.

How could one deprive millions of people of what, perhaps, they may need for their souls. I repeat: "perhaps." But even if there is the least possibility that what I have written is necessary to people's souls, then we must not deprive them of this spiritual food in order that Andrei can drink and indulge in debauchery and Lev daub and dabble[3] and . . . Well, God be with them. Mind your own business and do not judge . . . It is morning.

The day was like the previous ones; I felt ill but there is less unkindness in my soul. Waiting for what will come, which is bad.

Sofia Andreevna is quite calm.

July 30   I : 178

My health is a little better. I slept a lot. I received some very interesting letters, and did nothing except write letters. I rode over to Ivan Ivanovich's and gave him the proofs. Dinner at home. With my sons, same feeling of being strangers. Good thoughts about the need for silence; I will try. I will go to bed after seeing Zosia off. Sofia Andreevna was hurt that she had not been invited to play whist. I said nothing; this is how it must be.

Chertkov has drawn me into a struggle, and this struggle is painful and repellent to me. I shall try to carry it on with love (it is terrible to say how far I am from it).

In my present situation, what I seem to need above all is acting not, speaking not. Today I understood clearly that I must avoid spoiling my situation and must clearly remember that I need nothing, nothing at all.

I am still low, especially my mind. Writing nothing —all the better. Uninteresting letters. Sofia Andreevna spoke well about what happened, admitting that she had been too sensitive. It was very good. I went riding with Dushan. After dinner I wanted to read, but the Lodyzhenskis[1] came over and talked a lot, and so did I, a lot more than was necessary. Received a letter from Chertkov and wrote him a few words in answer. Everything is all right. I am going to bed.

August 1, i.I l.

An idle evening. The Lodyzhenskis came, and I talked too much. Sofia Andreevna again did not sleep, but she is not angry. I am waiting.

Alive, but in bad shape. I answered letters badly. The proofs from Ivan Ivanovich are bad. I rode over to Ovsiannikovo. Mentally sluggish and listless. I am quite successful in keeping silence. Sasha's health is growing weak again. I have something to note—later.

August 1 II : 4

Slept well, but I am still bored, sad, listless, acutely conscious of the lack of love surrounding me and, alas, in me. Lord help me! Sasha is coughing again. Sofia Andreevna told Posha all the usual things. It's all alive in her, her jealousy of Chertkov and her fear for the property. Very oppressive. I cannot bear Lev Lvovich, and he wants to settle down here. That would be an ordeal! Letters this morning. I wrote poorly, corrected one proof. I am going to bed, sick at heart. I am in bad shape.

August 2, i.I l.

August 2 I : 181

It is still just as oppressive in my soul, the same sluggishness. I walked a lot this morning. Few letters; I corrected the proofs poorly. There was a splendid letter from Tania; she is suffering for me, poor girl. I rode over for some seed-rye,[1] and Sofia Andreevna drove over to check on me.[2] She is the one who suffers, and I cannot help pitying her, however tormenting it is for me. Had a good talk with Posha in the evening. Now I am going to bed.

August 3, i.I l.

I understood my mistake only too well. I should have summoned all the heirs and declared my intention, not kept it secret. I wrote this to Chertkov.[1] He was very upset. I rode to Kolpna. Sofia Andreevna drove over to check, to spy. She rummages through my papers.[2] She has been questioning me about who brings letters from Chertkov. "You are carrying on a secret love correspondence." I told her I did not want to talk about it and left, but I was gentle. Unhappy woman, how can I help pitying her? Wrote Galia a letter.[3]

Alive. Sad. But I worked better on the proofs. There is a wonderful passage in Pascal;[1] I could not help being moved to tears when I read it, and felt in complete communion with this man, who had died hundreds of years ago. What other miracles could you want when you live with this miracle?

Rode to Kolpna with Goldenweizer. An awful scene in the evening, and I was extremely upset.[2] I did nothing, but I felt such a rush of blood to my heart that it was not only frightening but painful.

I go to bed with anguish in my heart, and I wake up with the same anguish. I just cannot overcome it. Went for a walk in the rain. Worked at home. Went riding with Goldenweizer. I feel uneasiness with him, for some reason. Letter from Chertkov.[1] He is very upset. I told him that I have decided to wait and not to start anything. It is

*a very good thing that I feel I am despicable. This eve-
ning an insane note from Sofia Andreevna, with a demand
that I read it. I glanced at it and handed it back. She
came and began to talk. I locked myself in, then ran
away and sent Dushan Makovitski. How will this end?
If only I do not sin myself. Going to bed. i.I l.*

August 4 I : 183

I still do not write down my thoughts. The day passed
peacefully; there were many worthless visitors. I feel
physically, and in my soul not well, unkind.
August 5, i.I l.

August 4 II : 7

*Nothing especially bad today, but I feel depressed.
Finished the proofs, but wrote nothing. I lost my temper
with a young fellow and for no reason, then gave a book
to a university student and his wife. A great deal of fuss.
Went riding with Dushan Makovitski to the Lodyzhenskis.[1]
Posha is leaving and Korolenko[2] is coming.*

August 5 I : 184

To be noted:
1) Habit is a great thing. What habit does is that
actions which used to require renewed effort and struggle
between the spiritual and the animal, do no longer require
effort or attention, and these may now be put to use for
the next task. It is like the mortar which binds the stones
that have been laid allowing new stones to be laid on top

of them. But this very same useful aspect of habit may be a cause for immorality, when the struggle is won by animality, thus: cannibalism, executions, wars, ownership of land, taking advantage of prostitution, etc.

2) Yes, faith, superstition, fanaticism give great strength for self-renunciation, but only because the doing of one single thing is held to be all-important, to be that which alone permits the whole law of life to be fulfilled; such are the observance of the laws of the church, self-imposed castration, self-immolation by burning, the destruction of unbelievers etc. But it is not superstitious faith, not anything single and limited that is needed for the fulfillment of God's law, but the resolving of all the most important problems in life on the basis of the universal law of God —of Love. Such behavior does not manifest itself in any of those striking deeds that are inspired by fanatical faith.

3) The more self-renunciation there is, the more difficult it is to remain humble, and *vice versa*.

4) (August 1) The words of a dying man are particularly significant. But are we not dying always, and particularly obviously in old age? Let the old man remember then that his words can be particularly significant.

5) "He threw himself on his knees, wept, wailed, and begged God to teach him how to be saved, but in the depths of his soul he felt that this was all nonsense and that no one would save him." [1]

6) What terrible, or rather amazing, insolence or folly those missionaries display who teach "savages" their churchly faith in order to civilize and enlighten them.

7) What we call the world is made up of two parts: our consciousness, and what we are conscious of. If there were no consciousness, then there would be no world, but we cannot say that if there were no world there would be no consciousness. (Is this true?)

8) Often one decides not to discuss with someone matters that are beyond his ken; but then restraint is forgotten, many words are wasted completely uselessly, and

148

one is irked when someone actually does not understand the things that he is not able to understand.

9) A completely egotistical life is an irrational, animal life. Such is the life of children and of unprocreative animals. But a life which is completely egotistical for an adult who is rational is an unnatural condition, or insanity. Such is the situation of many women, who lived an egotistical life legitimately in their childhood; then lived in the egotism of an animal family love; then in the egotism of conjugal love, then of motherhood; but then, when they part with what is not egotistic in family life, the children, they are left with their reason, but without general love, in the situation of an animal. This is terrible and very common.

10) You want to serve others; the workman wants to work. But to work usefully, one needs a tool, and it must be a good tool too. Now you, with your peculiarities, your character, your habits, the knowledge you possess, are you a good tool for the job of serving other men? What you must serve is not mankind, but God, and the way to serve Him is a clear one and a well-defined one. It consists in magnifying love within yourself. As you magnify this love, you cannot help serving other people, and will serve them in the way you need and others do, and God does.

11) The man who is hurt is not the unfortunate person, but the man who wishes to cause pain to others.

12) Every person is always in the process of growth, and therefore he may not be rejected. But there are people who in their present state are so alien, so remote, that you cannot treat them except as one treats children: affectionately, respectfully, protectively; but you don't place yourself on the same plane with them or demand from them understanding of which they are deprived. One thing makes such relations difficult: that instead of being curious and sincere as children are, these children are indifferent and reject what they do not understand, and above all, are so ponderously self-assured.

August 5. I feel rather fresher, but the bustle does not permit me to work; but no matter. I revised the letter to the priest.[2] Not very interesting letters. An American "globe trotter".[3] [In English in the original.] I went riding with Dushan. Sofia Andreevna is weak and nervous. Fokin was here; I still have my doubts.[4] "His holiness" [in English in the original] [5] wants to come; I do not know what to decide. I am glad that I prayed well this morning, being conscious of my love for all. Am going to bed.

August 6, i.I l.

August 5   II : 8

My thoughts are a little clearer. My renouncing Chertkov is regrettable, shameful, comic, and sad. Yesterday morning she was quite pathetic, and without malice. I am always so glad of this; it is so easy for me to pity and love her when she suffers and does not make others suffer.

August 6   I : 185

Alive. I walked through the fir grove. Read and wrote letters, and thought of writing "On Insanity," but did not feel like it. When I lay down I had an important thought, but I forgot it. Korolenko has come, a very pleasant, intelligent, and well-spoken man. But still all this talking and talking is painful.

August 6   II : 9

Today as I lay in bed I had a thought which—as it seemed to me—was very important. I thought I would jot it down later. And I forgot it, forgot and could not remember. Just now I met Sofia Andreevna right here, when I

*was writing this. She was walking very quickly and seemed
terribly upset. I became very sorry for her. I told them to
watch her secretly and see where she went. Sasha told me,
though, that she is not walking about without a purpose,
but that she is spying on me. I became less sorry for her.
There is malice in this and I am not yet able to be indifferent when it means that I must love what is malicious.
I think about going away, leaving a letter, and I am afraid
to do so, although I think that she would be better off. I
have just read letters and started to work on "Insanity,"
but put it aside. I have no real desire to write, nor the
strength. Now it is after midnight. This eternal hiding,
and fear for her, are depressing.*

August 7 I : 186

Am in a listless state. Tried to write "On Insanity," but
could not do anything. Asked Korolenko to go for a walk
with me this morning, and we had a good talk. He is
intelligent, but is dominated by the fallacy of science.
Then I went riding, got soaked through, and dried out
at the Sukhinins'.[1] Goldenweizer came over to see us, it
was depressing. To be given to Sasha for copying:

1) I have rarely met a man who is more endowed with
all the vices than I: voluptuousness, self-interest, malice,
vanity, and especially self-love. I thank God that I know
this, have perceived all this filth in myself, and am still
struggling against it. This is what explains the success of
my writings.

2) And this stupor is especially powerful and incurable
because people do not perceive it and cannot or will not
perceive it. And if they cannot or will not it is because
they are completely satisfied with themselves and their
situation. We are in evolution, in progress. We have airplanes, we have submarines. Isn't that enough? Just wait

a bit longer and everything will be wonderful. And indeed, unthinking people cannot help being overjoyed by airplanes, etc. There must be some reason for them to appear. And they did appear because the ninety-nine per cent who are slaves do what one per cent orders, and it is true that miracles are performed. And people believe that these miracles are really necessary and therefore they cannot and will not change the way of life which produces these miracles. Miracles support a bad way of life. A bad way of life produces miracles. Can we possibly improve life by continuing to live badly? Only one thing is needed: to put moral requirements in the first place, and if you do so, airplanes, etc., will be done away with immediately.

3) Masaryk wrote: The trouble is not that there is no religion, but that there is so stupid and false a religion. The religion of progress. And until it is abolished there can be no betterment. Faith in evolution, and therefore "to serve." I receive letters; there is general self-assurance, and in this case individual self-assurance. To serve what we want and know. True religion is to serve what we do not know, but we want to serve as we want and as we do, and the further it goes on the worse it is, but we say, "It will pass! We need faith in evolution."

4) It is difficult to imagine the revolution which would take place in the whole material life of people, not even if they began living by love, but simply if they stopped living a wicked, animal-like life.

5) If we talk of God the creator, then the God who, according to their understanding, has created man, a man who is incapable of understanding anything that is not limited spatially and temporally, this God, according to their understanding, would also be in space and time, meaning omnipresence (space) and eternity (time). Very good.

6) At first it seems that to live only in God's sight would be unstable, too limited, artificial, and unnatural.

But just try to live in this way, and you will see how easy and stable and natural it is. It is all that way.

Is life in time not given to men so that he may grow firm in his life in God?

Isn't it the same when people live only in other people's sight, as political leaders, scholars or artists do? However empty these activities are, however doubtful their results, people devote their whole lives to them. Then how can we help giving our whole lives to activity for the soul, which is always fruitful, always free, and always rewarded?

August 7   II : 10

Talk with Korolenko. An intelligent and good man, but completely under the superstition of science. The work I must write is very clear in my mind and it would be too bad not to write it, but I don't seem to have the strength. Everything is mixed up and I have no tenacity or persistence in a single direction. Sofia Andreevna is quieter, but she is irritable and hostile toward everyone. I read about paranoia in Korsakov's book. It is as if he had drawn her likeness. Sasha had the book, and passages in it are underlined, very likely by her. Korolenko said to me, "What a fine person Aleksandra Lvovna is." I was so touched that tears filled my throat, and I could not speak. When I recovered I said, "I have no right to speak, she loves me too much." Korolenko answered, "Well, then, I have the right."

It is still just as difficult for me with Lev, but thank God there are no bad feelings.

As soon as I got up, Sofia Andreevna ran outside. She
had not slept all night and she was upset and really sick.[1]
I went out and looked for her. I could not write anything.
Went riding with Bulgakov. The young people from
Teliatinki came over. But the five who had promised to
come did not come.[2] It all seems like a trick; thank God
I feel only pity for them. My liver is not working; I feel
dreary physically, but better spiritually, anyway. I had a
good talk with Sonia. I will probably go to Tania's. She
is coming here first. Now it is after eleven and I am going
to bed.

*Got up early. Many, many thoughts, but scattered. Well,
never mind. I pray and pray: Help me! And I cannot,
I cannot help wishing for death and waiting for it with
joy. My separation from Chertkov is more and more dis-
graceful. I am obviously at fault.*

*With Sofia Andreevna the same again. She wants Chert-
kov to come over. Again she did not sleep until seven in
the morning.*

*I have lost my memory entirely, and the strange thing
about it is that this loss is no loss at all: I have actually
gained a great deal by it, in clarity and strength of consciousness. I even think that one always has one at the
expense of the other.*

I am in a very serious, depressed mood. Again I cannot
even think of doing any mental work. I walked a lot, and

rode over to Maria Aleksandrovna's. Nice people. That terrible Ferre[1] came, terrible because of his impervious, naïve bourgeois nature. There was a Hungarian here too.[2] I behaved badly with them both. Sasha had another clash with Sonia. Tania is coming. I am going to bed, it is after eleven.

August 9 II : 12

I am more and more serious in my attitude toward life. Another upset. Talks with Ferre, Sasha. Sasha is harsh. Lev is a great and painful ordeal.

August 10 I : 18⟨

Very weak. I got up early and walked with difficulty. I jotted something down, well. Wrote letters. Had a pleasant ride with Dushan. Sofia Andreevna fell down. She did not sleep last night, but she is calm. Some soldiers came in the evening, three of them Jews and a Ukrainian,[1] a "political." My impression was that it was unnecessary and rather unpleasant.

1) How easy it is to forgive someone who is repentant and humble, and how difficult it is to extinguish *rancune* and ill will toward someone who has offended you and is self-assured and self-satisfied! And it is important to learn how to forgive these too.

For the first time yesterday, when I was writing a letter to the soldier, I felt the whole sin of this terrible business. (This is not it.)

2) Love is one's awareness that one is a manifestation of the Whole, the union of oneself with the Whole, and love for God and one's neighbor.

3) You need only to be conscious that you are humble, and you immediately stop being humble.

August 10

Everything is still depressing, and I am not well. It is good to feel that you are guilty, and that is how I feel.

Help me, Father, origin of life, universal spirit, source and origin of life, help me to live, if only the last days and hours of my life here, in Thy sight alone, serving Thee alone.

For the first time yesterday, when I wrote a letter to Galia,[1] I felt my guilt for everything, and a natural desire to ask forgiveness. The minute I thought of this, I felt "perfect joy." How simple and easy it is, how it liberates from desiring earthly fame, how it eases our relations with other people. Oh, if only it is not self-deception and can be maintained!

August 11

My health is worse and worse. Sofia Andreevna is calm, but just as estranged. Letters. Answered two. It is difficult with everyone. I can only desire death. Long letter from Chertkov, describing everything that has taken place. It was very sad and depressing to read and recall. He is completely right, and I feel guilty about him. Posha [Biriukov] was wrong. I shall write them both. I shall write all this.

August 11 and 12. I am amazed to see that I skipped yesterday. I had a letter, a very interesting one, yesterday, and I answered it today. Yesterday and today I did not write anything, only answered important letters. Today I did not go out. I am still very weak. It is after eleven and I am going to bed.

1) It is useful to learn, when you are by yourself, not to do anything which you would not do in the presence of others: not to kill flies, not to lose your temper with a horse, etc., but to do in the presence of others what you know you will be condemned for doing but do not consider bad.

2) God is the unlimited spiritual source, complete in Himself, which I am aware of as my "I" and which I acknowledge in all that lives.

August 13, i.I l.

I decided yesterday to tell Tania everything.[1] *Today since morning I had a depressing feeling, hostile toward her, toward Sofia Andreevna. And she must be forgiven and pitied, but I cannot as yet.*

I told Tanya. She is delighted and agrees. Chertkov was very pleased with my letter, according to Sasha.[2] *I did not go out all day. In the evening Gay*[3] *gave a good report on Switzerland. Sofia Andreevna is very upset, and she is always in that condition. Obviously she is ill. I am very sorry for her. Am going to bed.*

My health is a little better. It was pouring rain, so I walked along the terrace. A man walked up to me, wet through and with nothing over his shirt. I did not feed him or treat him in at all a brotherly fashion, but I shook hands with him, a stupid demonstration. I had some rather interesting letters, but still I have no desire to work. And what's the need? I feel well and kindly in my soul. A former "lady" was here, now a medical worker.[1] More of the same: service to others and sexual love. To be noted:

How good it would be to really debunk this love and show the falsity of it.

No change, and being with her, the same depression and the danger. Good letter from Chertkov asking me not to ride over to say goodbye if this might prevent my departure.[1] Tanechka is pleasant and sweet.

Sofia Andreevna has been in a very bad state since morning.[1] My health is better, though. I had a letter from Chertkov and wrote him. I walked through the fir grove, and went riding with Dushan. In the evening Khiriakov,[2] a pleasant fellow, Goldenweizer, and Dimochka were here. A conflict with Sasha; she came herself and made it up.[3] It is very difficult, but I am bearing up. Now it is after eleven and I am going to bed. Tomorrow we are leaving.

Worse and worse. She did not sleep last night. Rushed out in the morning. "Who are you talking with?" Then she told a dreadful thing, about excitation. A horrible thing to say: [3 words crossed out apparently by Sofia Andreevna, and undecipherable].[1]

Terrible, but thank God she is pitiful, I can pity her. I shall bear it. God help me! She has been tormenting everyone, and herself most of all. She will go with us. Apparently she is driving out [Varia Feokritova]. Sasha is distressed. Am going to bed.

[*Kochety.*] I woke up in poor health. Sofia Andreevna is going with us. We had to get up at six o'clock, and I had a hard trip. Trifling letters. It is very pleasant at Tania's. Now I am going to bed in a depressed condition, physically and spiritually. I read a book by Fedor Strakhov, *Search for Truth*.[1] It is very very good.

1) What a strange thing: I love myself, but no one loves me.

2) Instead of learning to live a loving life, people learn how to fly. They fly very badly, but they stop learning how to live lovingly in order to learn how to fly after a fashion. It is just as if birds stopped flying and tried learning how to run or build bicycles and ride on them.

On the way to Kochety I thought that if these disturbances and demands begin again I shall go away with Sasha. And I have said so. So I thought on the road. But

*now I don't. We arrived in peace, but in the evening she
saw me taking a notebook from Sasha. "What is it?"—
"A diary, Sasha is copying from it."*

August 16   I : 194

The same state of mental weakness. I read Strakhov's
Search for Truth with great joy and wrote him a letter.
I went walking twice; it was raining again. I had an explanation with Sonia which ended well, thank God. It is
very nice at Tania's. There are a mass of people and it is
too crowded and too luxurious. Am going to bed.

August 16   II : 19

*She did not sleep again last night. Brought me a note
saying that Sasha was copying my accusations against
her for Chertkov from the diary. Before dinner I tried to
calm her by telling her the truth, that Sasha is only copying out separate thoughts, and not my impressions of life.
She wants to be reassured and is very pathetic. Now it is
after three; what will come next? I cannot work. Nor,
it seems, do I need to. I do not feel badly in my heart.*

August 17   I : 195

Slept well, went walking. I noted something in the
notebook, but not well. I came home mentally weak; I do
not feel like writing anything, and that is good. Sleepiness,
weakness. The *skopets* Andrei Iakovlevich[1] came over;
talked about "Father" Peter Fedorovich.[2] Went walking
again and prayed very warmly and well, then slept. Din-

ner. Evening. Sofia Andreevna was calm the first day, but became a little excited toward evening. Played cards, did nothing.

August 17 II : 20

Today was a good day. Sonia was quite all right. It was also good because I was anguished. And my anguish was expressed in prayer and consciousness.

August 18 I : 196

The same, just as weak mentally. Did nothing. Sonia is grieved by the permission granted Chertkov to live at Teliatinki.[1] Uninteresting letters. I feel quite well in my soul, although sad, and that is a bad thing. Seriozha and Dmitri Olsufiev have come. I attended the performance at the school, which was very good.[2] Went riding.

August 18 II : 21

When Sofia Andreevna learned that Chertkov had received permission to live in Teliatinki, she became quite ill. "I'll kill him." I begged her not to talk and was silent myself, and this had a good effect, it seems. But now what? Help me, God, to be with Thee and do what Thou wishest. What shall be is not my affair. Often, no, not often but sometimes, I am in such a state of mind, and then how wonderful it is!

The same again. Weakness. I lack energy for work.
Trifling letters. I talked with Sofia Andreevna and was
wrong in agreeing not to be photographed.[1] I must not
make concessions. Do not feel like writing. Am going to
bed, it is after eleven.

August 20, i.I l.

*Sofia Andreevna has been begging me since morning
to renew my old promises and also not to have photographs made. I agreed, but it was a mistake. A good letter
from Chertkov. He is right in what he says about effective
methods of dealing with sick people. At dinner, for no
reason at all, I told about "Arago tout court."* [1] *And I
was ashamed. And ashamed that I was ashamed.*

Alive, even more so than I had expected. My head feels
a bit fresher. This morning I corrected the Preface. Very
trifling letters. There is a good socialist pamphlet, *Aux
antipodes de la morale. L'énergie et la matière. L'énergie
stationnaire et la matière dynamique.*[1] Amazing! And that
seems very clear to them! Sonia is still alarmed and
pathetic. I went riding with Diomidov;[2] he is *kind*. Am
going to bed. My stomach still does not work.

August 21, i.I l.

*I had a good talk with the watchman. It was bad that
I told about my situation. I went riding, and the sight of
this baronial domain so torments me that I am thinking
of running away and hiding.*

*Today I thought, as I recalled our marriage, that there
was something fatal about it. I was never even in love.
But there was nothing I could do but get married.*

[In S. A. Tolstoy's handwriting: "In the old diaries of
that time he wrote, 'Am in love as never before. I'll
shoot myself if she refuses me.' "]

More alive than yesterday. Made more changes in the
preface and corrected the proofs of the booklet "Humility"; it is good. Did not go riding, but walked to Veseloe
and talked with an old woman. Whist in the evening, and
feeling of shame.

*Got up late. Feel fresher. Sofia Andreevna is the same.
She told Tania that she had not slept all night because
she had seen a picture of Chertkov. A threatening situation. I want terribly to speak, that is, to write.*

I feel much better. Still no desire to work, and have
also been busy with the proofs of the booklets. I have

corrected all except one, "After Death." I rode over to the "Stalover";[1] yesterday he told good stories. Especially good the one about how his nephew "softened" after beating him up, his uncle, who offered no resistance. Sasha wrote it down well. This evening peasants were here and made a depressing, unpleasant impression, especially one, rich, a conservative, and a self-assured talker.[2] Sofia Andreevna is calm. Whist in the evening. Am going to bed.

August 22   II : 25

Letter from Rossolimo,[1] remarkably stupid, about Sofia Andreevna's condition, and a good letter from B.[2]
I am behaving quite well.

August 23   I : 201

I walked briskly and thought. Composed a little tale for children, on the theme "To All Equally," and the characters will be in it.[1] I outlined the story, then walked in the park and finished the "Booklets." Whist in the evening. Am going to bed. Sofia Andreevna is calm.

August 24   I : 202

I still feel well. This morning I read *Le Bab*. Very interesting and new for me. Then letters. I must write down the children's story; Tanichka retold it to me very well. For some reason I have no desire to write, but I should. Walked alone to Alexsandrovka, and in the evening I finished reading *Bab*. Am going to bed. Sofia

Andreevna is all right, if only she were not alarmed or suspicious.

To be noted: 1) I walk through the park and think of the conditions in which the Sukhotin children live, how many steps it is around the park, and whether I would drink coffee when I come back, etc. And it is clear to me that my walking, my bodily movement, and my thoughts are not life. What then is life? And I know only one answer: life is the liberation of the spiritual source of the soul from the body, which limits it. And therefore it is obvious that the same conditions which we consider misfortunes and of which we say, "This is no life!" (as I said and thought concerning my situation), that these alone are life, or at least the possibility of life. Only under the conditions which we call misfortunes and with which the struggle between the soul and the body begins, only under these conditions does there begin to be a possibility for true life and for life itself, if we struggle consciously and are victorious, i.e., our soul is victorious over our body.

2) Temporary life in space enables me to be conscious of my timelessness and spirituality, that is, of my independence of time and space.

3) If there were no movement in time or matter in space, I could not be conscious of my bodilessness and timelessness; there would be no consciousness.

4) Only consciousness of my unchanging, incorporeal "I" enables me to be cognizant of my body, of movement, time, space. And only the movement of matter through time and space enables me to be aware of myself. One defines the other.

5) What or whom to believe, or what or whom not to believe, that only one's reason can decide.

6) The external world is only matter in movement. In order that matter may be in motion, a separateness of material objects is necessary, and this separateness must first be in me. I am separated from the whole world, and therefore I recognize the separateness of other beings

165

from each other and from the whole world. The relation of material objects to each other is defined by measurements in space, and the relation of the movement of separate objects is defined by measurements in time (not good, unclear).

7) It is bad when the rich are not ashamed and the poor are not without envy.

8) *To All Equally* is the title of the character sketches.

9) I can be conscious that I feel like eating, that I feel like getting angry, that I feel like finding out . . . But who is this that is conscious?

10) First the government, with the help of the church alone, deceived the people in order to rule over them; now the government is preparing science little by little for this work, and science very willingly and diligently is taking up the task.

11) The clergy, both consciously and by tradition, unconsciously, try for their own advantage to prevent the people from emerging from the shadow of superstition and ignorance into which they have led them.

August 23 and 24   II : 26

I am reviving a little. Sofia Andreevna, poor thing, suffers without relief, and I feel that it is impossible for me to help her. I feel the sinfulness of my exclusive attachment to my daughters.

August 25   I : 203

I am writing before dinner. Nothing new. I wanted to think out the tale, but it did not turn out. A good letter, from Vladimir.[1] A depressing talk with my daughters.[2] I wrote a letter to Chertkov; he is sick, they say.

Varvara Mikhailovna [Feokritova] writes about the gossip at the Zvegintsev's. It upsets Sasha. It is all the same to me, thank God, but I feel less kind toward her. That must not be. Oh, if I only could be gentle but firm.

I feel well in my soul. The children's tale is not a success. I received letters and proofs. I read the *Vedic Magazine;* the account of the Vedas and *Areja Samai* is very good.[1] I rode to Trekhanetovo.[2] The luxury here is very depressing, the baronial domain and terrible poverty, the chimneyless huts. It is late; I am going to bed.

August 27, i.I l.

Last night Sofia Andreevna spoke heatedly with Tania.[1] The inconsistency of her thinking is completely hopeless. I am glad that I responded to her provocations and complaints with silence. Thank God, I have no bad feelings in the least.

Alive, but I am still not working. All day I was busy with Chepurin,[1] a worker who travelled to England, America and Japan. I read his book in manuscript, very badly written, and talked with him.

August 28, i.I l.

She is terribly pathetic and oppressive. This evening she began to talk about the photographs,[1] from her deranged viewpoint, of course. I tried to dismiss the matter and went away.

Alive, and well. I walked with the tutor[1] and had a good talk. Then apples for the children. At home I corrected "Truthfulness," and had some uninteresting letters. I walked to Trekhanetovo. It was very good in my soul. Gave apples to the children again. Said goodbye to Chepurin. This evening I could not restrain myself and objected to what Sofia Andreevna said, and it began. She won't let me go, and keeps talking. A letter from Lev, a very bad one. Lord help me.

It is more and more difficult to be with Sofia Andreevna. There is no love, but demands for love, which are near to hatred and are changing into hatred.

Yes, egotism is madness. The children used to save her —an animal love, but still selfless. But when that ended, only terrible egotism remained, and egotism is the most abnormal state. It is madness.

I have just talked with Sasha and Mikhail Sergeevich [Sukhotin], and both Dushan Makovitski and Sasha refuse to recognize that she is sick. But they are wrong.

Another empty day. Walks, letters. I am thinking and well, but I cannot concentrate. Sofia Andreevna was agitated, went walking in the garden, and did not return. She came in after twelve, and wanted explanations again. It was very painful. I restrained myself and she quieted down. She has decided to leave today.[1] It is good that Sasha has decided to go with her. She said goodbye very movingly, asking forgiveness from everyone. I am very, very lovingly sorry for her. There were good letters. Am going to sleep. I wrote her a note.[2]

It is sad without her. I am afraid for her. There is no tranquillity. I walked along the roads. I was about to start working when Mavor, a professor, came.[1] He is very lively, but a professor and a supporter of the government and irreligious, the classic type of the good scholar. A letter from Chertkov; he is sending some English articles. I did not even read anything. Cards in the evening. My head aches. A telegram from Sasha; they have arrived safely. Am going to bed. In the morning I thought over a work on insanity and irreligion—fine!

August 31, i.I l.

Yesterday morning was terrible, for no reason. She went out into the garden and lay down there. Then she calmed down and spoke sensibly. As she left, she touchingly asked forgiveness. Today, the 30th, I don't feel well. Mavor. Sasha telegraphed that all is well. What will happen?

Today is September 1. I did not write yesterday. I went walking in the morning as usual, had some useful thoughts, and wrote them down. Not very interesting letters. Then we went to the Matveevs.[1] A very strong impression of contrast between strong, sensible working people, worthy of respect, who are completely in the hands of idle, debauched people on the lowest level of development, at almost an animal level. I am tired of them, they are all on the verge of insanity. Dinner. Weariness, cards. There is a lot to write, but just one thing for now:

1) People gifted with reason and an awareness of the divine source in themselves which unites them, instead of developing this within themselves, want to move faster than horses or deer, or fly like birds. They stifle what has been given them for their well-being and try to develop what has not been given them and what they don't need. Amazing!

Today I got up early, had a good walk, and wrote down a prayer for children. I revised my correspondence with Anshina[2] and am sitting down, perhaps to work.

Worked a little. Wrote letters to Sonia and Biriukov after dinner. The Mamontovs[3] arrived. The madness of the rich is ever more striking, and I played cards with them until eleven, and am ashamed. I want to stop playing all games. Am going to bed tired.

August 31, September 1 II : 32

I wrote Sonia a letter that flowed from my heart.[1]

Got up early, slept little, wandered a long way, and am very tired. I wrote down something about the immobility of the spiritual ego in time, not badly, I think. I came home tired, read Posha's description of his exile,[1] and wrote him. I want to stop playing cards, I am ashamed of it somehow. I did not start working, and now it is two o'clock. I shall go riding. I should stop that too. To be noted:

1) At first it seems that my "I," my ego, moves along with all the world, but the more I live the clearer it becomes that my "I" does not move, but that my true ego is, that I am immobile, outside of time. And the whole world moves along past this "I," including my body, which grows bald, toothless and feeble, and the whole world, moving past my "I," freeing it from the delusion of life in time.

2) The more a man recognizes his spirituality, the more clearly he understands the delusion of his apparent movement in time. In the evening—I don't remember.

I received a very bad letter from her. The same suspicions, the same malice, the same demand for love, which would be ridiculous if it were not so horrible and tormenting to me.

Today in the Cycle of Reading: *Schopenhauer—"As the attempt to force love evokes hatred, so . . ."* [1]

Went walking in the morning but did not get as far as Obraztsovka. I returned and started to write with such enthusiasm as I have not felt for a long time. I rode to Trekhanetovo to see a peasant, whose horse died. A strong impression, an old man, older than I, they were threshing at his place. Mamontova. Sasha has come; it is as tormenting as ever at home. Bear up, Leo Nikolaevich. I am trying. I did not want to play in the evening, but sat in for others.

September 4

Early in the morning, having slept little, I rode to Trekhanetovo and Obraztsovka. Horrifying poverty. I can hardly refrain from tears. Letters, one abusive. I walked about the park and slept a while. Am going to dinner. To be noted:

1) An understanding of sin and committing or refraining from actions, not for any advantages or human glory but for fear of sinning, is an essential condition for a truly human, rational, good life. Those who live without an understanding of sin and without refraining from it live only an animal existence. And *all* so-called enlightened people live that way.

2) Life without an understanding of its meaning, i.e., without religion, is what is called insanity. When insanity is common to a great number of people, it emerges boldly and reaches the highest level of self-assurance. So sane people are actually considered insane, and are locked up or put to death.

3) According to the law of gravity everything strives to be united; so everything spiritual strives toward unity in accordance with the law of love.

4) I died, my spirit ceased to inhabit my body, but my true ego, my spirit, lives on and will continue to live in others who have understood me or understand me. "But that won't be your spirit any longer," people say. "All to the good, as individual personality will not be added to

what will continue to live after me," I answer. "Individual personality is what prevents the merger of my Soul with the Whole, and after death my soul will remain but not my personality."

September 4 II : 34

Sasha arrived. She brought bad news. Everything is still the same. Sofia Andreevna writes that she will come here. She is burning the photographs and is holding a prayer service in the house.[1] When I am alone, I am ready to be firm with her, and I can be, it seems to me, but when I am with her I am weak. I shall try to keep in mind that she is sick.

Today, the 4th, I was depressed; I wanted to die and I still want to.

September 5 I : 213

Today is September 5. Got up early, walked briskly in the park, had a lot of good thoughts and wrote them down. Now I want to write this also:

1) Materialists say outright that they have explained everything by their scientific experimental investigations and have reduced everything to general laws. There remains one psychic phenomenon, insignificant if compared to others, which has not yet been reduced to an explanation by the experimental method, but *ça ne tardera pas.*[1]

Amazing stupidity, or rather madness, or, in polite language, a deviation from common sense! That on which all life is based, which should be the basis of all learning, that alone is omitted in the hope that it may be explained almost any day now by some professor in Berlin or Hamburg. Amazing!

2) Oh, if you could only remember always that you stand before God Himself, before His highest form which is comprehensible to you, whenever you stand before a man.

September 5. Got up rather late; strolled through the park. I wrote rather well, I think, about movement, space, and time. Then I tried to go on with my work, but accomplished little, it did not go well. I rode over to Andrei Iakovlevich Grigoriev's[2] in terrible weather, rain. He saw me home. Sofia Andreevna has arrived. She is upset but not hostile. Then S. Stakhovich[3] arrived. Am going to bed, it is eleven o'clock.

September 6. Kochety   I : 214

I woke up sick, probably senile gangrene.[1] It was pleasant because it caused not only unpleasantness but a pleasant feeling of the nearness of death. Also weakness and lack of appetite. Good news from the Transvaal about a colony of nonresisters.[2] I ate nothing, now it is evening and the cinematographer has come.[3] I shall try to go and look. I talked with Sofia Andreevna and everything is all right.

To be noted: 1) Consciousness, the essence of conciousness, is something inaccessible, insurmountable, what we call the spirit, the soul. Consciousness is enclosed in a definite part of matter, this matter is our body, and here consciousness, by means of outward relations (the organs) with other bodies and matters, learns to know the world that surrounds it. In this lies the essence of human life.

September 8   I : 215

7-8. Yesterday my health was better. Only my foot aches, and *pas pour cette fois*.[1] As has been determined above, so let it be. It already exists, only I have not been permitted to see it.

I wrote letters, one to an Indian[2] and one about non-resistance to a Russian. Sofia Andreevna is becoming more and more irritable. It is difficult, but I am restraining myself. I cannot yet go so far as to do what should be done calmly. I am afraid of the letter we expect from Chertkov.[3] On the 7th the sweet Abrikosov couple and the cinematographer were here, and today, the 8th, all except for Mikhail Sergeevich [Sukhotin] and Zosia Stakhovich have gone to Novosil.[4] I went for a walk in the sun. Sofia Andreevna insisted that Drankov should film the two of us together. I do not think I shall work, I am restless. I have not written anything. I walked about the park and jotted down some notes. I had a letter from Chertkov and Sofia Andreevna received his letter. Just before that we had a painful talk about my departure. I defend my freedom. I shall leave when *I choose*. I am very sad, of course because I am in bad condition. Am going to sleep.

Sept. 9, i.Il.

September 5, 6, 7, 8   II : 35

Sofia Andreevna arrived. She was very talkative, but at first there was nothing that could hurt. But yesterday it began again, hints, looking for excuses to condemn. Very painful. This morning she ran to me to tell me some filth about Zosia Stakhovich. I am restaining myself and shall continue to do so, so long as I am able, and I shall pity her and love her. God help me.

September 9   I : 216

Alive, but in poor shape. Agitation, pathological agitation, started this morning. I myself am not completely well and am weak. I spoke from the bottom of my heart, but apparently none of it was accepted.[1] It is very painful. I walked twice for a little bit in the park and played cards in the evening. Dull, bad, and sometimes a strange feeling of something new. Am going to bed late, tired.

September 10   I : 217

Got up early. Slept little but am fresher than yesterday. Sofia Andreevna is still just as irritated. It is very painful. I rode with Dushan for a little while. A good letter from a peasant about faith; I answered it. And a very good one from an Italian in Rome about my philosophical outlook.[1] Sofia Andreevna has eaten nothing for the second day. They are about to dine, and I am going to ask her to come to dinner. Terrible scenes all evening.

September 8, 9, 10   II : 36

Yesterday, the ninth, she was in hysterics all day. She ate nothing and she wept. She was very pathetic. But she is inaccessible to any reasoning or persuasion. I made some comment, and, thank God, without any bitter feelings, and she took it in the usual way, unable to understand. I was in poor shape myself yesterday—gloomy and listless. She received a letter from Chertkov and answered him. A letter from Goldenweizer enclosing notes from V[arvara] F[eokritova] which are horrifying.[1]

Today, the 10th, still the same. She is eating nothing. I went into the room. Immediately reproaches about Sasha, that she ought to go to the Crimea. This morning I thought that I could not stand it and would have to leave her. There is no life with her. Only torment. As I told her, my misfortune is that I cannot be indifferent.

Slept badly, my heart is weak. I can do nothing. I walked twice into the park. Dushan is amazing with his hate for Jews since he acknowledges the principles of love.[1] Now I am going to dinner. It is sad and hard.

Toward evening she began making scenes—running out into the garden, sobs and screams. It went to the point that when I followed her into the garden she screamed, "He is a beast, a murderer, I cannot look at him," and she ran to hire a cart so that she could leave immediately. That was the way it was all evening. But when I lost control of myself and told her son fait, she immediately recovered, and so she remained today, the 11th. It is impossible to talk to her, because she does not recognize either logic or truth, or the need for accuracy in repeating what has been said to her or what she said herself. I am very close to running away. My health has become worse.

Sofia Andreevna left in tears.[1] She summoned me for a conversation, but I avoided it. She took no one with her. I am very, very tired. Read in the evening. I am alarmed for her.

Sofia Andreevna left after terrible scenes. I am becoming a little calmer.

Heart weak. I walked and wrote almost nothing down. I thought about Grot.[1] I must not write down what I think. I went riding with Dushan, a cold wind. A good letter from Gusev,[2] and a stupid one from Adadurov.[3] Answered them. Am going to sleep, tired. *E sempre bene.*

September 14, i.I l.

Alive, and I am even sleeping a great deal. Wrote nothing except for the letter to Grot. Weak. I rode to Golitsyna's[1] with Mikhail Sergeevich. I should write a great deal, but it is late, am going to bed.

1) I must remember that in my relations with Sofia Andreevna the point is not my own satisfaction or dissatisfaction but the fulfillment of the task of love, even in the difficult conditions in which she has placed me.

2) We are always trying to urge time on. This means that time is the mold of our perception, and that we wish to be liberated from this mold, which hampers us.

1) Yes, at first it seems that the world moves in time and I move along with it, but the longer one lives, and the more spiritual one's life becomes, the clearer it becomes that the world moves but the person stands still. Sometimes we are clearly aware of this, sometimes we fall again into the illusion that we are moving along with time. When we understand our immobility, our independence of time, we understand too that not only does the world move while we stand still, but that our body moves along

178

with the world. We grow gray, toothless, weak, sick, but this all happens to our body, to something which is not us. But we are just the same, the very same always, at eight or at eighty-two. And the more we are aware of this, the more our lives themselves pass outside of us into the souls of others. But this alone does not convince us of our immobility and independence of time; there is a more trustworthy means of knowing that the ego, what makes up our "I," is the same independently of time, always the same and undoubtedly so, and that is an awareness of our unity with the Whole, with God.

All right, the "I" is immobile, but it is liberated, i.e., a process of liberation occurs, and this process occurs necessarily in time. Yes, the removal of the covers, which is liberation, takes place in time. But the "I" is still immobile. The liberation of the consciousness takes place in time: there was more, now there is less, or there was less and now there is more consciousness. But consciousness itself is the same and immobile, it alone *is*.

2) Could I, had I preserved my memory, direct the greater part of my spiritual attention to consciousness and to checking on myself?

3) Vanity, the desire for human glory, is based on the capacity to pass into the thoughts and feelings of others. If a person lives only a bodily, egotistical life, this capacity will be used also for himself, in order to arouse praise and love for himself in others whose thoughts and feelings he will have tried to guess. But in a person who lives a spiritual life, this capacity produces only sympathy for others, knowledge of how to serve others; it evokes love in him. I experience this, thank God.

4) I have never experienced a hundredth part of the sympathy, sympathy to the point of pain and tears, which I feel now when I try at least to a small extent to live only for my soul, for God.

5) Today, September 5, 1910, I clearly understood the significance of matter, space, movement (time). Space is the measure of matter, time is the measure of move-

179

ment. If I say that a material object is hard, then I am only saying that it is harder than something else less hard: iron is harder than stone, stone than wood, wood than clay, clay than water, water than air, air than ether, ether than what? All these measures of hardness are related to hardness zero which I know within myself. The same with space. Sirius is further than the sun, the sun than the Earth, the Earth than the moon, the moon than Siberia, Siberia than Moscow, and so to my hand, my body, and to distance zero which I know within me. The same again with movement in time. The geological protozoa before the plants, the plants before the animals, animals before man, the Egyptians before the Jews, the Jews before the Greeks, and so on, to time zero within me, and also to zero movement in time which I know within myself. And therefore only what is incorporeal, nonspatial and immobile, meaning untemporal, actually exists, is reality. And this reality is what I am conscious of as myself. (Badly expressed, but good.)

6) Motherhood for women *is not the highest calling*.

7) The stupidest man is he who thinks he understands everything. It is a particular type.

8) To think and say that the world was produced through evolution is just as stupid as to say that it was created by God in six days. The former statement is still the stupider of the two. Only one intelligent statement can be made on this subject: I do not and cannot and need not know.

9) Instead of those for whom others work being grateful to those who do the work, those who work are grateful to those who force them to work for themselves. What madness!

10) I cannot get used to regarding her words as delirium. This is my whole misfortune.

I cannot speak with her because neither logic nor truth nor the words she has uttered nor her own conscience are binding on her. This is terrible.

11) Regardless of any love for me, of which not a trace

remains, she has no need of my love for her either. She needs only to have other people think *that I love her.* That too is really terrible.

12) We know beyond doubt one thing and one thing only, and that one and only thing, beyond doubt and known to us before anything else, is our "I," our soul, i.e., the incorporeal force which is connected to our bodies. And therefore any definition of whatever may be in life, any knowledge is founded on this one item of knowledge, which is known to all people.

13) Progress has no significance, either for the individual or for the human race, because it takes place in time, which is endless. Progress in time is only an essential condition for the possibility of being conscious of goodness and perfection.

September 17   I : 223

I skipped two days, the 16th and today the 17th.

Yesterday in the morning I revised the letter to Grot a little. And afterwards nothing in particular except for a letter from Iasnaia, very depressing.

Sixty letters, most of them worthless. I worked again on revising the letter to Grot; it is improving. Went riding with Dushan. A letter from Chertkov: his translation of the letter to Gandhi, a letter from Miss Mayo,[1] and a copy of the letter to Sofia Andreevna. All very good. There is a little to note down, tomorrow.

September 16-17   II : 39

But the letters from Iasnaia Poliana are dreadful. It is distressing that one of her crazy ideas is to claim that I am senile mentally and that therefore my will, if it exists, is invalid. In addition, the same stories about me and the admission that she hates me. I received a letter from Chertkov, confirming everyone's advice to remain firm in my decision. I do not know if I can hold out.

It is now the night of the 17th.

I want to return to Iasnaia on the 22nd.

September 20 I : 224

Did not write anything on either the 18th or the 19th. I revised the letter to Grot on the 18th and wrote some letters. I was unwell—my stomach. I walked a bit. In the evening I read an interesting book, *Those Who Seek God*.[1]

On the 19th still unwell, did not touch the letter to Grot but thought more seriously about it. Walked in the morning. An interesting story by Kudrin on serving his "punishment" for refusing service.[2] Kupchinski's book[3] would be very good if it were not for the exaggerations. I read *Those Who Seek God*. Telegram from Iasnaia asking about my health and the time of my arrival.

Today I got up almost well. Walked, read, and now it is after ten. I do not feel like writing, and I shall not sit down to work.

So I did not do anything. Read. The same in the evening. Went to bed late.

September 21 I : 225

Slept little and seem to be stirred up. Went walking. I feel like writing.

Revised the letter to Grot. Rode over to Vera Pavlovna [Golytsina's] with Tania and Mikhail Sergeevich. Nothing else.

I am going to Iasnaia, and horror seizes me when I think what awaits me there. Only fais ce que dois. The chief thing is to be silent and to remember that the spirit of God dwells in her.

[End of the first notebook of the *Diary for Myself Alone.* On the next empty page a sheet of clean paper has been pasted in, on which is written in Countess Tolstoy's hand:

"With a pain in my heart I have copied this sad diary of my husband. So much here is unjust, cruel, and—may God and Lev forgive me—untruthfully directed against me, dragged up and invented . . . Even about his marriage. Let good people read in his diary how he was when he courted me. '*I am in love* as never before . . . *I shall shoot myself if this continues,*' etc. Then he was *my* Levochka, and for a long time after. Here he is *Chertkov's.* Sofia Tolstoy."]

September 22   I : 226

Slept little again and feel stirred up. I revised the Grot letter very well before getting dressed. Some trifles to be noted:

1) Nowhere may the sinful life of the rich be so clearly seen as in the country, on a landowner's estate.

[Iasnaia Poliana] We had a very good trip. We dropped in on the dear Abrikosovs. I was sorry that I had not stopped by at Gorbov's[1] school; he came out with the boys. At home I found Sofia Andreevna upset: reproaches, tears. I was silent.

This morning Sofia Andreevna went out somewhere, then she was in tears.[1] It was very painful. A pile of letters, some interesting ones. Sasha is irritated and unjust.[2] Dined, read Max Muller on Indian philosophy.[3] What an empty book. I have lost my little notebook.[4]

Nikolaev was here with his nice boys.[5] Am going to bed at midnight. I am avoiding solitaire and want to avoid cards altogether. Life only in the present.

I walked to Nikolaev's and to the Kaluga men, who were making felt boots.[1] At home books; a German one by Smitt,[2] on "Science," "Letter to an Indian," and "On Law." Smitt is a scientific humbug. Maude is also lecturing me.[3] Went riding with Bulgakov. Dear Maria Aleksandrovna. Sofia Andreevna was unpleasant, but it passed away toward evening. She is sick, and I am sorry for her from my very soul.

Yes, I looked over "There Are No Guilty in the World," [4] I can continue it. To be noted:

1) For the first time I have clearly understood the whole significance of life in the present: to avoid whatever you think or do with the future in mind: games, fortune telling, worry about other's impressions of your actions, and especially at every moment, that it is now that can and should be good as it is under your control, and to regard whatever happens as your inner work. I have tested it several times, and always successfully.

2) The difference between knowledge and science. Knowledge is all, science is a part. Just the same as the difference between religion and the church.

*I lost the little diary. I am writing in this one. The day
began quietly. But at lunch there was talk of The Wisdom of Children, and assertions that Cherktov is a collector and has kept things.[1] What would he do with the
manuscripts after my death? I asked her rather heatedly
to leave me in peace. It seemed all right. But after dinner
she began to reproach me for shouting at her, and said
that I should pity her. I was silent. She went to her room
and now it is after ten and she has not come out. I am
depressed. A letter from Chertkov, full of reproaches and
accusations. They are tearing me to pieces. Sometimes I
think I should go away from them all. It turns out she was
sleeping, and when she came out she was calm. I went to
bed after midnight.*

Got up, wrote a letter, went walking. While out walking I wrote another letter to Malinovski[1] about the death
penalty. I corrected Ivan Ivanovich's proofs, which came
by mail. Dissatisfied, did not finish. Some unpleasant pic-
ture-taking.[2] Took a good ride with Bulgakov, and had
a good talk with Sasha. All evening read Malinovski's
book, a lot of good and necessary material. Am going to
bed, it is after eleven.

*I woke up early, wrote a letter to Chertkov. I hope he
will take it as I ask him to. Now I am getting dressed. Yes,
all my business is with God, and I must be alone. Another request to pose for a photograph as a loving couple.*

I agreed, and was ashamed all the time. Sasha was terribly angry. It was painful for me. In the evening I called her and said, "I do not need your stenography, but I need your love." And we both felt better and kissed and cried a bit.

September 26   I : 230

Slept badly, bad dreams. After getting up I hung the photographs in their places again and went walking. I began to write to the Czech youths,[1] and went on working on the booklets, "For the Soul." Am a bit more satisfied. An institute student, Chebotarev, was here, Military service lies ahead of him, and he does not know how he should act. A sincere person, I liked him. I went riding with Dushan. When we returned, I found Sofia Andreevna in an agitated state. She had burned the photograph of Chertkov. I came close to speaking out, but managed to remain silent; it is impossible to understand.[2] Khiriakov[3] and Nikolaev came in the evening. I am very tired. Sofia Andreevna attempted to speak again, but I stayed silent. I only said before dinner that she had rearranged my photographs in my room and had burned the photograph of my friend, and apparently I was to blame for everything. The culmination of the day was that Sasha and Varvara Mikhailovna [Feokritova] returned, summoned by Maria Aleksandrovna [Schmidt]. Sofia Andreevna met them violently, so Sasha has decided to leave.

September 26   II : 43

Scenes again because I had hung up the pictures as they used to be. I began to say that it was impossible to live in this way. And she understood. Dushan Makovitski told

*me that she shot from a toy pistol in order to frighten me.
I was not frightened and did not go to her. And it really
is better. But it is very, very difficult. Lord help me.*

September 27 I : 231

In the morning saw Sasha off; she has moved for good to
Teliatinki. Went walking, wrote an addition to the letter
to Grot. At home the booklets and letters, nothing else. I
rode horseback to Tula. My health is good. I am holding
my own. Something to note down. Khiriakov was here.
Sent the booklets to Gorbunov, and Anshina's letter to the
newspapers.[1]

September 28, i.I l.

September 27 II : 44

*How ridiculous the contradiction I am living in. With-
out false modesty I may say that I am conceiving and
expressing very important and significant ideas, and along
with this I am involved in a woman's caprices and am
devoting the greater part of my time to the struggle
against them.*

*In the matter of moral improvement, I feel myself a
complete child, a pupil, and a bad pupil, not very diligent.*

*Yesterday there was a terrible scene when Sasha re-
turned. She screamed at Maria Aleksandrovna [Schmidt].
Sasha left today for Teliatinki. And Sofia Andreevna is
very calm, as if nothing had happened. She showed me the
scarecrow-pistol, and shot from it, and lied. Today she
rode out after me on my ride, probably spying on me.
Pathetic but difficult. Lord help me.*

Alive, but unwell, weak. Sasha came over. I did absolutely nothing and did not start anything, except for letters and few of them. Rode to Maria Aleksandrovna [Schmidt]; Nikolaev was there. On returning home, as I was leaving the village, I met Chertkov and Rostovtsev.[1] We talked a while and parted. He was obviously very glad, and so was I. Read in the evening, one book by a writer from the people, a competitor of Gorky's,[2] and an interesting book, *Antoine le Guérisseur*.[3] A truly religious outlook, only poorly expressed. Yes, I forgot to note that there was this officer, terrible.[4] I first thought that his conscience was burdened by his position as a soldier, but he talked about the root[?]-weakness, *lache;* then about physiology and hereditary cells. I lost patience and said that first of all one should stop bearing weapons of murder, and then that I had covered a lot of paper with my scribbling and whoever needs me will find all that I can say in my writings, and I took my leave and went away.

Very difficult. These expressions of love, this loquaciousness, and constant interference. It is still possible to love, I know it is. But I cannot. I am in bad shape.

Got up early. Frost and sunshine. Still weak. Went walking, have just returned. Sasha ran over. Sofia Andreevna did not sleep and also got up around seven, very nervous. I must be more careful. Just now, as I was walking, twice I caught myself feeling dissatisfied, because I had renounced my freedom of will, and because the new edition will be sold for hundreds of thousands,[1] but both times I corrected myself, remembering to be pure only in the sight of God. And immediately one is aware of the joy of life. To be noted:

Yes, I also prayed well; Lord, Master of my life, and King of Heaven. To be noted:

1) If there is any sort of God, then there is only the One whom I know within myself as I know myself, and also in everything living. People say, there is nothing material, no matter. No, there is, but it is only that through which God is not nothing, is not unliving, but a living God, by means of which He lives in me and in everything. Why—I do not know, but I know that it is so.

I must remember that my soul is not "divine," as they say, but is God Himself. As soon as I am God and am aware of myself, then there is no evil, no death, nothing except joy.

2) Now I am in a bad mood: everything is bad, everything torments me, everything is contrary to my wishes. And then I recall that my life only consists of being liberated from what conceals me from myself, and immediately everything shifts around. Everything that tormented me seems like trifles, unworthy of attention, while what life consists of, and what its joys are, are immediately apparent to me. Just take them. And instead of irritation I have a calm turning upon myself, and what tormented me becomes material to be reworked. And reworking is always possible and always gives the best joy in life.

September 29. Iasnaia Poliana. 1) What terrible mental hell modern literature is, especially for young readers from the people. First, it stuffs their memories with the obscure, self-assured, empty chatter of writers who write for their contemporaries. The main peculiarity and harm of this chatter is that it all consists of allusions to and quotations from the most various writers, the most recent and the most ancient. They quote phrases from Plato, Hegel, Darwin, about whom the writers do not have the least con-

189

ception, and along with them are phrases of some Gorky, Andreyev, Artsybashev,[2] etc., about whom it is not worth while having any conception. Secondly, this chatter is harmful because, by filling their brains, it leaves no room or leisure for them to become acquainted with those writers who have withstood the test of time, not only for decades, but for hundreds and thousands of years.

Sasha had come. Sofia Andreevna said that she is ready to make peace with Varya [Feokritova]. Then I was very much moved by her thanking me for showing affection for her. I am frightened, but I would like to think that even she can be overcome by kindness. I went riding with Bulgakov along the Zaseka, near Miasoedov. Very good. No work at all, and it is not necessary. Only worthless letters, and in the evening I read over, making marks, a book of proverbs, and also a wonderful book by a Belgian worker, sixty-five years old, almost illiterate, who has a circle of those who believe in him and preaches a very profound and true doctrine about the divinity of the soul: we must not believe in God, but must believe that we are God. His whole doctrine is in this belief and in love, love for one's enemies, only this love is real. There is much that is superfluous, unclear, the connection with the Biblical legend of Adam, Eve, and the surpent interpreted allegorically, but the main principles are very profound and true. Am going to bed.

September 29   II : 46

Sasha still wants to live away from home. I am afraid for her. Sofia Andreevna is better. Sometimes I feel false shame for my weakness, and sometimes, as now, I rejoice in this weakness.

Today for the first time I saw the possibility of taming her with kindness and love. Oh, if only . . .

Feel very bad, weak. Did nothing except letters, and those badly. I had a pleasant ride with Dushan. In the evening I read my biography, and it was interesting. Very much exaggerated. Sasha was here. Sofia Andreevna was calm. To be noted:

1) (I think I have written this before, but I feel it especially strongly today:) God breathes through our lives. I could, in my confusion, tell myself that I am I and God is Himself, or does not exist, and then I could understand that I am He, and then everything is easy and I feel joy and freedom.

2) Sofia Andreevna says that she cannot understand love for one's enemies, that it is an affectation. She, and many others, do not understand it, mainly because they think that the partiality they feel for other people is love.

Today the same. She talks a lot for the sake of talking and does not listen. Today there were difficult moments because of my weakness; I saw unpleasantness and pain where it did not exist and could not exist for true life.

The same listlessness. [Received] from Cherktov Lentovskaia's[1] letters and his article and some other things. I read it; his work about the soul is interesting and good. Few letters, and not very interesting ones. I wrote a bit about socialism for the Czechs. Sofia Andreevna spoke about arranging a meeting with Chertkov. I said that there was no use talking, that we must simply stop being foolish and live as always. Went riding with Bulgakov, and spent the evening with Goldenweizer. And I also read Maupassant; "The Family" is a gem. Let Sasha copy in about matter and happiness.

1) I meant to ask Sasha to copy it and forgot.

October 1

My hostile feeling toward her is terribly depressing, but I cannot overcome it when she begins this talking, endless talking without end and without sense or purpose. Chertkov's article on the soul and God is, I fear, a bit too clever.[1] It is a joy that all who are truly religious by nature have one and the same element in common. Antoine le Guérisseur, too.[2]

October 2

Got up ill, went walking. An unpleasant north wind. Did not note anything, but thought well and clearly during the night about how good it would be to depict artistically all the vulgarity of the rich and bureaucratic classes and of the peasant workers, and to put down at least one person who is spiritually alive in the midst of both of them. It could be either a woman or a man. Oh, how good it might be, and how it attracts me! What a great work it might be! And now I am thinking of it without any idea of the consequences, and this should be the case in any real work, including genuine artistic work. Oh, how good it might be! Yesterday, reading Maupassant's story made me want to portray the vulgarity of life as I know it, and during the night the idea came to my mind of placing a spiritually alive person in the midst of this vulgarity. Oh, how good! Maybe I shall do it. I wrote two short letters to Iakovleva and Preobrazhenskaia.[1] I suddenly felt like sleeping after lunch, and slept an hour. Then I had a good talk with Pavel Ivanovich [Biriukov] and Goldenweizer. Now it is time for dinner. Sasha was here. She is in low spirits. She shouldn't. Everything is for the best, just try not to foul things up yourself. I am trying to live only for my soul, and I feel how far I am from this. Sofia Andreevna's health is bad. Seriozha is coming, and Tania tonight.

To be noted:

1) God breathes through our lives and through all life in the world. He and I are one and the same. As soon as I understood this, I became God.

2) A materialistic explanation of life is just as much a consequence of ignorance as the invention of machines of perpetual motion (I get letters from peasants with projects such as this). *Perpetuum mobile* is a result of ignorance of mechanics, while a materialist explanation of life results from ignorance of wisdom. "You just keep oiling it, you can put tar in it, or put oil in it, it'll run all right."

3) God breathes through us and is blessed. His main attribute is the good. He is understood by us as the good. We seek the good, and our whole lives consist of this search, and therefore, whether we want it or not, our whole lives consist of a search for God.

If we seek good for ourselves, for our corporeal self, we will not find it; instead of good we shall find grief and evil, but our errors, whatever the consequences, shall lead to the happiness of others in other generations. So the life of all always consists of a search for happiness and always the attainment of it, although in a wrong way of living it means the attainment of good for others, for all except oneself, while in a right way of living it means the attainment of good for oneself as well. If we seek God, we shall find goodness. If we seek true goodness, we shall find God. Love is only the striving toward the good. And therefore it is truer to say that God is the good than that God is love.

In the morning the first thing she spoke about was her health, then denunciations and talking without end, and interfering in the conversation of others. And I feel ill. I cannot overcome a hostile and unkind feeling. Today I felt very strongly the need for creative work and I see the impossibility of devoting myself to it, and this because of her, of my persistent feeling about her, and of my inner struggle. Of course this struggle and the possibility of victory in it are more important than any conceivable work of art.

I did not finish writing about yesterday evening. I had a good talk with Seriozha and Biriukov about Sonia's illness. Then Goldenweizer played magnificently, and we had a good conversation with him. I did not wait up for Tania but went to sleep late. Last night, strangely enough, I kept having horrible dreams. I woke up early, went walking in good weather, and Sasha came over. All is well with her. I do not feel like writing.

To be noted:

1) I have told myself many times that on meeting and communicating with anyone I should keep in mind that a manifestation of the spiritual source stands before me, and I should treat him accordingly. To keep this in mind means to be aware of yourself, i.e., to summon God who is within you. And if you have summoned Him, and if it is no longer you who will be dealing with this person, but God who is within you, then all will be well.

2) Music, like every art, but music especially, stimulates a wish that everyone, as many people as possible, might participate in the pleasure you are experiencing. Nothing demonstrates the true significance of art more emphati-

cally than this transferral of yourself into others and your wish to feel through them.

3) The Venus de Milo, the beauty of the female body. It is all nonsense; it is lust, given the form of so-called art. (This is poor.)

4) Forgot what.

October 5   I : 238

I was seriously ill for two days, since the 3rd. Fainting spells and weakness. This began the day before yesterday, October 3, after my nap before dinner.[1] A good result of it was Sofia Andreevna's reconciliation with Sasha and Varvara Mikhailovna. But Chertkov is still just as far away. I am particularly sorry for him and Galia, for whom this is very painful. There were few letters, which I answered. Yesterday I stayed in bed all day without getting up.

October 5   II : 50

I handed over my leaflets and now I am beginning again. And it seems to be necessary to begin again: on the 3rd, after my nap before dinner, I became unconscious. They undressed me, put me to bed, gave me an enema, and I spoke about something. I remember nothing. I woke up and recovered consciousness at eleven. Headache and weakness. Yesterday all day I lay in a fever with a headache, ate nothing, and the same weakness. Also last night. It is now seven in the morning, my head and liver still ache, and my legs, and I am weak, but I am better. The main result of my illness is that it reconciled Sasha with Sofia Andreevna. Sasha was especially wonderful. Varya came. We shall see. I am struggling to overcome my hostile feelings toward her, but I cannot forget these

*three months when she has tormented those near to me
and myself as well. But I shall overcome it. Last night
I did not sleep, and, while I cannot say I thought, ideas
wandered through my head.*

October 6

Got up more cheerful, not very weak, and went walking. I noted something which Sasha will copy. To be noted now:

1) As I was walking I felt especially clearly and vividly the life of calves, sheep, moles, trees: each, which has put roots down in some way, does its own bit, to put out a sprout during the summer. The little seed of a fir tree, or the acorn, have turned into a tree, a young oak, and they grow and will live hundreds of years, and new ones will come from them, and the same with sheep, moles, people. And this has gone on for an infinite number of years, and will continue for the same infinite time, and it will happen in Africa and India and Australia and on every spot on the globe. And there are thousands and millions of such globes. And when you understand this really clearly, how ridiculous it is to talk of the majesty of anything human or even of man himself. Of all the creatures that we know, man is higher than the others, that is true, but as there are creatures infinitely below man, which we know of in part, so there must be creatures which are infinitely above us, which we do not know because we cannot. And when man is in such a situation it is ridiculous to speak of any majesty he may have. All that we may desire of ourselves as men is that we may not behave foolishly. Yes, only that.

1) God breathes through us and is blessed. We seek bliss, meaning that whether we want to or not we seek God. If we seek bliss for ourselves (physical, personal bliss), we shall not find it, but involuntarily we shall

help bring bliss to others, by our example or the consequences (struggle, technical perfection, scientific or religious delusions). If we are aware of ourselves as God,
seeking bliss for all (love), then we shall find our own
bliss. If we seek God we shall find bliss; if we seek true
bliss, we shall find God. Yes, love is a consequence of bliss.
The first thing is not love but bliss. It is truer to say that
God is bliss than that God is love.

2) Man is aware of his life as something that always
is and always has been, and not even always because
"always" indicates time, while that is, is, and only is. My
body was given me from my mother's womb, but I am a
completely different "I."

3) The reproach most commonly made to those who
express their convictions is that they do not live according
to them and that therefore their convictions are insincere.
But if you thought about it seriously, you would understand that it is completely the reverse. Could an intelligent
man, who has expressed convictions which do not accord
with his way of life, avoid seeking this discrepancy? If
he still continues to express his convictions, which do not
accord with his way of life, then this only demonstrates
that he is so sincere that he cannot help expressing what
exposes his weakness and that he does not do what the
majority do, fit his convictions to suit his weakness.

October 7   I : 240

1) Religion is the establishment of one's relations to
the world in a manner providing guidance in all one's
acts. Usually people established their relationship to the
source of all, to God, and they ascribe to this God their
own characteristics: punishments, rewards, the desire to
be respected, love, which is essentially only a human
attribute, not to mention the absurd legends which describe God as a man. They forget that we can recognize

or rather cannot help recognizing, the source of all, but we cannot form any sort of concept about this source. But we have invented a human God of our own and address Him as a familiar, ascribing our own characteristics to Him. This chumminess, this diminution of God, distorts the religious understanding most of all, and for the most part deprives people of any religion whatever or of guidance in their actions. If you establish such a religion, it is best to leave God in peace and not attribute to Him not only the creation of paradise and hell, wrath, the wish to redeem sins, and similar stupidities, not even attribute to him will, desires, or love. Let us leave God in peace, understanding that He is something completely inaccessible to us, and construct our own religion and our own relationship to the world, using the qualities of reason and love that we possess. This religion would also be a religion of truth and love just as all the religions have been in their truest sense, from the Brahmins to Christ, but it will be more precise, clearer, more obligatory.

2) What a terrible blasphemy it is, for anyone who understands God as he can and should, to identify a certain Jew, Jesus, with God!

On the sixth I did not feel like working and could not, so I did not work. Not very interesting letters. I am depressed at heart. Still I went riding. Many people in the evening: Strakov[1] and his daughter, Bulygin, Boulanger. It is difficult and dull for me to speak.

October 7. Slept little, the same weakness. I went walking and noted down about chumminess with God. Sasha copied it in. Did nothing except letters, and few of them. Tania rode over to Chertkov's. He wants to come at eight, right now.[2] I shall remember what I must remember, that I live for myself in the sight of God. Yes, the trouble is that when I am alone I remember, but when I meet someone I forget. Read Schopenhauer. Must tell Chertkov. That is all until eight o'clock.

Chertkov was here. He was very simple and clear. We

talked a lot about everything except our difficult relations.
It is better that way. He left after nine. Sonia had an
hysterical fit again; it was painful.

October 7   II : 51

*Yesterday, October 6, I was weak and gloomy. Every-
thing was depressing and unpleasant. A letter from Chertkov. He thinks this is no use. She has been trying to get
him to come over and has invited him. Today Tania rode
over to the Chertkov's. Galia[1] is very upset. Chertkov
decided to come at eight, and it is now ten minutes of.
Sofia Andreevna asked me not to exchange kisses with
him. So repulsive. She had an hysterical fit.*

October 8   1 : 241

Got up early, went to meet the horses coming to take
dear Tania away. Said goodbye to her. Sasha and Varvara
Mikhailovna [Feokritova] also saw her off. Afterward I
came home and revised "On Socialism," a worthless article.
Then I read Nikolaev.[1] At first I liked it very much, but
later less, especially the summary of Part I. There are
defects, inaccuracies, far-fetched interpretations. Sonia
came and I told her everything I wanted to but I could
not keep calm.[2] I became very much upset. Then went
riding with Dushan, slept, and had dinner. In the evening
I read Nikolaev again, the summary of Part I, which I
did not like. Now it is after ten, and I am going to bed.

October 9, i.I l.

October 8

Today is the 8th. I told her all I thought necessary. She objected and I became upset. And that was bad. But perhaps something will still remain. It is true that my only concern should be not to behave badly myself, but I am sincerely sorry for her, not always but most of the time. I spent the day better, and I am going to bed.

October 9

My health is better. Went walking and had good thoughts in the morning, as follows:

1) The body? Why the body? Why space, time, causality? But the very question "why?" is a question about causality. And the mystery of why we have a body remains a mystery.

2) We must ask, not why I live, but what I should do.

I shall not write in anything more. I wrote nothing except a worthless letter. I feel well in my soul, significant, religious and well for that reason. Read Nikolaev: it was worse. Went riding with Dushan. Wrote a note to Galia. Spent the evening quietly and calmly, read "On Socialism," and about the prisons in *Russian Wealth*.[1] Am going to bed.

October 9

She is quiet, but is preparing to talk about herself. I read about hysteria. Everyone is guilty except for her. I did not go to the Chertkovs and I shall not. Tranquillity is the most precious thing of all. I feel stern and serious at heart.

Got up late, at nine, a bad sign, but I passed the day well. I am becoming accustomed to working on myself, to summoning my own highest judge and obeying his decisions on what appear to be minor problems of life. I was only able to read the mail and the *Cycle of Reading* and *For Every Day.* Then I corrected the proofs of three booklets "For the Soul." I like them. Went walking before dinner. Ilia's Sonia and her daughter were here,[1] Boulanger and Nazhivin later on. We had a good conversation; he is very close to me. Am going to bed. To be noted:

1) Our task is only to maintain ourselves as a tool by means of which the master performs some task which I cannot know, and to keep ourselves in the best condition, so that if I am a plow, the plowshares are sharp, or if I am a lamp there would be nothing to prevent me from burning. Also what is done with our lives is not given to us to know, and we do not need to know.

2) The concept of God in even the most primitive form, far as it is, of course, from corresponding to a rational conception of Him, is still very useful for our lives in that the conception of Him, even the most primitive, transfers our consciousness into an area where a man's assignment may be perceived, and therefore all deviations from it, errors and sins, become clear.

3) When revolutionaries achieve power, they inevitably must act as all rulers do, they must commit violence, in other words act in ways without which there can be and is no power.

Quiet, but strained and frightening. No peace.

The days fly by without work. Got up late and went walking. At home Sofia Andreevna was upset again by my imaginary secret meetings with Chertkov;[1] I am very sorry for her, she is ill. Did nothing except letters and looking over the "Preface."

Had a very good ride with Dushan. After dinner had a discussion with Nazhivin. To be noted:

1) Love for our children, our spouse, our brothers, is a sample of the love which we should and must feel for all.

2) One must be like a lamp, closed to outside influences, such as wind or insects, and also be clean, transparent, and brightly burning.

More and more often, on meeting people, I remember who I really am and what I demand of myself, only in God's sight, and not in the sight of others.

Since morning she has been saying that I met secretly with Chertkov yesterday. She did not sleep all night. But, thank goodness, she is struggling with herself. I behaved well and remained silent. Whatever may happen she interprets as a confirmation of her mania. Never mind.

Got up late. A painful conversation with Sofia Andreevna. I was silent most of the time. I worked on the revision of *On Socialism*. Went riding with Bulgakov to meet Sasha. After dinner I read Dostoevsky;[1] the descriptions are good, although all sorts of little jokes, wordy and not very funny, hinder the reader. The dialogues are impossible, completely unnatural. In the evening again there were hard words from Sofia Andreevna. I remained silent. Am going to bed.

October 12   II : 56

Again talking and a scene since this morning. Something or someone told her that I have left my diaries to Chertkov in my will. I remained silent. An empty day; I could not work well. This evening the same talk again. Hints, investigations.

October 13   I : 246

I am still at a low point intellectually, but spiritually alive. Revised *On Socialism* again; it is all very trifling, but I started on it. I shall be more restrained in my work, more economical, for there is little time left to me, and I waste it on trifles. Perhaps I may write something useful.

Sofia Andreevna is very much upset and is suffering. It would seem that what lies ahead of her should be so simple: to live out the years of old age in harmony and love with her husband, not interfering in his work or in his life. But no, she wants—God knows what she wants, she wants to torment herself. Of course it is an illness, and one cannot help pitying her.[1]

October 13   II : 57

It turns out that she found my little diary and took it away. She knows about some will, leaving something to someone, obviously concerning my works. What torment she suffers over their money value—and she is afraid I shall interfere with her edition. And she is afraid of everything, poor thing.

October 14 I : 247

The same as ever. But today I am physically very weak. There was a letter on the desk from Sofia Andreevna with accusations and an invitation to repudiate something.[1] When she came in I asked her to leave me in peace, and she left. I had an oppressive feeling in my chest and my pulse was over 90. Again revised *On Socialism*, a worthless occupation. Before going out I went in to see Sofia Andreevna and told her that my advise to her is to leave me in peace, not to interfere with my work. It was depressing. Went riding. Mrs. Lodyzhenskaia[2] was here; I completely forgot her.

Slept. Ivan Ivanovich was here. I had a good talk with him and Belinki.[3] I read over my old letters, very instructive. How can I blame youth, and how can I help rejoicing that I have lived to an old age?

October 14 II : 58

A letter reproaching me for some paper about rights, as if she were mainly concerned with the financial question; that is better and more understandable. But when she speaks exaggeratedly about her love for me and kneels down and kisses my hands, I find it very painful. I still cannot definitely announce that I shall go to the Chertkovs.

Got up early, thought about space and matter; I shall write it in later. Went for a walk. Letters and my booklet on sexual desire. I do not like it. Stakhovich, Dolgorukov with another gentleman, Gorbunov and Seriozha have arrived. Sofia Andreevna is calmer. Went riding with Dushan. I wanted to go to the Chertkovs, but changed my mind. Conversations in the evening, not too boring. Am going to sleep.

There was a clash with Sasha and general disturbance, but it was bearable.

Not too well, listless. I went walking, did not think of anything. Letters, revised *On Socialism,* but I soon felt weak and put it aside. I said at lunch that I would go to the Chertkovs. A stormy scene, she rushed out of the house and to Teliatinki. I rode out and sent Dushan to say that I would not go to the Chertkovs, but he did not find her. When I came back, she was not yet there. Finally we found her after six. She came and sat motionless in her outdoor clothes, eating nothing. And this evening she attempted an explanation of her conduct. Late in the night she very movingly asked forgiveness, admitting that she was tormenting me, and promised not to do it any more. Will something come of it? [1]

Today it was decided.

I wanted to go to Tania's, but I am hesitating. She had an hysterical fit, angry.

The fact of the matter was that she proposed that I go to the Chertkovs, she requested me to go, but today, when I said I would go, she went wild. Very, very painful. God help me. I told her that I was not going to make any promises, and am not making any, but I shall do all I can not to anger her. I shall hardly be able to make my departure tomorrow. But I must. Yes, it is an ordeal, and my part is to do no unkindness. God help me.

Got up at eight, walked through the Chepyzh oak wood. Very weak. I thought well about death and wrote Chertkov about it. Sofia Andreevna came and was still treating me gently and kindly, but she is very excited and talks a lot. Did nothing except letters. Cannot work, or write, but thank God I can work on myself. I am making progress. I read Sri Sankara;[1] not the right thing. Read Sasha's diary; it is good, simple, truthful. Perper[2] and Bez. [?] were here from Tashkent. I talked badly with Perper and got angry for no reason. Am going to bed, feeling weak. Death is near and I will offer no resistance.

Wake. Sofia Andreevna is better, seems to repent, but there is an hysterical exaggeration in that too. She kisses my hands. She is very excited and talks continuously. I feel well morally. I remember who I am. I read Sri San-

kara. The basic metaphysical idea of the essence of life is good, but the doctrine as a whole is confused, worse than mine.

October 18 I : 251

Still weak, and the weather is bad. Thank God, without wishing to I feel a good *readiness for death*. Walked little. Was depressed by two petitioners; I do not know how to deal with them. I do not behave rudely, but I feel that I am guilty and it is depressing. And for good reason. Walked about the garden. Had few thoughts. Slept, and got up feeling very weak. Read Dostoevsky[1] and was amazed by his slovenliness, his artificiality, his fabrications, and read Nikolaev's *Concept of God*.[2] The first three chapters of Part I are very, very good. Now I am getting ready for bed. Had no dinner and feel very well.

October 18 II : 62

The same depressing atmosphere of fear and alienation. Nothing happened today. She began to talk about faith tonight. She simply does not understand what faith is.

October 19 I : 252

Sofia Andreevna came in during the night. "Another conspiracy against me." "What are you talking about, what conspiracy?" "Your diary was given to Chertkov. It is not here." "Sasha has it." It was very painful. I could not go to sleep for a long time, because I could not overcome an unkind feeling.[1] A pain in my liver. Molostvova[2] has come. I walked through the fir grove, barely able to move. To be noted:

1) The conception of the world as material in time and space has nothing that is actually real about it, but it is only our conception. This is so because this conception is internally self-contradictory. Matter cannot be understood except within the limited confines of space, whereas space is infinite, i.e., unlimited. Everything, in order to be a thing, must be limited in some way, limited by some other thing: the earth by the air, particles of air by gases, gases by thinner gases. And these? . . .

Exactly the same is true of time. Time defines the duration of occurrences, whereas time itself is infinite, and therefore every attribute as to its infinitude has no significance. The life of a micro-organism is less prolonged than the life of a man, and the life of a man than the life of a planet, and the life of a planet than? So that all measures of prolongation have only a relative meaning, they are only $\frac{x}{\infty}$, and therefore are all equal to each other, whatever x may be.

2) To live in God's sight does not mean to live in the sight of some God in heaven, but it means to evoke the God who is within you and live in His sight.

3) Militarism arouses the demand for patriotism, which in turn justifies the baseness of militarism. Patriotism arouses the demand for militarism, which in turn supports patriotism.

4) You may recognize God within yourself. When you recognize Him in yourself, then you may recognize Him in other beings (and especially vividly in people). When you recognize Him in yourself and in other beings, then you recognize Him within Himself.

Again did nothing except letters. My health is bad. A change is near. It would be good to live out the remaining days better than I have. Sofia Andreevna said that she regretted what happened yesterday. I expressed some of my thoughts, especially that if there is hatred even for one person, then there can be no true love. I talked with Molostvova, or rather listened to her. I finished reading and skimming through the first volume of the *Karamazovs*. There is a great deal that is good, but so clumsy. The Grand Inquisitor at Zosima's farewell. Am going to bed, it is twelve o'clock.

20, i.I l.

October 19

II : 63

Very painful conversation last night. I bore it badly. Sasha talked of a sale for a million.[1] We shall see what will happen. Maybe that would be best. If only I may appear before the highest Judge and deserve His approval!

October 20

I : 253

Alive, and even somewhat better, but still did no serious work. Revised *On Socialism*. Was depressed by the petitioners. Went for a long ride with Dushan. Mikhail Novikov has arrived.[1] I talked a lot with him, a seriously intelligent peasant. Perevoznikov and Titov's son, a revolutionary, came as well.[2] Said goodbye to Molostvova this morning. Everything is calm.

October 20

II : 64

There is no use writing down what is bad. Things are bad. I shall write only one thing: of how Sasha gives me joy and how sweet and dear she is to me.

Walked without having thoughts. At home there were many letters, which I answered. I tried to continue *On Socialism* and decided to discard it. It was badly begun, and there is no need for it. There will only be repetitions. Then the Iasnaia Poliana conscripts arrived, and I talked with them.[1] We are too far apart; we cannot understand each other. Went walking in the garden. Dinner. Dunaev came in the evening and talked a lot.[2] I am tired. I long painfully for solitude. I had something to write down, but forgot it. In a condition such as mine now it is good, even very good, to feel scorn for oneself. Sofia Andreevna is all right.

I am bearing my ordeal with great difficulty. I keep remembering Novikov's words, "When I used the whip, she got a lot better," [1] and Ivan's "It's our way to use the reins," [2] and I am displeased with myself. Last night I thought about leaving. Sasha talked a great deal with her, and I am holding back my hostility with difficulty.

I'm still doing no work. Dunaev is generous, ardent, and affected, but naturally so. A good letter from Chertkov. I did not go riding, but went for a walk and talked with some latrine-cleaners. Did not note down anything. In the letter to Dosev there is much truth, but not the whole of it.[1] There is also weakness. I do not even feel like writing my Diary. Nikolaev's book is excellent.[2]

There is nothing hostile on her part, but I am depressed by the pretense on both sides. A letter from Chertkov to me, enclosing the letter to Dosev and the announcement. Everything is very good, but it is annoying that the secret of my diary has been violated. Dunaev talked well.[1] What he repeated to me of her statements to him and to Maria Nikolaevna [Tolstoy] [2] is terrible.

The letter to Dosev is for me above all that program which I am still so far from fulfilling.[1] My talks with Novikov[2] suffice to make this obvious. The mitigating circumstance is supposed to be my liver. But my liver should not only obey but should serve. *Je m'entends.* To be noted:

1) I have lost my memory of everything, of almost all the past, of all my writings, of everything which has brought me to the state of awareness in which I now live. Formerly I could never have imagined this condition of thinking every minute of my spiritual self and its demands, in which I now live almost all the time. And I am experiencing this state without effort. It is becoming habitual. Just now after my walk I stopped in to ask Semion[3] about his health and was as pleased as Punch with myself, and then, as I was walking by Aleksei,[4] I barely answered his "hello." This I immediately noticed and reproached myself. That is a real joy, and it would not have happened if I lived in the past or even was aware of it or remembered it. I could not live a timeless life in the present, as I now do, most of the time. How can I help rejoicing in my loss of memory? Everything that I worked out in the past (even if only my inner work in my writings) I live by, and make use of, but the work itself I do not remember. Amazing! But I think this joyous change takes

place in the lives of all old people: life is entirely concentrated in the present. How wonderful!

Dear Bulgakov has come. He read his essay, and vanity is already pecking at him.[5] A good letter from a priest, which I answered.[6] I made a little progress on the article *On Socialism,* which I have taken up again. Went riding. All evening I spent reading over the penny booklets and sorting them. I wrote a note to Galia[7] in the morning. A letter from Gusev about Dostoevsky;[8] he feels just as I do.

October 23

II : 67

The pretense on both sides is just as painful as ever. I try to be natural, but it does not work. I cannot stop thinking about Novikov. When I went riding, Sofia Andreevna followed me on foot to see whether I was going to Chertkov's. I am ashamed to admit my foolishness even in my diary. Yesterday I began doing exercises—the old fool wanted to get younger—and I pulled a cupboard over on myself and hurt myself for nothing. There's an eighty-two-year-old fool for you!

October 24

I : 257

Received two letters today, one, on Merezhkovski's article, exposing me,[1] and the other from a German from abroad, also exposing me,[2] and this hurt me. I immediately thought in perplexity, why should people be abused and condemned for their good efforts? And I immediately understood that this was not exactly justified, but was inevitable, essential, and beneficial. How conceited and proud a man would become if it were not for this, how imperceptibly he would substitute satisfaction of popular opinion for fulfillment of the work of his soul. How instantly such undeserved hatred and scorn of others liberate us from concern with popular opinion, transferring us to the only stable ground for life, the fulfillment of the duty of one's conscience, which is the will of God.

Gastev[3] and Miss Almedingen[4] arrived. Read letters and answered them, did nothing else. This morning I made a real fool of myself. I began to do some gymnastics unsuited to my years, and pulled a cupboard over on myself. What an oaf. I feel weak, but I remember myself, thank goodness for that. I worked a bit on *Socialism.* Gastev talked very well about Siutaev and the Cossack.[5] It is essential for the people to have a guide in the religious sphere and a leader in the secular sphere.

1) I imagined very vividly a story of how a priest is converting a man of free religion and of how the converter is himself converted. A good subject. Went riding with Bulgakov. Evening depressing.

October 24   II : 68

Sasha was crying because she had quarrelled with Tania. I cried too. Very painful, the same tension and unnaturalness.

October 25   I : 258

Got up very early, but did nothing all the same. Walked to the school[1] and to Prokofi's, and talked with his son, a conscript in the army.[2] A good lad, he promised not to drink. Then worked a little on *Socialism.* Rode to the school with Miss Almedingen and then for a long ride with Dushan. Read Montaigne in the evening. Seriozha has come; he is a pleasure for me. Sofia Andreevna is still just as agitated.

The same depressed feeling. Suspicions, spying, and on my part a sinful desire that she would give me an excuse to leave. I am in such bad shape. I think of leaving, and then I think about her situation, and I feel sorry and can't do it. She asked for a letter to Galia Chertkov.[1]

Had a dream. Grushenka, a novel, it seemed by Nikolai N. Strakhov.[1] A wonderful subject. Wrote a letter to Chertkov. Made some notes for *On Socialism.* Wrote "On the Death Penalty" for Chukovski.[2] Went riding with Dushan to Maria Aleksandrovna's. Andrei has come. It is very hard for me in this madhouse. Am going to bed.

More and more I am oppressed by my life. Maria Aleksandrovna [Schmidt] does not want me to leave, and my conscience does not allow it.[1] *I must bear her, bear her without changing the outward situation, but working inwardly. Lord help me.*

Got up very early. Had bad dreams all night. Took a good walk. At home wrote letters, worked a little on the letter to N.[1] and on *On Socialism,* but have no mental energy. Went riding with Dushan. Dinner. Read about Siutaev.[2] A marvellous letter from a Ukrainian to Chertkov.[3] I made corrections on the article for Chukovski. Nothing to note. Things seem bad, but actually all's good. The burden of our relations keeps increasing.

October 27 II : 71

On October 25, the whole night my tormenting struggle with her haunted me. I would wake up, then doze off, and it would start all over. Sasha told me what is being said to Varvara Mikhailovna [Feokritova].[1] I feel both sorry and unbearably disgusted.

On October 26, nothing special happened. Only my feeling of shame increased, and so did the need to take some step.

October 28, Optina Pustyn I : 261

[Oct. 27]

Went to bed at 11:30. Slept until after two. Woke up, and again, as on previous nights, I heard doors opening and footsteps. On previous nights I did not look at my door, but now I looked and saw through the crack a bright light in the study and heard rustling. It was Sofia Andreevna hunting for something, probably reading. The day before she had asked and demanded that I should not lock the doors. Both her doors stay open, so that my least movement is audible to her. Day and night all my movements and words must be known to her and under her control. Again footsteps, the door carefully opened, and she went out. I do not know why, but this aroused an uncontrollable aversion and indignation in me. I wanted to go back to sleep but could not, I twisted and turned for about an hour, then lit a candle and sat up. The door opened and Sofia Andreevna came in,

215

asking about my "health" and expressing surprise at the light which she had seen in my room. My aversion and indignation increased, I was choking, and I counted my pulse: 97. I could not lie down, and suddenly I came to the final decision to leave. I wrote her a letter[1] and began to pack the most necessary things, only so as to get away. I woke up Dushan, then Sasha, and they helped me pack. I trembled at the thought that she would hear me and come out. There would be a scene, hysterics, and I would never be able to leave without a scene. Soon after five everything was somehow packed and I started for the stable to tell them to harness the horses, while Dushan, Sasha and Varia finished packing. The night was pitch black, I lost the path to the wing of the house, and fell into a thicket, pricking myself, knocked against a tree, fell down, lost my cap, could not find it, got out of there with an effort, went home, took another cap, and with a lantern I got to the stable and ordered them to harness the horses. Sasha, Dushan and Varia came. I was trembling, expecting pursuit, but then we were on our way. We waited an hour in Shchiokino, and every minute I expected that she would appear. But now we were in the train, we started, and the fear passed and instead I felt pity for her, but not doubt that I had done what I should. Perhaps I may be mistaken, in justifying myself, but I do think that I was rescuing myself; it was not Leo Nikolaevich that I was rescuing but that which sometimes and to a very small extent is within me. We reached Optina. I am well, although I did not sleep and ate hardly anything. The journey from Gorbachev in a third-class carriage jammed with working people was very instructive and good, although I took it in weakly. Now it is eight o'clock and we are in Optina.[2]

*On the night of the 27 the event occurred which im-
pelled me to take this step. And now I am at Optina, on
the evening of the 28th. I sent Sasha a letter and a telegram.*

Slept fitfully. Alesha Sergeenko came in the morning;
I greeted him gaily, not understanding. But the news he
brought is terrible: Sofia Andreevna, when she had read
the letter, screamed and dashed to the pond. Sasha and
Vania ran after her and pulled her out. Andrei is at home.
They guessed where I am, and Sofia Andreevna asked
Andrei to find me at all costs. And now, on the evening
of the 29th, I am awaiting Andrei's arrival. A letter from
Sasha. She advises me not to lose hope. She has written
for a psychiatrist and is waiting for the arrival of Seriozha
and Tania. I was very depressed all day, and physically
weak too. Went walking, and yesterday finished my note
to *Rech* (Speech) about the death penalty. I went to
Shamardino. Mashenka was a great comfort and joy for
me, in spite of her story about the "evil one," and so was
dear Lizanka.[1] Both understand my situation and are
sympathetic. On the way here I kept thinking of some
way out of the situation for her and for me, and could not
think of any, but it will come, whether we want it or not,
and it will not be what we foresee. Yes, I should think
only about acting so as not to sin. And what will be will
be. That is not my business. I found *A Circle of Reading*
at Mashenka's, and as I was reading the 28th I found
just the right answer to my situation: the test is necessary

and beneficial for me. Now I shall go to bed. Lord, help me. A good letter from Chertkov.

October 30, i.I l.

October 29, Optina Pustyn   II : 73

Sergeenko came.[1] Everything is the same, even worse. If only I do not sin, and do conceive no malice. Now I am not.

October 30, Shamardino   I : 263

i.I l.

Alive, but not entirely. Very weak and sleepy, and this is a bad sign.

I read Novoselov's "Philosophical Library" book; "On Socialism" is very interesting.[1] My article *On Socialism* is lost; it's a pity. No, it is not. Sasha has come. I was very glad, but it was painful. Letters from my sons. The letter from Sergei is good, brief, to the point, and kind.[2] I went to rent a hut in Shamardino and am very tired.[3] Wrote a letter to Sofia Andreevna.

October 31, Astapovo   I : 264

When we were still in Shamardino, Sasha and [?] were afraid that they would overtake us, so we left. In Kozelsk Sasha caught up with us and we rode on together. We had a good trip, but after four I began to shiver, then my temperature was 104°, and we stopped in Astapovo.[1] The kind station master has given us two fine rooms.

God is that unlimited Whole, of which man acknowledges himself to be a limited part.

Only God truly exists. Man is a manifestation of Him in matter, space, and time. The more the manifestation of God in man (life) unites with the manifestations (lives) of other beings, the more he exists. The union of this life of one's own with the lives of others is accomplished through love.

God is not love, but the more love there is, the more man reveals God, the more truly he exists.

Astapovo, Oct. 31, 1:30 p.m.

If we wish by the concept of God to clarify our understanding of life, then there can be nothing solid or reliable in our concept either of God or of life. These are only idle speculations, leading nowhere. We recognize God only by being conscious that He is manifested in us. All that derives from this consciousness and the rules of conduct based on it never fails to satisfy man fully both in comprehending God and in managing his own life on the basis of this consciousness.

November 3, Astapovo   I : 265

The night was bad. I lay in a fever two days. On the 2nd Chertkov came.[1] They say that Sofia Andreevna . . . On the 3rd Tania. Seriozha came during the night, which moved me very much.[2] Today, the 3rd, Nikitin,[3] Tania,[4] then Goldenweizer and Ivan Ivanovich. So much for my plan: *Fais ce que doit, adv. . .*

And all is for the good of others and chiefly for me.[5]

Notes

January 2 (N-I:1)

1. A sketch added as an epilogue to "Three Days in the Country," a trilogy of sketches designed to dramatize the miseries of peasant life. "Dream" was first published in 1911.

2. Wanda Landowska (1881-1959), famous harpsichordist and pianist; made several visits to Iasnaia Poliana between 1907 and 1910; her husband, Henryk Leo Landowski, a journalist.

3. Count Dmitri Adamovich Olsufiev (1862-?), an old friend of the family; he was member of the Council of State and was more than once requested by Tolstoy to intervene on behalf of his persecuted friends.

4. The offices of the local rural administration. Tolstoy made the trip to look into the complaints the peasants were making about the harsh measures taken to exact payment of taxes from them. The trip provided material for "Taxes," the third of the "Three Days" sketches.

5. René Marchand, correspondent of the Paris daily *Le Figaro*.

January 3 (N-I:2)

1. "Poverty of the People," or "Poverty," finally entitled "The Living and the Dying," the second part of "Three Days in the Country."

1. Sergei Lvovich Tolstoy took a very active part in organizing and supervising the migration to Canada and the resettlement there of several thousand members of the Dukhobor sect in 1898.
2. A. I. Solovov, one of Tolstoy's very many correspondents who wrote to him seeking enlightenment on various religious and moral matters.

1. Eugen Heinrich Smitt (1851-1910), Austrian journalist and writer on religious and moral problems.
2. Mahomet Fatih Murtazin, a Mulla in the town of Samara: Tolstoy answered his questions on religious matters.

1. Aleksander Drankov (1880-?), owner of a cinematographic studio in Moscow, the first in Russia; he came to show some films he had made at Iasnaia Poliana and to make new ones.
2. See Jan. 3, n. 1.

1. Zaseka, or Kozlova Zaseka (now Iasnaia Poliana), the local railway station, two miles from Tolstoy's estate.
2. A town twenty-three miles from Iasnaia Poliana.
3. Yegor Pavlovich Kuzevich, a peasant from Iasenki, a village near Iasnaia Poliana.

1. Nikolai Nikolaevich Gusev (b. 1882), Tolstoy's secretary in 1907-1909, devoted follower and author of important biographical works on Tolstoy. He was arrested in August 1909, at Iasnaia Poliana, and exiled for two years to the remote Perm province for spreading illegal Tolstoyan literature.
2. Aleksandra Lvovna and Chertkov had been in disagreement as to who would publish *For Every Day*.

3. *Coenobium, Rivista internazionale de liberi studi,* published in Lugano, Switzerland.

January 10 (N-I:9)

1. A petitioner from Demenki, a village about a mile from Iasnaia Poliana. Tolstoy formulated a prayer for help in dealing with people, which is stated on January 13, n. 4.

January 11 (N-I:10)

1. A reference to Tolstoy's prayer on communicating with people, see January 13, n. 4. Natalia Zharova was a widow from Iasnaia Poliana.

2. The forester's house known at Iasnaia Poliana as "the lieutenant's" because it was once occupied by a forester who was a retired army lieutenant. There was a telephone there.

January 13 (N-I:12)

1. "Three Days in the Country," the sketches.

2. Philip Petrovich Borisov (1878-1918), groom at Iasnaia Poliana.

3. A petitioner who showed Tolstoy the indictment against her husband. He had killed a seventy-five-year-old man who while drunk had tried to rape her.

4. Halley's Comet, which could be observed in 1910; there was much talk at the time that it would bring the end of the world.

5. Tolstoy read Maxim Gorky's "Varenka Olesova," and in marginal notes pointed out the artificiality of the language, the falseness of the descriptions and of the figures of speech.

6. *A Cycle of Reading. Thoughts of many writers on the Truth of Life and Conduct, selected, collected, and arranged for each day.*

7. *For Every Day.* A similar collection, but not following the topical arrangement of the *Cycle.*

January 14 (N-I:13)

1. Sergei Mikhailovich Bulygin (1889—), oldest son of M. V. Bulygin.

1. Tolstoy attended the assizes of the Moscow Court for criminal cases in Tula. He attended the trial of peasants from Denisov, who were accused of robbing the mail, and the closed trial of I. I. Afanasiev for belonging to the illegal Socialist-Revolutionary Party and holding literature from it. According to a Tula newspaper, Tolstoy defended the accused merely by his presence, and the peasants were acquitted, while Afanasiev was given the minimal sentence, three years.

2. Tomáš Garrigue Masaryk (1850-1937), Czech political leader and scholar, at that time a professor of philosophy at the University in Prague, later the first president of Czechoslovakia.

1. Alexander Mikhailovich Kuzminski (1845-1917), Sofia Andreevna Tolstoy's first cousin and husband of her sister Tatiana, was presiding judge in the Senate (Supreme Court). In response to a letter from Tolstoy on behalf of one of his followers, who was to be tried by the Senate for spreading Tolstoy's illegally published works, Kuzminski wrote that he "always endeavored to protect himself from any outside influences whatever."

1. Baron Schilling; no information on him is available.

2. Professor Vahan Fomich Totomiants (1871-?), an authority on the cooperative movement. Tolstoy's reply to him, praising the cooperative movement, was widely published.

3. Alexander Vladimirovich Golitsyn (1876-?), physician, active in the Zemstvo and the cooperative movement; a relative of Tolstoy's by marriage. He also wrote about cooperatives.

1. Iliusha—Tolstoy's son Ilia Lvovich.

2. Mikhail Pavlovich Skipetrov (1888-1911), ex-student who had left Petersburg University under the influence of Tolstoy's views.

1. Peter Alekseevich Sergeenko (1854-1930), writer and old acquaintance of Tolstoy. He brought a gramophone and records, including some of Tolstoy reading from *A Cycle of Reading.*
2. Tolstoy's son Andrei was on his way to St. Petersburg where he had been given a position in the Ministry of the Interior.

1. A peasant from Iasnaia Poliana. Tolstoy liked to walk along the Kiev highway, less than a mile from his house, and talk with pilgrims and passers-by on the road.
2. Samuil Ivanovich Smirnov (1880-?), Iaroslav peasant who refused military service and was sentenced to four years in a disciplinary battalion.
3. Fedor Khristoforovich Grauberger (1857-1919), follower of Tolstoy, a former teacher.
4. Iakov Aleksandrovich Tokarev (1860?-?), a member of the Molokan religious sect.

1. Mary Shanks (1866-?), an Englishwoman, daughter of the owner of a fashionable store in Moscow and sister of the wife of Tolstoy's English biographer and translator, Aylmer Maude.
2. Prince Pavel Dmitrievich Dolgorukov (1866-1927), Chairman of the Society for Peace in Moscow, a public figure. He arrived for the opening of a "People's Library," commemorating Tolstoy's eightieth birthday. He brought a catalogue of books and asked Tolstoy to choose the books for the library.

1. These booklets were Tolstoy's last important work, later entitled *The Way of Life.*
2. The "People's Library," which was opened in a grand ceremony that day.
3. Helen Keller.

1. Second issue of *The Way of Life*.

2. Sofia Emmanuilovna Dmitrieva-Mamonova was a friend of Tolstoy's older daughters.

3. Countess S. A. Tolstoy was returning from Moscow.

4. Third issue of *The Way of Life*.

5. Tolstoy rode to a nearby town to arrange for two orphans to enter an orphanage. Ozerki, a village about six miles from Iasnaia Poliana.

6. I have done what I could; let those who can do better.

1. Dr. Makovitski ran a clinic where he tended the local population without charge.

2. One of many letters which Tolstoy received, reproaching him for the discrepancies between his avowed principles and his way of life.

1. M. V. Shmelkov, an assistant railroad mechanic, who came to consult Tolstoy about changing his profession to agriculture. Tolstoy advised against it.

2. Nikolai Evgenievich Felten, was arrested in 1909 for distributing forbidden books by Tolstoy. Felten wrote Tolstoy describing his trial; he was sentenced to six months in prison; the sentence was appealed.

3. This was an article entitled "The Last Stage of My Life," which was published in several dailies on February 6. It was an excerpt from Tolstoy's diary of 1889, which had been translated into French and then retranslated into Russian becoming unrecognizable in the process.

1. In *The Way of Life*, thoughts on a single theme are presented for each day. Tolstoy gathered material for them by going through *For Every Day* to select thoughts related to these themes. On this day he had completed gathering material for two themes, or two "days."

2. (See January 12, I-11). Tolstoy wrote this preface in the form of a letter to V. A. Posse, the editor of a monthly.

3. "The Notes of a Lackey" was written by A. P. Novikov, who had been a manservant in the employ of Prince G. P. Volkonski. Excerpts from it had been published by Chertkov in 1905, under the title "The People and the Gentry."

4. "Dorik"-Fedor Mikhailovich Sukhotin (1895-1920), younger son of M. S. Sukhotin by his first marriage. Tolstoy's daughter Tatiana was his stepmother. Dorik, Tatiana's daughter Tania, and Aleksandra Tolstoy all had measles.

5. Baron d'Estournelles de Constant, a pacifist leader and member of the French parliament, was in Moscow at the head of a French parliamentary delegation. He sent Tolstoy a telegram of greeting.

6. Tolstoy's First and Second *Readers* for teaching Russian. A teacher in St. Petersburg had written him complaining that the price of the *Readers* had been raised (from ten to fifteen copeks). Tolstoy replied that as the *Readers* had been written before 1881, they were the property of his wife and he had no control over them, but promised to do what he could.

February 14 (N-I:37)

1. i. I l.: "If I live." Tolstoy often ended a diary entry with the next day's date and this abbreviation, and started the next day's entry with the comment "Alive."

February 15 (N-I:38)

1. Aleksander Modestovich Khiriakov (b. 1863), author of articles and books about Tolstoy. In 1909 was sentenced to a year in prison as editor of the newspaper *The Voice* in St. Petersburg. He corresponded with Tolstoy while in prison.

2. A former workman came to see Tolstoy and explained that he wanted to settle on the land and get two hoboes to come and work with him; later he would increase the number of such settlers, hoboes changed to ploughmen. Tolstoy liked the young man, but showed skepticism as to the success of his scheme.

3. Thoughts from *The Way of Life,* chapter 6, "Sins, Temptations, and Superstitions," and chapter 17, "False Beliefs."

1. The article for Boulanger's book on Buddha.

1. Mitasha—Prince Dmitri Dmitrievich Obolenski (1844-?), an old acquaintance of the Tolstoys.

1. The "Danish [actually Norwegian] Jew": M. Levin, formerly a Russian subject, at that time a correspondent of a Norwegian newspaper in Oslo.
2. Boris Osipovich Goldenblat (1862-?), an attorney at law in Tula who had taken on some cases for peasants at Tolstoy's request.
3. The article on Buddha.

1. Vladimir Germanovich Molostovov (1859-1918), a landowner from Kazan; had traveled widely in the Orient; marshal of the nobility of his district. His wife Elizaveta wrote on Russian sectarians.

1. "Political" here: one sentenced or exiled for a political crime, such as belonging to an illegal party. The "sailor" (or former sailor), unidentified, seems to have been a Social-Revolutionary; he asked Tolstoy for money to leave the country. Tolstoy took an interest in him and sent him to rest at the Chertkovs, then collected the money he needed from the members of his household.
2. Adrian Pavlovich Eliseev, the Tolstoy's coachman.
3. Philipp Petrovich Borisov, the stableman, who had apparently gone for the mail.
4. Tolstoy rode over to pay a call on Maria Aleksandrovna Schmidt, who was ill.
5. Paul Bourget's play, *La Barricade,* Tolstoy had received an article from Paris about this play.

6. Elias Lehr, an Austrian writer on religious and moral questions. Tolstoy thanked him for sending him his books.

7. Tolstoy wrote to the Executive Committee of the Czech Progressive Party on the occasion of Masaryk's sixtieth birthday.

8. See n. 5 above.

9. Ilya Danilovich Galperin-Kaminski, a Russian writer settled in France, translator of Tolstoy into French; he sent the article on Bourget to Tolstoy.

February 25 (N-I:46)

1. Literally, "in a dog's mood," in a rotten mood.

2. A story based on a tragic incident during the coronation of Tsar Nicholas II in 1896; about a thousand persons were trampled to death on the Khodynka field outside Moscow in a stampede caused by a badly organized distribution of gifts to the populace.

3. E. Melnikov, a schoolboy in the seventh grade, who had written Tolstoy about a vice which tormented him.

4. Karel Jonaš on putting into practice the principles of the fifteenth century Czech moralist Peter Chelčicki.

February 26 (N-I:47)

1. An expression Tolstoy used when he was asked to write more imaginative literature. "It is like the two peasants," he explained. "One asked the other to go to the baths with him; the other answered, 'I don't need to; I once had a bath.' "

February 27 (N-I:48)

1. Mark Ostakhov and Aleksei Eliseev; conscientious objectors. Ostakhov wrote a story of his life in which he told about the ordeal he suffered upon refusing military service.

2. "Lapshin"—Probably Iu. A. Lokshin, who had written Tolstoy that after reading his works he had become indifferent to death or money.

3. K. P. Slavnin, was put on trial for publishing in the newspaper *New Russia* Tolstoy's ideas on teaching children the law of God, from *For Every Day*.

1. W. H. Davies' *The Autobiography of a Super-tramp*, with an introduction by George Bernard Shaw.

1. Probably the seventh chapter of *The Way of Life*, finally entitled "Overindulgence."

2. Tolstoy accompanied Dr. Makovitski on a medical call to a village about six miles away. He started back home on foot in very cold weather, and Dr. Makovitski overtook him and brought him home when he had finished his visit.

1. Lev Shestov, pseudonym for Lev Isaakovich Schwarzman (1866-1938), writer, author of the book *The Good in the Teachings of Tolstoy and Nietzsche* and other philosophical and critical writings. An antirationalist influenced by Dostoevsky and Kierkegaard.

2. While Aleksandra Tolstoy was ill, Bulgakov had helped Tolstoy with the work she had been doing; Aleksandra feared that he would take it over altogether.

1. Nadezhda Pavlovna Ivanova was an acquaintance of the Tolstoys in Tula.

1. A thirty-year-old peasant, a former artillery noncommissioned officer, a revolutionary, and finally again a peasant; had been influenced by Tolstoy's writings and came to "make his life clearer."

2. Christo Dosev (1886-1919), a Bulgarian Tolstoyan.

3. Sergei Mikhailovich Popov (1887-1932), at one time a zealous Tolstoyan.

4. A German novel by Josef Baitz, *Ecce Sacerdos, Ein Zeitroman* (1909).

1. Mikhail Aleksandrovich Stakhovich (1861-1923), an old acquaintance of the Tolstoys, a member of the Duma. Tolstoy frequently asked him to intercede with the government on behalf of various victims of persecution.

1. Countess Aleksandra Andreevna Tolstoy (1817-1904), a second cousin of Tolstoy's, was a lady-in-waiting at the court. A close friendship developed between Tolstoy and Countess Aleksandra, a very brilliant woman prominent in high society; they met in St. Petersburg, then abroad, in the 1850's. Tolstoy had corresponded with her for many years, and his letters and her memoirs were to be published. Stakhovich brought a typed copy of the manuscript with him.

1. Kinosuke Shiraishi, a pastor in Kofu, Japan. He had written to Tolstoy asking him to elaborate some of his views on religion, refusal of military service on Christian principles, and refusal to pay taxes. Tolstoy worked on the letter from March 9-19.

2. "15,000"—Vsevolod Iulievich Shimanovski, a former officer who, under the influence of Tolstoy's ideas, had left military service to become a teacher, had written Tolstoy asking for what good cause he could use a sum of 15,000 rubles; Tolstoy suggested the publication of a popular encyclopedia.

3. Zosia—Sofia Aleksandrovna Stakhovich, the sister of Mikhail Stakhovich and old friend of the Tolstoy family.

1. Tolstoy answered this letter, which has not been preserved, "You say that you love science and music, but you do not love anything except your animal nature. Your letter is terrible. I am very sorry you wrote it."

2. Tolstoy sent to I. I. Perper, editor of *The Vegetarian Review,* the manuscript of a Russian translation, done by the wife of his friend Goldenweizer, of a book by Bruno Freidank, *Die Schrecken der Civilisation.*

1. Swami Dayanand Sarasawanti, *Light of Truth,* an English translation of the *Satyarth Prakasa.*

1. Tolstoy intended this Preface to be a clear, compressed statement of his philosophy. He worked on it from 1907 to October, 1910; it was rewritten more than a hundred times.

2. Aleksander Aleksandrovich Stakhovich, the older brother of Mikhail and Sofia (Zosia) Stakhovich, a member of the second Duma.

3. Vladimir Aifalovich Molochnikov, a metal worker from Novgorod, a Tolstoyan. He had been imprisoned for a year for distributing Tolstoy's forbidden works, and arrested again in March 1910 for "enticing" two soldiers to refuse military service, but was found not guilty.

4. Fedor Semenovich Perevoznikov, a metal worker living at the Chertkovs.

5. Nikolai Semenovich Leskov, (1831-1895), famous Russian writer, who toward the end of his life came under the influence of Tolstoy's ethical ideas.

1. Ivan Aleksandrovich Bodianski, son of an old friend of Tolstoy's; had sent Tolstoy an article asking him to recommend a publisher.

2. Prokofi Vlasovich Vlasov, a peasant from Iasnaia Poliana befriended by Tolstoy. The occasion for this particular visit to Prokofi was the following: A peasant from a distant town had come to see Tolstoy, asking him to intervene on his behalf; he had been found guilty of horse-stealing; he told Tolstoy, however, that he had bought the horse from Prokofi, who, apparently, was prepared to confirm this. Tolstoy rode over to ascertain the facts, and asked Prokofi how old the horse had been. Prokofi said it was six years old, but the peasant had claimed it was two. In view of this discrepancy, Tolstoy refused to intervene.

3. "A Letter to an Indian," Tarakute Das, then a student in America, written in 1908.

1. Arvid Iärnefelt, a Finnish writer. His drama was *Titus, the Destroyer of Jerusalem.*

1. This letter grew into the article "On Madness."
2. The young people at Teliatinki wanted to put on an amateur performance and asked Tolstoy to write a play. He started one but did not finish it.
3. A. P. Voitichenko came to Iasnaia Poliana to play Ukrainian national songs on the cembalom, a stringed instrument resembling the zither.

1. Aleksander Nikiforovich Dunaev (1850-1920), a friend of Tolstoy's who shared his views.
2. Vladimir Galaktionovich Korolenko (1853-1921), a well-known writer and publicist, his article, entitled "An Everyday Occurrence," opposed capital punishment.

1. Archpriest Aleksander Rudanski, a priest of the Greek church in Mogilev-Podolski, wrote Tolstoy asking whether "Christ the Saviour had risen from the dead in the flesh."

1. Fedor Alekseevich Strakhov (1861-1923), a close friend and follower of Tolstoy's, a philosopher.
2. Masaryk spent two days at Iasnaia Poliana, March 29 and 30.
3. Mikhail Stakhovich and his sister, Maria Aleksandrovna Rydzevska.

1. P. Olberg, a correspondent of *Hufvudstadsbladet,* the Swedish-language newspaper published in Finland; Tolstoy argued that the Finnish people had only to assert their rights not to pay taxes or serve in the army in order to possess these rights.

2. Samuil Moiseevich Belinki was living at Teliatinki and assisting Chertkov with Tolstoy's correspondence. He was friendly with Molochnikov, who was still in prison.

3. Tolstoy asked Mme. Rydzevski, who was leaving for St. Petersburg, for her help in the Molochnikov affair.

1. Sergei Terentievich Semionov, a peasant writer (1868-1922). In 1894, Tolstoy wrote a preface to a volume of stories about peasant life. His admiration for Semionov's literary work was hardly justified.

1. "And I feel fine."

2. Lev Petrovich Sergeenko, a fourteen-year-old boy who was staying with the Chertkovs at Teliatinki.

3. Grigori Konstantinovich Gradovski (1842-1915), a liberal journalist and writer had asked Tolstoy to send a few words of greeting to the second Congress of Russian Writers. Tolstoy replied that, although he sympathized with the general purposes of the Congress, he could not participate in it because it was sanctioned by the government. He agreed to having the letter made public, but only on condition that it be read in its entirety. The leaders of the Congress, Gradovski and Mikhail Stakhovich, did not respect Tolstoy's terms and read only the first, congratulatory, part of the letter, omitting the reference to the government.

4. Vladimir Vladimirovich Filosofov, who had come to ask Tolstoy for a signed portrait which could be hung in a home for aged writers and their families. He also discussed with Tolstoy the coming Peace Congress in Stockholm.

5. Apparently from Prokhor Afanasievich Melnikov, a former soldier, who wrote that he had been "awakened from a sinful sleep" by reading Tolstoy's works.

1. This collection of booklets was finally entitled *The Way of Life*.

2. Aleksandra Lvovna had developed tuberculosis and was going to the Crimea for a cure. Point 3 in this entry also refers to this event; Tolstoy wrote Chertkov, "If it were not for the money which I left the children she could have stayed on here, but now she cannot help leaving. But this is all as absurd as the comet."

1. The prayer formulated on January 13, "Help me in all intercourse with people to see myself in them."

1. Joseph Ivanovich Petrozhitski (1851-1910), a former village school-teacher, was a member of the terrorist "Will of the People" group and had been imprisoned several times. After reading Tolstoy's writings, he repudiated violence and settled in the Caucasus. He had written Tolstoy only a few days previously that he had had a premonition of death.

2. Traditional Lenten food when eaten without butter.

1. Aleksandra Petrovna Kurnosenkova, a peasant widow in Iasnaia Poliana whom Aleksandra Tolstoy had been helping.

2. Probably Peter Pavlovich Shintiakov, a landless peasant.

3. A woman whose husband, Bodianski by name, had been condemned to hard labor for participating in the so-called "Novorossiisk Republic." During the peasant disturbances connected with the Revolution of 1905, particularly in the south and southeast of Russia, the peasants organized small "republics," seized land and carried out raids on the property of the landowners. The petitioner claimed that her husband was innocent and asked Tolstoy to intervene either with the Empress or with the Prime Minister, Stolypin. Tolstoy wrote Count D. A. Olsufiev, an acquaintance of Stolypin's (see January 2, note 3).

1. George Bernard Shaw. Tolstoy wrote on the envelope of his letter, "Intelligent stupidities from Shaw."

2. Tolstoy's letter to the secretary of the "First Universal Races Congress," in which he condemned pacifism. It was not sent.

3. Semen Mikhailovich Solomakhin, a sectarian who shared Tolstoy's views and printed and distributed his forbidden books.

4. Shakhaev. Tolstoy observed of him, "Whatever you start to say, he will finish for you."

1. Vasili Vasilievich Suvorov, a peasant in Iasnaia Poliana who was about Tolstoy's age.

2. Vasili Petrovich Mazurin, a teacher who had arrived at views similar to Tolstoy's.

3. Mikhail Osipovich Menshikov (1854-1918), once a friend and sympathizer of Tolstoy's later had turned against him and became a prominent staff member of the reactionary daily, *New Times*. In a venomous article, "Is Count L. N. Tolstoy Suffering?" quoting a statement of Tolstoy's that he was suffering" for the fate of Finland, as well as for the Jews, the Poles, the Lithuanians, and others, Menshikov commented that Tolstoy was suffering either "from the lack of suffering," or from the hatred of an anarchist for all social reality, the immediate object of his hatred being Russia.

1. *The World Chinese Student's Journal*, published in English. Tolstoy observed after reading it, "If I were young I would go to China."

1. Tolstoy listened to both these boys and thanked them for their urgent advice, "which I have lived without for such a long time."

2. Harada, a Christian who had been educated in America and was director of the first institute in Japan. He knew of Tolstoy's ideas but did not agree with him in all respects. Kadju Midzu-

taki, a young Japanese attending Moscow University, who had been sent by his government to learn Russian and obtain technical information about Russian industry.

3. *Indian Home Rule*, by Mohandas Gandhi, and a letter from Gandhi to Tolstoy. At the end of the book, there is a list of Tolstoy's works which Gandhi recommended: *The Kingdom of God is within You*, "What is Art?" and *What Then Must We Do?*

April 20 (N-I:88)

1. Trotski-Seniutovich, a retired colonel, who came to argue with Tolstoy about religion and autocracy.

2. Tolstoy did not go riding again until after May 11. He stopped because of the impression his riding horseback made, when some peasants were without horses to do their farmwork. Eventually he was persuaded to go riding again, as it was necessary for his health.

April 21 (N-I:89)

1. Antonina Mikhailovna Shcheglova had brought her two daughters to Tolstoy so that he could talk to them and influence them to better behavior.

2. A biography of Gandhi by Joseph J. Doke.

3. Leonid Andreev (1871-1919), writer of stories and plays, extremely popular at that time.

4. An article by D. N. Zhbankov, "Modern Suicides," in *Contemporary World*, III, 1910. Zhbankov was a doctor and social worker whom Tolstoy knew.

April 22 (N-I:90)

1. Tolstoy customarily walked alone in order to think by himself; he declined Andreev's offer to accompany him.

April 24 (N-I:92)

1. The young people at Teliatinki had put on Tolstoy's comedy, *The First Distiller, or How the Devil Earned a Crust*, written in 1886.

1. Olga Konstantinovna Tolstoy, first wife of Tolstoy's son Andrei and sister of Chertkov's wife.

2. Aleksei Petrovich Sergeenko, older son of Chertkov's assistant, P. A. Sergeenko. Aleksei Sergeenko witnessed Tolstoy's will on July 22, 1910, went to see Tolstoy at Optina Pustyn after he left home in October, and was present at Tolstoy's bedside in Astapovo at the end of his life.

1. S. T. Semionov's story, "The Offense."

2. Aleksei Sergeenko spent two evenings at the Tolstoys.

1. Mikhail Weinberg, a young man from Repin's agricultural colony in Tashkent, a pharmacist. Weinberg told Tolstoy about Repin's insanity (see June 30).

1. Vasili Vasilievich Pliusnin, a Siberian who shared Tolstoy's views. He had helped Tolstoy occasionally in his work.

1. Orest Dmitrievich Durnovo, a former officer, who had made an arrangement of the Gospels, treating them as literally true and interpreting every word. Tolstoy refused to endorse the opus, and when Durnovo and his wife started to argue with Tolstoy about it, he walked away without further ado.

2. "That is no reason to behave badly."

3. Sergei Petrovich Spiro, a writer and contributor to the *Russian Word*. He had visited Iasnaia Poliana several times previously.

4. An answer to the pupils of a rural school in Kliuchitsi, Nizhni-Novgorod Province. Tolstoy never sent the letter, but forwarded some books to the school.

5. Aleksander Petrovich Ivanov, a former officer who had be-

come a pilgrim. He had come several times to Iasnaia Poliana and had done copying for Tolstoy. He was always wandering and had no permanent home.

6. Kochedykov, formerly a weaver, mentally ill, kept asserting that "in this world there are two truths, the force of inertia and the Apocalypse."

May 1 (N-I:99)

1. Tolstoy went over to the Kiev highway to watch an automobile race between Moscow and Oriol. Tolstoy commented, "Some people don't even have bast shoes, and these automobiles here cost twelve or thirteen thousand rubles!"

2. A group of students from a scientific institute in Tula.

May 2 (N-I:100)

1. For Kochety, where his daughter Tatiana Sukhotina and her family lived.

2. "Tanias": Tolstoy's daughter Tatiana (Tania) and her daughter, Tolstoy's granddaughter, also named Tatiana.

May 3 (N-I:101)

1. Masaryk's book on suicide, *Der Selbstmord als sociale Massenerscheinung der Modernen Civilisation*. Tolstoy wrote Masaryk that the book was splendid and on the whole accorded with his views.

May 6 (N-I:104)

1. Chertkov had been forbidden by the government to live in the Tula Province since March 1909. As Kochety, the Sukhotin estate, was on the boundary of Oriol Province, Chertkov was planning to move to a nearby village so that he could see Tolstoy, but the government unexpectedly gave him permission to visit Tolstoy in Kochety.

2. A Latvian ex-Baptist and Tolstoyan, who had learned about Tolstoy from his brother who had died in prison. Tolstoy had known the brother, so he sent this man books and a letter in answer.

1. The article "On Madness"; see March 28.

1. Tolstoy had been planning to write a novel under this title since 1908 but he never finished it; two versions of a story by that name were published among his posthumous works, the first written in 1909 and the second in August and September 1910.

2. Chertkov had written to the newspapers protesting Gradovski's distortion of Tolstoy's letter about the Congress of Writers (see April 7). Gradovski wrote an answer justifying his action, and aroused Tolstoy's indignation.

3. Tolstoy rode on horseback, for the first time since April 20.

1. He talked with teachers from a local school about going barefoot, which he said was good and nothing to be ashamed of.

2. Lev Mikhailovich Sukhotin and Sergei Mikhailovich Sukhotin, the two sons from the first marriage of M. S. Sukhotin, the husband of Tolstoy's daughter Tatiana.

1. V. V. Veresaev (pseudonym of Vikenti Vikentievich Smidovich) (b. 1867), physician and writer; Tolstoy was reading his *Notes of a Physician* (1901), a book that had a quite sensational success.

2. S. T. Semionov, author of *Peasant Stories*.

3. Nikolai Mikhailovich Gorbov, a neighbor of the Sukhotins', who had translated some of Thomas Carlyle's works into Russian and had a valuable library on history of art. He was a patron of educational institutions for peasant children.

4. Leonid Dmitrievich Semionov (1880-1917), a religious freethinker who was in correspondence with Tolstoy.

1. "All Qualities Come from Her," the comedy Tolstoy began for the young people at Teliatinki (see March 23). The play was never completed, and it was presented at Teliatinki only after Tolstoy's death.

1. Albert Réville, a French Protestant theologian and historian of religions; at the Collège. Tolstoy was reading his book, *Les religions des peuples noncivilisés*.

1. A mistake: The correspondent was Maria Nikolaevna Iakovleva, a children's writer and translator. She had gone to see Tolstoy at Iasnaia Poliana, but as he was not there she wrote him a letter.
2. To live dying and to die living.

1. An English photographer, Thomas Tapsell, took a motion picture of Tolstoy as he was leaving for a walk. He was using a camera which Thomas Edison had sent to Chertkov. The films were sent to the United States to be developed, but were found to be damaged.

1. Countess S. A. Tolstoy had forbidden the village women to go by way of the Iasnaia Poliana gardens to the meadows where they got grass for the cattle. Tolstoy persuaded Sofia Andreevna to cancel her orders.

1. "Mitasha," Prince Dmitri Obolenski.
2. The potential conscientious objector, one David Maksimchuk, who had come from Podol Province to talk with Tolstoy.

3. Aliosha, Aleksei Sergeenko; see April 26, n. 2.

4. Skipetrov, see January 25, n. 2.

5. Ilia Vasilievich Sidorkov, an old servant in the Tolstoy house.

May 25 (N-I:121)

1. N. N. Gusev; see Jan. 8, n. 1.

2. Apparently H. Weinel, *Das freie Christenthum in der Welt,* 1909.

May 27 (N-I:122)

1. Robert Vipper, Professor of History at Moscow University; his article, "The Twilight of the Peoples" drew a parallel between the downfall of the Roman Republic, that of the Roman Empire and the contemporary situation.

2. Tolstoy's son Sergei told about a soldier who had bayonetted a convict who was trying to escape. The soldier was tormented by nightmares about the occurrence and eventually became insane.

3. Pavel Nikolaevich Orlenev (died 1932) famous actor, tragedian; toured extensively in Russia and abroad. Chertkov wrote to Tolstoy about Orlenev's interest in popular theater.

4. "Kolichka" Gay, Nikolai Nikolaevich Gay, the son of the famous artist, Tolstoy's friend.

May 29 (N-I:123)

1. When the Countess Tolstoy complained to Tolstoy that she could not go on any longer managing the estate, he asked her why she went on with it. She asked what else could she do, and he answered, "Go away somewhere, anywhere, to Odoev, to Paris." She had hysterics and rushed out of the house. Tolstoy was afraid that she would harm herself, and his heart began to beat very irregularly. She was found and brought home, but he remained weak.

2. Prince Pavil Petrovich Trubetzkoi (Paolo Trubetzkoi, b. 1867), a famous sculptor; was raised in Italy and lived abroad, visiting Russia from time to time; his mother was American. Paolo Trubetzkoi made three busts of Tolstoy and two small sculptures of Tolstoy on horseback. Goldenweizer heard from Tolstoy that during one of Trubetzkoi's visits, Sofia Andreevna

asked him whether he had read *War and Peace*. The sculptor, who spoke French with an Italian accent, replied, "J'ai jamais rien lou." (I never read anything).

May 30 (N-I:124)

1. Larisa Dmitrievna Nikolaeva, wife of Sergei Dmitrievich Nikolaev (See "List of Characters").

June 1 (N-I:125)

1. Nikolai Gavrilovich Chernyshevski (1828-1889), famous literary critic, political theorist, author of two novels and of numerous writings on philosophical, social and economic problems. A social and political radical and a materialist philosopher; had a wide audience in the 1860's, until his banishment to Siberia. His work is very highly regarded in the Soviet Union, and was a significant factor in Lenin's version of Marxism.

June 3 (N-I:126)

1. Lydia Alekseevna Ivanova, a landowner. She described the advantage of using oil-burning engines, for agriculture.

June 4 (N-I:127)

1. A letter to one Nikolai Stepanovich Chernov, a peasant. Tolstoy wrote him that he received about a thousand letters a year from correspondents asking whether they should become authors. "It is not only far more respectable but far more necessary to be a blacksmith, working seventeen hours a day, than it is to write compositions which no one needs, thousands of which appear every day, and my own among them."

2. The Cherkess guard, hired by Countess Tolstoy to protect the property, had arrested Prokofi Vlasov, a local peasant who had been a pupil in Tolstoy's school. Prokofi was taking away some timber.

1. Olga Konstantinova Klodt, a Finnish admirer of Tolstoy.
2. The story "By Chance" was originally intended to be included in *The Wisdom of Children*. Shortly afterward Tolstoy wrote it as an independent story.
3. Parasha, a Iasnaia Poliana village idiot, had become pregnant, and jokes were told in the village about this event.

1. Zakaz, the woods that started near the house at Iasnaia Poliana; Tolstoy was buried there according to his wish.
2. About 26 workers who attended the Prechistenski Workers' School in Moscow.
3. This was Trinity Day, which the villagers celebrated with music and dancing.

1. The "mother of a murderer," Snetkova, whose son was accused of murdering his friend.
2. A letter stating that Tolstoy could not give financial help to anyone. The letter was not sent.
3. Doctor Dmitri Vasilievich Nikitin, formerly Tolstoy's personal physician. He stayed at Iasnaia Poliana from June 7-9.

1. On June 8 Tolstoy got up after ten A.M.; he had obviously had a fainting fit during the night.
2. The doctors examined Tolstoy after his illness, and this annoyed him.
3. Orlenev; see May 27, n. 3.
4. Ivan Dmitrievich Sytin (1851-?), publisher of the Moscow newspaper *Russian Word* and head of a very important publishing business. He specialized in large cheap editions for mass circulation.
5. Babism, a religious movement which arose in Persia in 1844; Tolstoy showed a strong interest in this movement.

1. Chertkov, forbidden to enter Tula Province, was at the time of Tolstoy's visit, at "Otradnoe," in Moscow Province. Tolstoy went to visit him, accompanied by Aleksandra Tolstoy, D. P. Makovitski, V. F. Bulgakov, and I. V. Sidorkov, his valet.

1. The town of Meshcherskoe, close by Otradnoe, the estate that Tolstoy was visiting. It was a center of welfare activity; there was an orphanage and psychiatric hospitals there.

1. A reference to the preface of *The Way of Life.*

2. There was an asylum in the village of Liubuchany for non-violent and convalescing mental patients.

3. Karel Veleminský, a Czech educator, translator of Tolstoy's works into Czech. The conversation was taken down verbatim by at least four persons.

1. The Meshcherskoe Psychiatric Hospital.

2. Alexander Ivanovich Kuprin (1870-1938), a prominent writer of short stories and novels.

1. Troitskoe District Psychiatric Clinic; there were about a thousand patients in this hospital.

1. A mistake for Sofia, Bulgaria. Tolstoy dictated a letter for the Slavic Congress that was to convene there.

2. In the village of Ivino, women, formerly inmates of the Meshcherskoe Hospital, were living in peasant homes during their convalescence.

3. Sergei Timofeevich Kuzin (1864-?), a peasant and self-taught writer. The course of his life had been influenced by Tolstoy.

June 19 (N-I:139)

1. On June 19 Chertkov learned that he would be permitted to stay at Teliatinki, close to Iasnaia Poliana, while his mother was there.

June 20 (N-I:140)

1. Alexander Sergeevich Buturlin, an old acquaintance of Tolstoy's, a doctor and formerly a member of the "People's Will," a terrorist group.

June 21 (N-I:141)

1. Aleksander Petrovich Surin. Tolstoy sent a story based on his encounter with this peasant to the newspapers *The Russian Herald* and *Speech*. It was also published as a separate booklet under the title, "Favorable Soil (Out of My Diary)."

2. Fedor Alekseevich Strakhov; see March 5, no. 1.

3. Andrei Iakovlevich Grigoriev. The Skoptsy, a sect that practised castration.

4. Doctor Grigori Moiseevich Berkenheim; lived with the Tolstoys in 1903, as their family physician.

5. The article later entitled "On Madness."

6. Ivan Savvich Nikitin (1824-1861), a poet who wrote particularly about the hardships of peasant life.

7. To the District Mental Hospital at Troitskoe.

June 22 (N-I:142)

1. Tolstoy and Chertkov visited a silk-weaving factory in Liubuchany. The owner of the factory, an Old Believer, showed them the factory.

2. The telegram, from V. M. Feokritova in Iasnaia Poliana, read: "Countess Tolstoy has serious nervous upset, insomnia, tears, pulse hundred, asked me to telegraph. Varia." The telegram was dictated by Countess Tolstoy, except for the last

phrase. Sofia Andreevna Tolstoy wrote of this telegram, "Varvara Feokritova has telegraphed Leo Nikolaevich, but he will not come! This senile love for the false deceiver Chertkov, who has separated us, is repulsive, and I hate him for it."

June 23 (N-I:143)

1. Tolstoy answered this telegram, "More convenient to come tomorrow afternoon, send telegram, if absolutely necessary shall come tonight." This telegram caused the Countess Tolstoy to have an hysterical outburst; she immediately had another telegram sent, "Think absolutely necessary. Varia." V. Feokritova (Varia) asserts that Sofia Andreevna wrote the telegram herself, including the signature, "Varia."

2. From S. A. Tolstoy's *Daybook,* June 23rd: "They arrived this evening. A depressing argument. Everything which we have lived by our long lives is lost! Our love is lost, smashed to bits."

June 25 (N-I:145)

1. From S. A. Tolstoy's *Daybook,* June 25: "This morning I completely lost my head and suffered terribly. I begged Leo Nikolaevich to help me restore my balance, but he is helpless because he does not love me but loves Chertkov. Against his wishes but at my request he drove to Ovsiannikovo with me. Everything about me was in pain: my stomach, my legs, my heart. Leo Nikolaevich kept trying to get out and leave me. I cried. I do not know if he saw, but he did not leave me and we finished the ride together, and I felt a little better afterwards."

2. See May 30, n. 1.

June 26 (N-I:146)

1. The cause of the new crisis was that Sofia Andreevna had read the entry in Tolstoy's diary for June 20, "I want to try to contend consciously with Sonia, using goodness and love." She rushed in to Aleksandra Tolstoy and Vera Feokritova, shouting, "What am I, an evil woman, that he should struggle with me! What does he have to struggle with me about? What am I doing? . . ." When she challenged Tolstoy he explained that he meant that he must try to be kind to her in every way. She

immediately began to ask him where his diaries were, as she only had the ones up to 1900. When he said that they were in Chertkov's keeping, she was still more upset. She rushed outdoors, got soaking wet, and sat under Tolstoy's balcony, protesting that she wanted to catch a chill and die.

From S. A. Tolstoy's *Daybook*, June 26, "Another tormenting day. It is four A.M., and I have not even undressed. I keep thinking what I am to do. But I can find no answer. I feel very ill. Can it possibly be that I shall not die? Leo Nikolaevich is just as distant and angry. I am tormenting him, I am sorry for him, but he is in good health and has spiritual strength while I am perishing."

June 27 (N-I:147)

1. *A Course in Psychiatry*, by S. S. Korsakov, Moscow, 1901. Tolstoy used the book both for his article "On Madness," and to interpret what he had seen at the mental hospitals he had visited. He also hoped to find in it an explanation of Sofia Andreevna's condition.

June 28 (N-I:148)

1. To Sergei Tolstoy's, to celebrate his birthday. Sofia Andreevna was anxious that her husband go with her, but as she knew he was very tired she told him he need not come. He decided to go anyway.

2. Chertkov wrote the Countess Tolstoy, trying to clarify the dispute between them and settle it, if possible. He had come to live in Teliatinki, near Iasnaia Poliana. Chertkov brought the letter in person, and he and Tolstoy were so deep in conversation that they walked in the wrong direction and Tolstoy almost missed the train.

3. Sergei Tolstoy had not received the telegram announcing their arrival, so there were no horses to meet them.

June 30 (N-I:149)

1. Vasili Akimovich Repin, a former artillery officer, who had followed Tolstoy's ideas and organized an agricultural community in Tashkent. Beginning in 1909, showed signs of mental deterioration. Since June, 1910, stayed with M. A. Schmidt at Ovsiannikovo.

2. Nikolai Grigorievich Sutkovoi, who had left government service to work on the land.

July 4 (N-I:151)

1. The Countess Tolstoy wrote in her *Daybook* for July 1: "Chertkov came over and there was a stormy explanation. Made an effort to be reconciled with him for Leo Nikolaevich's sake." She observed in her *Diary*: "What can I do now? Alas! I must pretend that Leo Nikolaevich has not been taken from me completely."

2. Tolstoy's son, Lev, arrived from Paris. Tolstoy often used the terms *numerator* and *denominator* to express his opinion of people, the numerator standing for the spiritual qualities and capacities, and the denominator for self-evaluation. The smaller the numerator and the larger the denominator (which was infinity in the case of his son Lev), the smaller the actual number expressing the value of the individual.

3. Mother of Vladimir Grigorievich Chertkov, who was staying at Teliatinki.

4. See June 30, n. 1. Many of Miss Schmidt's copies of Tolstoy's manuscripts and letters were destroyed in this fire.

5. See June 30, n. 2.

6. Peter Prokofievich Kartushin (1880-1916), a rich Don Cossack who sympathized with Tolstoy's views and contributed financially to their dissemination. He was working with the peasants at Iasnaia Poliana with Sutkovoi and his sister.

July 5 (N-I:152)

1. See May 27, n. 4.

July 6 (N-I:153)

1. Maria Aleksandrovna Schmidt had spent four days at Iasnaia Poliana after her house was burned down.

2. Anna Evgenievna Zvegintseva, a neighbor who was influential in St. Petersburg. According to Feokritova, Countess Tolstoy had gone to ask her to use her influence to have Chertkov sent away.

1. A chapter from a story by Pierre Mille, *La Biche Ecrasée,* 1909.

1. Ivan Kopylov, a poor peasant from Iasnaia Poliana.
2. Nikolai Vasilievich Davydov (1848-1920), an old acquaintance of the Tolstoys; a jurist, docent at Moscow University.
3. See May 27, n. 4.
4. Charles Salomon, French author of articles on Tolstoy and translator of his works; he had brought with him the book by André Gide, *Le retour de l'enfant prodigue,* at Gide's request.

1. The events of the "terrible night" are partly recorded in Sofia Andreevna's own *Diary,* under July 10: "There was another clash, and again I saw the same cruelty and alienation, the same shielding of Chertkov. I was completely ill, and once more was overcome by despair; I lay down on the balcony on the bare boards and remembered that forty-eight years ago on this same balcony, still a girl, I had had the first experience of Leo Nikolaevich's love . . . Leo Nikolaevich heard me stirring and came out shouting at me that I was keeping him from sleeping and that I must go away. I went out into the garden and lay on the damp ground for two hours in my thin dress . . . Then the alarm was given, Dushan [Makovitski], Gay and Liova came and began shouting at me to get up and trying to pick me up from the ground. I was trembling all over from the cold and damp. If any of the foreigners had seen in what condition the wife of Leo Tolstoy had been brought, lying at two or three o'clock in the night on the damp ground, stiff with cold and at the limits of despair, how amazed these good people would be!" Sofia Andreevna refused to rise and go into the house unless Leo Nikolaevich came himself to fetch her. This he did, yielding to the rather rough urging of his son Lev.
2. The ninth chapter of *The Way of Life,* finally entitled "Parasitism."

1. Filia, the stable boy, had been sent to the Chertkovs to invite Goldenweizer to go riding, but he invited Chertkov instead. As the Countess Tolstoy saw the latter arrive, she became hysterical and Tolstoy had to send him away without explanation.

2. See July 10, n. 4.

1. Tolstoy's letter dated July 14, 1910, made five points: "1) I shall keep my present diary for myself and give it to no one."

"2) I shall take the old diaries from Chertkov and shall keep them myself, probably in the bank."

In point 3 Tolstoy tried to explain his relationship to his wife: "As I have loved you since youth, I have never stopped loving you, despite various reasons for my becoming cooler to you: . . . First, my greater and greater withdrawal from the interests of a worldly life and my feeling of disgust for it, while you did not want to and could not part from it, since you did not have in your soul those foundations which led me to my convictions; but this is only natural and I do not reproach you . . . Secondly, . . . your personality in recent years has become more and more emotional, despotic, and uncontrolled. . . . Thirdly, the main reason, the fatal one, for which neither you or I could be blamed, is our completely contradictory understanding of the meaning and purpose of life. . . . But regardless of all the misunderstandings that there have been I have not ceased loving and valuing you.

"My judgment of your life with me is as follows: I, a debauched man, sexually depraved, no longer in my first youth, married you, a pure, good, intelligent, eighteen-year-old girl, and in spite of my soiled past you have lived with me almost fifty years, loving me, living a hard laborious life, bearing children, feeding, raising, and looking after the children and me, without yielding to the temptations which might so easily have captured any woman in your situation, strong, healthy, and beautiful. . . .

"4) If at present my relations with Chertkov are hard for you, I am ready not to see him. . . .

"Now 5) if you do not accept these conditions for a good and peaceful life, then I shall take back my promise not to leave you. I shall go away. . . ."

The diaries were brought back from Chertkov's the same day, in conformity with point two of the letter.

2. A town 6 miles from Iasnaia Poliana.

1. From S. A. Tolstoy's *Daybook*, July 15. "I have been upset again since this morning by Leo Nikolaevich's refusal to give me the keys or the receipt from the bank to keep, as otherwise I am afraid that he would give the diaries back to Chertkov. He refused rudely. I had another serious nervous attack. I wanted to drink opium but lost my courage again; I vilely deceived Leo Nikolaevich into thinking that I had drunk it but immediately admitted my deceit, wept, sobbed, but made an effort and gained control of myself. How shameful, painful, but . . . no, I shall say nothing more. I am sick and tormented."

2. Matthew Gering, an American from Nebraska, had a letter of introduction from William Jennings Bryan who had corresponded with and visited Tolstoy.

1. See July 15, n. 2.

2. Gavriil Akinfievich Komarovskikh. Tolstoy said of him, "He is a very interesting person, and, as often happens, he lives alone with his religious ideas. He wants to express them and he is beginning to write. He showed it to me: the very best thoughts, but clumsily written."

1. Tolstoy went to Teliatinki and copied his Will in his own hand; this was Tolstoy's last visit to Teliatinki.

1. From S. A. Tolstoy's *Diary*, July 18. "I have been very depressed, languid, and gloomy since this morning and felt like crying. I thought that if Leo Nikolaevich is hiding his Diaries so carefully just from me, which he never did before, then

there must be something that he has to hide only from me, since Sasha and Chertkov have had them, and they are now locked up in the bank. I was tormented by doubts all night and all day, and I told Leo Nikolaevich about this and expressed my suspicion that he had been unfaithful to me in some way and was now concealing it and hiding them. He began to assure me that it was untrue, that he had never deceived me. . . . [Then he shouted,] "I have given up everything, my property, my works, I have left myself only the Diaries, and I should give them up too; I wrote you that I would go away, and I shall go away if you torment me."

2. The truth about himself.

July 19 (N-I:166)

1. Tolstoy had been invited to a Peace Congress in Stockholm, and decided to write a supplement to his "Report to the Peace Congress in Stockholm," written in 1909.

2. Dr. D. V. Nikitin, a family physician of the Tolstoys, brought with him a neuropathologist, Dr. G. I. Rossolimo, professor at Moscow University. Dr. Rossolimo examined Countess Tolstoy and recommended that she and Leo Nikolaevich separate for a while.

July 20 (N-I:167)

1. St. Francis, anticipating a rebuff from a gatekeeper of a town, counsels his followers to believe that God inspires even the gatekeeper's hostile actions.

2. Vera Sergeevna Tolstoy, who was visiting Iasnaia Poliana, a niece of Tolstoy's; she was the common-law wife of a Bashkir, Abdurashid Abulfak Sarafov.

July 22 (N-I:170)

1. See Appendix.

2. From S. A. Tolstoy's *Diary*, July 22:
During dinner, I expressed my displeasure and bewilderment at the fact that I was never given, if only to read, a copy of L.N.'s latest works because Chertkov takes hold of all the manuscripts. L.N. again became angry, raised his voice and began saying unpleasant things. Again, I began to cry, left

the dinner table and went upstairs to my room. He realized
what had happened, followed me and the conversation again
became unpleasant. But in the end he suggested that we go
for a walk together in the garden which I always appreciate and
enjoy and the tone of mutual hostility seemed to have dis-
appeared.

As a consequence of my note to him and my agreeing to his
visiting L.N., Chertkov arrived. I want to be generous toward
him with all his rudeness and unpleasantness. I overcame myself when I sat down to play checkers with my granddaughter
Sonichka and managed to forget Chertkov."

July 23 (N-I:171)

1. From S. A. Tolstoy's *Diary,* July 22:

Chertkov came again. L.N. and he were whispering to each
other but I overheard. L.N. asked: "Do you agree with what
I wrote?" The other said: "Of course I agree." Again a conspiracy of some sort. God have pity on me.

When, with tears in my eyes, I started to beg L.N. to tell me
what agreement they had spoken of, L.N. again made a wicked,
unfamiliar face and denied everything, stubbornly, insistently.
I don't recognize him! Again I am in despair and the jar of
opium is on my table. If I have not drunk it yet it is only
because I do not wish to make them all, including Sasha, happy
by my death. But how miserable they make me! L.N.'s health
is better. He'll do everything he can to survive me and to go
on living with Chertkov. I am longing to swallow the contents
of that jar and leave L.N. a note saying: "You are free."

Tonight, L.N. told me, wickedly: "Today I have decided
that I wish to be free and that I am not going to pay any
attention to anything." We shall see who is the winner if he
too declares war on me. My weapon is death and it will be my
revenge and the shame will be on him and on Chertkov for
having killed me. They will say: she was mad. But who was it
who drove me mad?" . . .

July 25 (N-I:173)

1. From S. A. Tolstoy's *Daybook,* July 25: "Decided to leave
home. Packed, took poison along so that I could take it in solitude if I could not stand it. I cried as I left my home and left
my place to Chertkov. I met Andriusha and his family at the
station in Tula. He understood my state and brought me home.

Leo Nikolaevich's joy and mine, I felt his love when I returned."

Under the same date, July 25, Sofia Andreevna wrote in her *Diary:* "Having discovered that there is a secret agreement between L.N. and Chertkov and some plot against me and the family, of which I am absolutely certain, has made me, of course, profoundly miserable. Never in my life have there been any secrets between me and my husband. [The last addition by S. A. Tolstoy: "This secret plot was the testament and Chertkov's letter accompanying it and signed by L.N., both secretly from me."] And aren't these asides, mysteries and plots insulting to a loving wife? In any case, all the recent moves by L.N. have caused a sharp antagonism between his children and that wily, wicked Pharisee Chertkov. And this is terribly sad! Why is L.N. arranging such a posthumous memory for himself and why is he perpetuating such evil? And all these people speaking and writing about I don't know what love. And they always denied that there were any documents, saying that they'd never write them, and all L.N.'s denials were nothing but words: private ownership—during his lifetime he reserved author's rights for himself; documents—he announced in the newspapers that he was renouncing his works starting from 1881 and now he has handed in his diaries and received a receipt from the National Bank, he wrote something with Chertkov and I believe with Bulgakov and today handed him large sheets, probably his testament depriving the family of the rights to his works after his death.

July 26 (N-I:174)

1. As the Countess Tolstoy was becoming more and more upset about Chertkov, Tolstoy decided to stop seeing him and wrote him about it. Chertkov agreed, so long as Tolstoy's freedom would not be limited by this, and therefore he urged him to make no promises.

July 27 (N-I:175)

1. Rudolf von Ihering (1818-1892), German legal theorist. This thought is from his book, *Die Schuld im Römischen Civilrecht*, 1867.

1. Sofia Aleksandrovna Stakhovich, see March 9, n. 3.
2. There had been rumors of a plot to have the will invalidated on the ground that Tolstoy was senile.

1. *The first entry in a new diary, "a diary for myself alone," which Tolstoy kept with him at all times and did not let anyone see. His main diary was read by close friends and passages were copied from and into it by various people.*
2. *See July 28, n. 2.*
3. *Allusion to Lev Lvovich's modeling.*

1. Mitrofan Vasilievich Lodyzhenski, a writer on religious questions living not far from Iasnaia Poliana. He talked with Tolstoy about Indian philosophy, Yogis, theosophy, hypnotism and science. He was accompanied by his wife and an acquaintance, S. V. Chirkin, formerly a consul in Bombay.

1. Tolstoy used the money that Aylmer Maude had sent him for the publication of *Resurrection* in English to buy new seed rye for the Iasnaia Poliana peasants. Their own seed grain had been spoiled by worms.
2. Countess Tolstoy wrote in her *Daybook:* "I rode in the cabriolet to meet Leo Nikolaevich, who had gone over to Kolpna to look for rye for the peasants. I met him; I was terribly afraid that I would meet him with Chertkov."

1. *After Tolstoy's conversation with P. I. Biriukov, he began to believe that he had made a mistake in making a secret will and that he should have announced his decision openly to all the family.*
2. *Sofia Andreevna had taken his diary and had copied out*

passages from it. She had been very much upset by the references to his feelings against her. When Tolstoy discovered this, he decided to hide the diary in another place.

3. *Anna Konstantinovna Chertkova, née Dieterichs, wife of Vladimir Grigorievich Chertkov. Tolstoy wrote apologizing to her for the state of their relations.*

August 3 (N-I:182)

1. The passage from Pascal ran, "One's own will never satisfies one, even if all its demands are satisfied. But a man need only renounce his free will, and immediately he will experience complete satisfaction. When one lives for one's own will, one is always dissatisfied; when one renounces it, one cannot help being satisfied. The only true benefactor is hatred for oneself, because every man is worthy of hatred for his lust. But while he hates himself, man seeks a being worthy of love. But as we can love nothing outside ourselves, we are forced to love a being which is within us but not of us, and there can only be one such being: universal being. The Kingdom of God is within us (Luke 17:21); universal good is within us but it is not of us."

2. Sofia Andreevna recalled, and read aloud, a passage from Tolstoy's Diary for 1851, "I have never been in love with women . . . I have fallen in love with men very often . . . [Followed the names of these men.] There was voluptuousness in this, but it is impossible to judge why this was so, because, as I have said, my imagination had never produced any lubricious pictures; on the contrary, I felt a terrible revulsion." Countess Tolstoy tried to interpret her husband's alleged love for Chertkov in terms of this passage.

In her *Diary*, under August 3, she notes that she brought Leo Nikolaevich the page from his Diary for 1851 with the passage about his infatuations with men; the passage, she thought, would make Leo Nikolaevich better understand her reasons for being jealous of Chertkov. But Leo Nikolaevich would not understand; instead he flew into a violent rage, told Sofia Andreevna to get out, threatened to leave, and finally locked himself in his room.

August 3 (N-II:6)

1. *Chertkov answered Tolstoy's letter of August 2 and pointed out the reasons for making a will and keeping it secret.*

1. *See July 31 (first diary), n. 1.*
2. *See March 25, n. 2.*

1. This may be a reference to some uncompleted literary work.

2. Father Dmitri Nikiforovich Renski, priest in the Birth of Christ Church in Moscow. Tolstoy worked three days on this letter.

3. A Mr. Freeman, son of the director of an oil syndicate(?)

4. (See May 22.) Fokin and five or six of his fellow-villagers, would-be conscientious objectors. Tolstoy suspected that their intention of talking with him might be a provocation on the part of the government, giving it an excuse to act against Chertkov.

5. Sri Paramahamsa, an Indian, who intended to visit Tolstoy. Tolstoy finally decided not to see him.

1. Tolstoy had gone to see Korolenko off and was riding home on horseback when it started to rain. He took shelter at the house of L. G. Sukhinin, a doctor in Tula.

1. According to V. M. Feokritova, Countess Tolstoy did not sleep all night and at 7:30 went out into the fir grove to find Tolstoy. She tried to persuade him to see Chertkov, but she was so upset that Tolstoy immediately refused on the grounds that her peace of mind was most valuable. She returned only at lunch time.

2. See August 5, n. 4.

1. Vasili Iulievich Ferre, a neighbor of the Tolstoys, formerly vice-governor of Smolensk.

2. An unidentified correspondent of a Hungarian newspaper.

Tolstoy was quite indignant when he learned that he was interested in the land question but had not heard of Henry George.

August 10 (N-I:189)

1. Two battalions of soldiers were encamped opposite the entry to Iasnaia Poliana. The officers had forbidden the soldiers to speak with Tolstoy, but four came, one of whom was an officer.

August 10 (N-II:13)

1. *Chertkov's wife, A. K. Chertkova.*

August 12 (N-II:15)

1. *Tolstoy told his daughter Tania about the will.*
2. *The letter that Tolstoy wrote Chertkov, agreeing with him that Biriukov was wrong and the will was justified.*
3. *See May 27, n. 4.*

August 13 (N-I:191)

1. E. D. Iazykova, formerly a rich woman who had changed her way of life under the influence of Tolstoy's writings. She had passed examinations to be a doctor's assistant (*feldsher*) and was working in this capacity.

August 13 (N-II:16)

1. *For Kochety.*

August 14 (N-I:192)

1. Tatiana Lvovna Sukhotina had decided to take her father to Kochety for a rest, but Countess Tolstoy decided to come too. She wrote in her *Daybook:* "Felt poorly, had no dinner, worrying about the arrangements Leo Nikolaevich and Sasha are making for going to Kochety, and I have decided to go myself."

2. See February 15, n. 1. Khiriakov had only just been released from prison.

3. Tolstoy said that his wife was completely ill and that he was ready to be a nurse for her to the end of his life. His daughter Aleksandra said rather ill-temperedly that she could not do that. A couple of hours later she came to ask her father's forgiveness for her lack of restraint.

August 14 (N-II:17)

1. *Sofia Andreevna came to her husband in the morning, and, speaking loudly and hysterically, had asked him whether she could go to the Maslovs and would not her husband be jealous of Taneev, who would be there?* Sergei Ivanovich Taneev was a composer and pianist to whom Sofia Andreevna had been passionately attached some years previously. He was living at the Maslovs', landowners in Orlov and friends of Sofia Andreevna. She went on to say something still worse, which Tolstoy would not repeat. T. L. Sukhotina wrote, "Could a sane person ask these things at the age of 66? . . . No, I am convinced that she is sick, and we shall soon have to have a doctor for her and put her under guardianship." Goldenweizer found Tolstoy weeping after this scene.

August 15 (N-I:193)

1. F. A. Strakhov, *The Search for Truth,* a collection of articles and thoughts with an introductory letter by Tolstoy. Tolstoy was reading it before publication.

August 17 (N-I:195)

1. See June 21, n. 3.

2. There was a legend among the *Skoptsy* that the founder of the sect was actually the Russian emperor Peter III (1728-1762).

August 18 (N-I:196)

1. On August 14 Chertkov had received permission to live permanently at Teliatinki. The Countess wrote in her *Daybook* that this news "plunged me in despair."

2. Tolstoy and others staying at Kochety visited the local school

and saw a presentation of Chekhov's *Malefactor*. Tolstoy enjoyed it.

1. Countess Tolstoy wrote in her *Daybook:* "At eight in the morning Leo Nikolaevich came in and said that I should not be upset, that he promised me, 1) not to see Chertkov at all, 2) not to give away the diaries, and 3) not to allow any more photographs of himself to be taken [by Chertkov]. 'But I shall correspond with him, as I need it for my work,' Leo Nikolaevich added." Tolstoy wrote Chertkov justifying these promises on the grounds that he did not regard them as binding but rather as acts of mercy.

1. "Arago tout court": *the great chemist Arago preferred to be addressed only by his last name; he thought everyone should know who he was.*

1. Dr. Faust, *Aux Antipodes de la Morale. Critique de la Morale bourgeoise,* Paris: Edition de la Maison Jacques, 1910.
2. Ivan Mikhailovich Diomidov, a young student who was a tutor for Sukhotin's younger son.

1. A local name for the *skopets* Grigoriev; see June 21, n. 3.
2. Four peasants came to talk with him; one of them, the one described in this passage, wanted to talk all the time and interrupted Tolstoy, which upset him.

1. *Rossolimo who had examined Countess Tolstoy on July 19, diagnosed her condition as "degenerative characteristics of a double nature: hysteria and paranoia. The first may be discerned in the particularly vivid nature of all her experiences,*

in the concentration of all her interests around her own person,
even sacrificing the interests of truth and her best feelings and
being completely unscrupulous in the means she employs to
attain her purposes. The second condition may be perceived
in her excessive suspiciousness and the incorrect conclusions
founded on this in everything that affected Leo Nikolaevich, his
teachings, his relations to Chertkov, etc." (From Rossolimo's
letter to *Aleksandra Tolstoy).*

2. Possibly Kasum Bairomov, a former Babist who was disillu-
sioned with Babism. Tolstoy received a letter from him that day.

August 23 (N-I:201)

1. Tolstoy told his children's tale to his granddaughter Tania
and her cousin. Aleksandra Tolstoy took it down stenographi-
cally. It was first published posthumously as a "Story for Children." Tolstoy had planned to write a cycle of stories or
sketches under the title, *All the Same,* which he was thinking
of in the summer and autumn of 1910.

August 25 (N-I:203)

1. From a peasant in Vladimir, Vasili Andreevich Voronov, on
the concept of God.
2. Tatiana Sukhotina had received a letter that an influential
neighbor and friend of Countess Tolstoy, A. E. Zvegintseva,
was spreading rumors about the abnormal closeness between
Tolstoy and Chertkov, and that she was using influence to have
Chertkov again expelled from Tula Province.

August 26 (N-I:204)

1. Tolstoy read an article about the *Areja Samai,* an Indian
national-religious society antagonistic to English influence.
2. A village about five miles from Kochety.

August 26 (N-II:28)

1. *Sofia Andreevna wrote in her* Diary: *"My talk yesterday*
into the night with my daughter Tania explained much to me.
She, Sasha, and Leo Nikolaevich are carrying on a busy corre-
spondence with Chertkov. They are so afraid I will read some-

thing (*although I have never had the vile habit of opening other people's letters*) *that in Iasnaia they send the letters to Chertkov only through intimates and here they put them in the mailbag last of all and carefully lock them up, or they write to Goldenweizer or Bulgakov. Leo Nikolaevich also locks up his Diary from me very carefully; but the Diary is at home; somehow it still may fall into my hands.*"

August 27 (N-I:205)

1. Ivan Chepurin. He had begun to write the story of his life at Tolstoy's suggestion.

August 27 (N-II:29)

1. *Countess Tolstoy wrote in her* Daybook: "*Suffered all day, physically and spiritually. There are fifty-eight photographs here, at Tania's, taken of Leo Nikolaevich from all angles, in all poses and places, and with various smiles and grimaces. . . . This is no spiritual communion.*"

August 28 (N-I:206)

1. Diomedov; see August 20, n. 2, in first diary.

August 29 (N-I:207)

1. Countess Tolstoy received a telegram from her son Lev, informing her that his trial for printing Tolstoy's legend, *The Restoration of Hell*, in 1906 had been set for September 3 in St. Petersburg. This was earlier than she had expected, and she hurried home so that she could see him off.

2. Tolstoy's note ran, "You touched me deeply, dear Sonia, with your good, sincere words at parting. How wonderful it would be if you could overcome in yourself—I do not know how to call it—that which is within you and torments you. How wonderful it would be, both for you and for me. All evening I was sad and desolate. I never stop thinking of you. I am writing what I feel, and I do not want to write anything unnecessary. Please write. Your loving husband, L.T. Am going to sleep, it is after 11."

1. James Mavor, Professor of Economics at Toronto University. He had helped the Dukhobors settle in Canada in 1889 (see January 4, n. 1), and had been in correspondence with Tolstoy since 1897. They discussed the economic situation in China, which Mavor had just visited, and the theories of Henry George, which Mavor opposed.

1. *Tolstoy wrote his wife on September 1 as follows: "I was expecting a note from you today, dear Sonia, but thanks even for the brief one which you wrote Tania. I never stop thinking of you and feeling you, despite the distance. You are concerned about my physical state, and I am grateful to you for it, but I am concerned about your spiritual state. How is it? May God help you in the work which I know you are doing on your soul. Although I am more occupied with the spiritual side, I would like to know about your physical health too. As for me, if it were not for the alarming thoughts about you which never leave me, I would be completely satisfied. My health is good, as usual I take walks in the morning which are so very dear to me, during which I note down the thoughts that come into my fresh mind and give me joy, then I read and write at home. Today for the first time I have begun to go on with the article I began long ago on the causes for the immoral life which all people in our time are living. Then a ride on horseback, or more frequently a walk.*

"Yesterday Dushan and I rode to Matveeva's, and I was weary, not so much from the trip over (she brought us back in her carriage) as by her very senseless chatter. But I do not regret the trip. It was interesting and even instructive for me to observe these circles, coarse, base and rich, in the midst of poor people. The day before yesterday Mavor was here. His stories of China and Japan were very interesting, but I was very tired from the tension that comes of speaking an unaccustomed language little used by me. Went walking today. Now it is evening, and I am answering letters, yours first of all. How are you making use of your time? Are you going to Moscow, and when? I have no definite plans, but I want to do what would be pleasant for you. I hope and believe that it will be as well for me in Iasnaia as it is here. Am waiting for your letter. I kiss you. Leo."

1. Varvara Dmitrievna Matveeva, a landowner who sympathized with Tolstoy's ideas, and her relative, Vladimir Aleksandrovich Matveev. They lived about 11 miles away.

2. A. F. Anshina, a schoolteacher with whom Tolstoy corresponded about teaching in elementary schools according to his books *Thoughts of Wise People,* and *For Every Day.*

3. Vsevolod Savvich Mamontov and his wife, neighbors of the Sukhotins.

1. P. I. Biriukov's memoirs of his exile in 1897, entitled "The Story of My Exile," published in *A Historical Almanach of the Past,* 1909.

1. *The full quotation from Schopenhauer in the* Cycle of Reading *runs, "Faith, like love, cannot be summoned by force. Therefore it is risky to try to introduce it or strengthen it by governmental measures, since, as the attempt to force love evokes hatred, so the attempt to force faith evokes skepticism."*

1. *Countess Tolstoy returned to Iasnaia Poliana in a distraught mood. She asked V. M. Feokritova to remove all the pictures of Chertkov from Tolstoy's bedroom and she was planning to burn them. She told Feokritova, "Now I shall send for the priest. I want to have a prayer service and have holy water spinkled in Leo Nikolaevich's rooms, or else the spirit of Chertkov will rule there; it must be smoked out. I have taken down his pictures, and now let the priest sprinkle holy water." A prayer service was held that afternoon in the bedroom.*

1. It will not be long.
2. See June 21, n. 3.
3. See March 9, n. 3.

1. Dr. Makovitski had diagnosed Tolstoy's illness, first and most likely, as stiffness and chill from yesterday's trip in the rain; secondly, as podagra, a disease common to the Tolstoys, and finally, Tolstoy insisting that every possibility be considered, Makovitski mentioned the least probable, senile gangrene. Tolstoy looked up the latter disease in the medical encyclopedia and decided that he was suffering from it.

2. Gandhi had sent Tolstoy an issue of a magazine, *Indian Opinion*, published in English and several Indian languages in South Africa.

3. A. I. Drankov, who made films of Tolstoy and showed some earlier ones.

1. It's not for this time.

2. Gandhi, about the journal *Indian Opinions*.

3. Chertkov had written Tolstoy that he was writing a letter to the Countess Tolstoy. He wrote her a 3000-word letter, explaining his position in detail.

4. To the country fair in Novosil, the capital of the district.

1. The Countess Tolstoy wrote in her *Daybook:* "My extreme nervousness broke out again. In vain I had created for myself a dream that Leo Nikolaevich would return to Iasnaia with me, and when he pitilessly smashed it, I went to pieces again. I must be completely free of the dependence of my heart on my husband, and it would be easier . . . Leo Nikolaevich today still tried very hard to be kind, and I am grateful for that."

1. Giulio Vitali, an Italian writer, author of a number of books on Tolstoy. He was writing a biography of Tolstoy and set forth Tolstoy's philosophical outlook in seven points.

1. *Tolstoy received some notes which Feokritova had taken of a conversation between Countess Tolstoy and Miss Schmidt about her plans for his writings after his death. If Tolstoy were to die without leaving any notarized will, Sofia Andreevna would immediately publish them all. "Even if he left everything to Chertkov, or to the general public, I still will not hand over the unpublished works, for the years are not written on them. They will just have to guess when they were written. Everyone will believe that they were written before 1881. And in any case we shall not leave the Will undisputed, neither I nor my sons, we have a very strong argument, we shall prove that he has been mentally weak recently, that he frequently fainted, and that's true, and everyone knows it, and we shall prove that at a moment of mental weakness he was forced to write a Will, and that he himself never wanted to hurt his children."*

Tolstoy wrote of these notes to Chertkov: "However depressing it is to know all this and to know that so many outsiders know about it, it is useful for me to know it. Although there is great exaggeration in a bad sense in what Varvara Mikhailovna writes and what you think of it. You do not take into account her sickness and the mixture of good impulses with bad."

1. In a conversation about the Jewish Pale, Tolstoy asked Makovitski, "Are you really in favor of the Jewish Pale?" Makovitski answered, "Not in favor, but I recognize the right of people not to let Jews into their midst."

1. Sofia Andreevna returned to Iasnaia Poliana alone.

1. Nikolai Iakovlevich Grot, professor of philosophy and a friend of Tolstoy's; died in 1899. A collection of articles was to be published in his memory.
2. January 8, n. 1. Gusev was in jail for having "arbitrarily left" his place of exile.

3. M. Adadurov, from Saratov, wrote Tolstoy a long letter, reproaching him for using "parables" and "symbols" in his writings, whereas "real, irrevocable truth is so splendid that it does not need tinsel."

September 14 (N-I:221)

1. Princess Vera Pavlovna Golitsyna, a neghboring landowner. She was fervently Orthodox and refused to read Tolstoy's more recent writings. They discussed morality, religion, and also drunkenness.

September 17 (N-I:223)

1. Isabella Fyvie Mayo, an English writer who sympathized with Tolstoy's views.

September 20 (N-I:224)

1. *Seekers after God,* a book by A. S. Pankratov.
2. Andrei Ivanovich Kudrin, a peasant from Samara who had been influenced by Tolstoy's ideas and had refused military service on religious grounds.
3. Philip Petrovich Kupchinski, writer, author of *The Curse of War,* 1911. He had been at Iasnaia Poliana previously and sent Tolstoy his book before publication. Tolstoy wrote him, that, although the book had value, there were some defects, particularly his exaggerated descriptions of "the horrors of war."

September 22 (N-I:226)

1. N. M. Gorbov, a landowner living near Kochety, who had built an experimental school on his place.

September 23 (N-I:227)

1. Countess Tolstoy wrote in her *Daybook:* "Our wedding day; I cried all morning for the forty-eight years of my married life! And for all my love and selfless life, what is there? He returned yesterday evening, not sacrificing *even a single day* of playing

whist and living an Epicurean life at the Sukhotins to do me a favor, and he is even becoming hateful to me with his pity. Toward evening and in the middle of the day Leo Nikolaevich became kinder, and it became easier for me. As if I, finally, really had found my other half."

2. Aleksandra Lvovna Tolstoy was upset because her father had agreed to have his picture taken with Sofia Andreevna on the occasion at their forty-eighth wedding anniversary.

3. Max Müller, *Six Systems of Indian Philosophy*, 1901.

4. Tolstoy had lost the first notebook, which he called "A Diary for Myself Alone." Two weeks later the Countess Tolstoy discovered it in a boot. She read it and did not return it.

5. S. D. Nikolaev and his sons.

September 24 (N-I:228)

1. Itinerant craftsmen who made the rounds of the villages in the fall, making felt boots for winter out of the wool the peasants brought them.

2. See January 5, n. 1. He wrote Tolstoy about Tolstoy's articles, the titles of which are given here.

3. Aylmer Maude. He had sent Tolstoy the second part of his biography of Tolstoy, in English.

4. See May 10, n. 1.

September 24 (N-II:41)

1. *Countess Tolstoy's* Daybook, *"Again Leo Nikolaevich shouted at me for wanting to read his unpublished manuscript,* The Wisdom of Children [*see June 5, n. 2*], *of which there was not a single copy in the house. Chertkov had grabbed the manuscript, and I called him a collector. This drove Leo Nikolaevich wild, and I cried all day again."*

September 25 (N-I:229)

1. Ioaniki Alekseevich Malinovski (1868-1932), historian of law and professor at the University of Tomsk at that time. He had sent his book, *Blood Vengeance, or the Death Penalty*, to Tolstoy.

2. As the photographs taken on September 23 did not come out, Countess Tolstoy insisted on a repetition. This picture is the last photograph taken of Tolstoy.

269

1. The young Czechs belonging to the Party of Populist-Socialists were planning to publish a *Reader*, containing articles on socialism and popular economics. They asked Tolstoy to contribute. He started a letter to them which grew into the article "On Socialism," on which he continued working until he left Iasnaia Poliana.

2. Tolstoy had rehung the photographs which the Countess Tolstoy had displaced during his absence at Kochety. His wife, enraged by this, tore Chertkov's portrait to shreds and prepared to set fire to it, then shot several times from a toy pistol, pretending to kill herself. Maria Aleksandrovna Schmidt, a frightened observer, telegraphed Aleksandra Tolstoy and her friend Feokritova to return immediately. When they did so, around midnight, an argument flared up between them and the Countess, in consequence of which they both left to live in Teliatinki. The Countess wrote in her *Daybook*, "I chanced to go into Leo Nikolaevich's study, and I noticed that Chertkov's portrait was hanging over Leo Nikolaevich's chair again. I was very much upset and indignant. I tore this hateful image into pieces, and of course a whole series of incidents followed this; and again unbearable suffering from jealousy and despair at losing my husband's love. Sasha and Varvara Mikhailovna Feokritova returned during the night and abused me for practicing with the toy pistol, which was the reason Maria Aleksandrovna Schmidt had sent for them. All these good-for-nothing women are spoiling my life and my relations with my husband."

3. See February 15, n. 1.

1. See September 1, n. 2. Tolstoy sent his correspondence with Anshina to the newspapers.

1. Nikolai Dmitrievich Rostovtsev (1845-1921), former artillery officer who later turned to agricultural and Zemstvo work. He was a close friend and a house guest of Chertkov's.

2. Mikhail Sivachev, a metal worker, author of *Let the Reader Judge: Notes of a Literary Makar*.

3. *Culte Antoiniste. Révélation d'Antoine le Guérisseur*. Tolstoy said of it, "A wonderful book. His religious and moral teaching

completely accords with my views, and, as I read the book, I meet my own thoughts: that the world is illusion, that God is in the soul." Antoine was an uneducated Belgian metal worker who left the Catholic Church and began to interpret the Bible independently, using a moral standard of judgment. He had many followers, and had been successful as a healer.

4. Unidentified.

September 29 (N-I:233)

1. Probably a reference to the edition of his works which the Countess Tolstoy was preparing.

2. Mikhail Petrovich Artsybashev (1878-1927), a writer of the early twentieth century whose novels and plays were rather crudely sensational and exploited the theme of free love. His novel *Sanin* (1907) was extremely popular.

October 1 (N-I:235)

1. Maria Andreevna Lentovskaia, formerly a doctor's assistant. She was an enthusiastic follower of Tolstoy.

October 1 (N-II:48)

1. V. G. Chertkov, *"On Free Thinking," an article which Chertkov never finished. Tolstoy wrote him that the first three parts were good, but the fourth was too complex and unclear.*

2. See September 28, n. 3.

October 2 (N-I:236)

1. See May 18, n. 1, Tolstoy wrote Iakovleva about perfecting one's life, and V. Preobrazhenskaia, a medical student, about the meaning of life.

October 5 (N-I:238)

1. Countess Tolstoy's *Daybook:* "In the morning Leo Nikolaevich went walking, then went for a short ride; when he returned he complained that his feet were numb with cold, and he lay down without taking off his boots. During our dinner I

went into his room and saw with horror that he had forgotten everything and that he was drowsy and was talking at random. Then something terrible happened. There were convulsions in his face and terrible twitchings of his legs, which could not be held. Horror, despair, and repentance filled me. Toward night the convulsions stopped. All night I sat on a chair beside Leo Nikolaevich. He slept and groaned a lot. Our daughter Tania came during the night."

October 7 (N-I:240)

1. See March 30, n. 1. His daughter was Natalia Fedorovna Strakhova, by marriage Pyrikova.

2. Countess Tolstoy agreed to have Chertkov come to see Tolstoy after his illness. He came on October 7 at eight o'clock; this was his last visit to Tolstoy in Iasnaia Poliana.

October 7 (N-II:51)

1. *Chertkov's wife. Chertkov wrote Tolstoy, "I am very sorry for Galia. She suffers very much day and night in spirit from the artificiality of this separation from you, and I understand her fully, but I do not suffer. On the contrary, I repeat, I feel very well in my soul."*

October 8 (N-I:241)

1. Peter Petrovich Nikolaev (1873-1928), formerly a Don Cossack, an amateur philosopher. He wrote *The Concept of God as the Perfect Basis of Life*. He had sent Tolstoy the book before publication and asked his opinion.

2. Countess Tolstoy had been upset by Chertkov's visit. She wrote in her *Daybook*, "When I got up, Leo Nikolaevich gave me a long lecture, excitedly and in part maliciously, about Chertkov, and said that what I was doing was nonsense. He wants to associate with him, but the price is too high for me, but it would suit Leo Nikolaevich, of course."

October 9 (N-I:242)

1. V. A. Miakotin, "Modern Prison and Exile," *Russian Wealth*, 1910, no. 9.

1. Sofia Nikolaevna Tolstoy, *née* Filosofov, wife of Ilia Tolstoy. She was visiting Iasnaia Poliana with her nine-year-old daughter Vera.

1. Countess Tolstoy's *Daybook* for October 10: "I am tormented by curiosity and the desire to read Leo Nikolaevich's diaries, but alas! they are inaccessible. He walked a lot today. Perhaps to a meeting with Chertkov?"

1. Tolstoy read the first volume of the *Brothers Karamazov.*

1. Countess Tolstoy's *Diary* for October 13: "More unhappy than ever, and I am tormented. Leo Nikolaevich holds a knife over me all the time (in a symbolic sense, of course): 'If I want I'll kill you right off.' And I hold poison all the time and more than ever before I think: 'If I want I shall kill myself.' And these are our lives, or rather mine. The news, a confirmation of an earlier report, that Leo Nikolaevich had written a paper renouncing his rights as author after death, secretly from the family, and had secretly transferred them to Chertkov, utterly killed me. All day I think of suicide. . . . Leo Nikolaevich repudiates the State, and now with his diaries, which are now in a State Bank, and with his Will, he is hiding behind the State along with Chertkov! So many theories, and how little practice! It is not my personal profit that torments me, but the fact that it is a secret from me, and the malice which gave birth to this will."

1. "Every day you ask me, as if you were interested, about my health, how I slept, but every day there are new blows which consume my heart to ashes, cut short my life, and torment me unbearably, but cannot prevent my sufferings. Fate allowed me to discover this new blow, your malicious act depriving your

numerous descendants of royalties, although your accomplice in this did not want it disclosed to the family. He threatened that he would smirch our family and has succeeded magnificently in doing so by extracting that paper from you depriving them of everything. The government, which you and he have abused and denied in all your pamphlets, will by law take from your heirs the last piece of bread and will hand it over to the Sytins and other rich printers and swindlers, while Tolstoy's grandchildren, by his vain and evil wish, will die of hunger. The government, the State Bank, guards Tolstoy's diaries from his wife. Christian love is consistently killing, by these various acts, the person who is closest to you (not in your sense, but in mine), your wife, who had never committed any malicious actions all this time, and is not doing so now, except from very profound suffering. But various threats are still hanging over me even now. And here you are, Levochka, going out to pray as you walk; as you pray, think hard about what you are doing under the pressure of that villain, suppress your malice, open your heart, awaken your love and kindness, not your hatred and bad deeds and vain pride (concerning the royalties) and hatred for me, the person who has loved you and given her whole life and love for you, and has helped you in every way. If you think that I am guided by self-interest, I am ready, like my daughter Tania, to refuse my rights to inherit from my husband. What use would it be to me? Obviously I shall soon depart from this life one way or another. If I survive you, I am horrified to think what evil I shall see arising from your grave and in the memories of your children and grandchildren. Put it down, Levochka, while you are alive. Awaken and soften your heart, and awaken in it the love of God, which you proclaim so loudly to others. S. T."

2. Wife of Mitrofan Vasilievich Lodyzhenski; see July 31, n. 1.

3. See March 31, n. 3.

October 16 (N-I:249)

1. Countess Tolstoy's *Diary*, October 16: "Got up calm, although unwell. I did not sleep this morning and kept thinking how to get Leo Nikolaevich's diaries out of the State Bank in Tula. I came out to lunch, and suddenly Leo Nikolaevich announced that he was going to Chertkov's." In her *Daybook* for the same day, "Was upset by Leo Nikolaevich's intention of going to Chertkov's. Ran through the fields and woods for four hours straight. Suffered unbearably. He did not go, but I did not know that. I was at Teliatinki, had no dinner. Toward evening my heart rejoiced being with Leo Nikolaevich."

1. Sri Sankara Acharia (788-820?), Indian Religious philosopher and writer.
2. Iosif Iosievich Perper, a vegetarian, editor of the periodical *Vegetarian Review*.

1. *Brothers Karamazov.*
2. See October 8, n. 1.

1. Countess Tolstoy's *Daybook,* October 19: "I was very much upset yesterday evening by the disappearance of Leo Nikolaevich's Diary from his desk. Last night, when he woke up, I asked him, 'Where is the diary?' 'Sasha has it.' Well, I was somewhat relieved, although it is upsetting that I do not have it. She has been copying out thoughts for Chertkov, obviously."
2. See February 21, n. 1.

1. *Aleksandra Tolstoy told her father that Sofia Andreevna had been negotiating with Miss Almedingen to sell Tolstoy's works to the* Enlightenment *publishers for a million rubles. Tolstoy was very much upset by these rumors and spoke of writing an announcement for the newspapers that he forbade anyone to sell the rights for publication of his works.*

1. Mikhail Petrovich Novikov, a peasant living about forty miles from Iasnaia Poliana and author of stories and articles about peasant life. Tolstoy told Novikov about his relations with his wife and said that he would go away. On October 24 he wrote Novikov, as follows:
"Mikhail Petrovich: In connection with what I told you before your departure, I am writing you with this request: if it should really happen that I came to you, would it be possible for you to find for me in your village some separate, warm

cottage, even a very tiny one, so that I would bother your family for the shortest possible time? I am also informing you that if I should have to telegraph you, I would telegraph you not in my own name but in that of T. Nikolaev. I shall await your answer. I press your hand as your friend. Leo Tolstoy.

"Keep in mind that all this should be known only to you alone. L.T."

2. F. S. Perevoznikov; see March 17, n. 4. Mikhail Titovich Polin, a peasant from Iasnaia Poliana, belonging to one of the Socialist parties.

October 21 (N-I:254)

1. Four conscripts from Iasnaia Poliana who were going into the army. One was the young Socialist, Polin.
2. See March 25, n. 1.

October 21 (N-II:65)

1. *When Tolstoy told Novikov about his difficulties with his wife (see October 20, first diary), Novikov told of how his brother had a wife who would be drunk for a week or more at a time. After twenty years he suddenly could stand it no more and took a whip to her just twice and cured her.*
2. *Aleksandra Tolstoy told her father of how the coachman Ivan Matveev had once commented about the events at Iasnaia Poliana that things were bad, and he added, "We do it country fashion; if the woman makes a fool of herself, her husband takes the reins to her. Then she's like silk."*

October 22 (N-I:255)

1. K. F. Dosev (see March 5, n. 3) had written Chertkov's wife that Tolstoy was a slave to his wife and that he was amazed that Tolstoy had not been able to break with her and with the life of a "rich landowner" as yet. Chertkov wrote Dosev a long answer, saying that Dosev had not understood Tolstoy and that actually his decision to stay with his wife demonstrated "the greatest freedom—freedom from concern about public opinion."

2. *The Concept of God;* see October 8.

1. See *March 25, n. 1, and October 21, first diary. Dunaev talked about Germany, which he had just been visiting. He also talked with the Countess Tolstoy about her relations with her husband.*
2. *Wife of Sergei Tolstoy.*

1. See October 22, first diary.
2. See October 20, first diary, and October 21, second diary.
3. Semion Rumiantsev, the cook.
4. Aleksei Borisov, the yardman.
5. Bulgakov had read a paper entitled "On Higher Education and Science," attacking university education, before an audience of 250 interested listeners. Afterwards he withdrew from the University of Moscow.
6. Archpriest Dmitri Egorovich Troitski. He wrote Tolstoy from time to time, on the instructions of the Synod, to persuade Tolstoy to change his mind about the established church.
7. Chertkov's wife. Tolstoy wrote her about his opinion about Dostoevsky.
8. Chertkov's wife had sent Tolstoy a letter from N. N. Gusev (see January 8, n. 1), attacking Dostoevsky, especially his *Diary of a Writer.* He comments on Dostoevsky's criticism of Tolstoy's attitude toward the war against the Turks in 1877-78 at the end of *Anna Karenina,* where Dostoevsky ascribes a fatalistic and pacifistic attitude to Vronsky instead of the passionate enthusiasm which Dostoevsky advocated. Tolstoy was much interested in these comments and asked to have the *Diary of a Writer* sent to him.

1. Dmitri Sergeevich Merezhkovski (1865-1941), poet, and critic. The article here referred to was from his book, *Leo Tolstoy and Dostoevsky, Life and Work,* 1909. A student from St. Petersburg, Alexander Barkhudarov, had written Tolstoy an accusatory letter based on this book.
2. Johannes Albrecht, from Breslau.
3. Peter Nikolaevich Gastev, a follower of Tolstoy's who worked in agricultural communes.

4. Natalia Alekseevna Almedingen, daughter of A. N. Almedingen, a journalist and editor of children's magazines. Miss Almedingen had continued her father's work and participated in the Enlightenment Publishers. See Oct. 19, n. 1.

5. Vasili Kirilovich Siutaev (1820?-1892), a peasant of Tver who had left the Orthodox Church and had espoused a free Christian religion. Tolstoy had known and admired him. Gastev told about the Cossacks M. S. Astakhov and A. I. Eliseev (see February 27, n. 1), who had visited Tolstoy. Apparently Astakhov was a stern, direct sectarian, who believed that some person should be at the head of spiritual life. He had hoped to have Tolstoy as the leader, but when Tolstoy told him that he was sinful and that no man was perfect, he was very depressed. But when he remembered that Tolstoy had also said that once the Russian peasant begins to seek God he will seek with all his soul, stopping for nothing, he was glad.

October 25 (N-I:258)

1. Tolstoy brought a children's magazine, *The Sun*, to the school in Iasnaia Poliana to distribute it to the children. Copies of it had been brought by Miss Almedingen.

2. Prokofi Vlasov; see March 19, n. 2, and June 4, n. 2. His son Peter was on leave.

October 25 (N-II:69)

1. *Countess Tolstoy's* Daybook: *"Leo Nikolaevich corresponded with Galia Chertkov, not saying what the subject was, and he does not give me her letters."* Tolstoy told his daughter Aleksandra that his wife came in the middle of the night to ask what Chertkov's wife was writing him.

October 26 (N-I:259)

1. Apparently an unrealized idea for a novel. Grushenka is one of the heroines in the *Brothers Karamazov* by Dostoevsky. Nikolai Nikolaevich Strakhov (1828-1896) philosopher and literary critic, had been a close friend of Tolstoy and also Dostoevsky.

2. Kornei Ivanovich Chukovski, poet, critic, and literary scholar, had written Tolstoy, asking him to contribute to a collection of brief statements protesting against capital punish-

ment. These statements were to be published in the most-read newspapers and would be written by well-known public figures. Tolstoy wrote an article in response, "The Real Means," which he finished on October 29 in Optina Pustyn.

October 26 (N-II:70)

1. *Tolstoy remarked to Maria Aleksandrovna, "I am thinking of leaving Iasnaia." She exclaimed, "Leo Nikolaevich, dear friend, that will pass, that is just a passing weakness!" Tolstoy answered, "Yes, yes, I know it is a weakness, and I hope it will pass."*

October 27 (N-I:260)

1. Probably his farewell letter to Countess Tolstoy.
2. See October 24, n. 6, first diary. He was reading P. N. Gastev's memoirs of Siutaev.
3. One Ivan Ovdiuk, who wrote that he had been spiritually transformed after a visit from Chertkov and after reading Tolstoy's books.

October 27 (N-II:71)

1. *Dr. Makovitski reported that Countess Tolstoy told V. M. Feokritova that she agreed to allow Chertkov into the house and she would behave as she used to if they would give her the Diaries from 1900 to the present. But she would not let Leo Nikolaevich go to the Chertkov's in case Chertkov might invite a notary public and make him write a will.*

October 28 (N-I:261)

1. "My departure will upset you. This I regret, but you must understand and believe me that I could not act otherwise. My situation at home is becoming—has become—unbearable. Aside from everything else, I can no longer live in the condition of luxury which I have been living in and I am doing what old people of my age usually do: they withdraw from worldly life to live their last days in solitude and quiet. Please understand this and do not follow after me, even if you do find out where I am. Your arrival would only worsen your position and mine,

but it would not change my decision. I thank you for the forty-eight years that you lived with me in honor and I beg your forgiveness for everything of which I have been guilty in regard to you, just as with my whole soul I forgive you everything of which you have been guilty in regard to me. My advice to you is that you reconcile yourself to this new situation in which my departure places you, and that you have no unkind feelings against me. If you wish to communicate anything to me, tell Sasha; she will know where I am and will send me whatever is necessary. She cannot say where I am, because I made her promise to me not to speak of this to anyone. Leo Tolstoy. October 28, 1910. I have instructed Sasha to gather my things and my manuscripts and to send them to me. L.T."

2. A famous monastery founded in the fourteenth century, in the province of Kaluga. Tolstoy had made several trips to this monastery in the past and had talked with the elders there.

Dr. Makovitski observed of Tolstoy on that day, "In the evening, as he was writing, he hurried more than usual. But in the daytime he did not cherish his time as he usually did. This was very obvious to me. He did not write down any thoughts all day."

October 29 (N-I:262)

1. Tolstoy's sister Maria Nikolaevna and her daughter Elizaveta Valerianovna Obolenski. Maria Nikolaevna Tolstoy, a nun, was at the Shamardino convent. She told of how one night the door had banged and someone had started to walk along the corridor and knock on the wall with a stick, yet when the door was opened in the morning there was no sign of this intruder. Maria Nikolaevna and her cell-mate, who had been frightened by the sounds, decided that it had been the devil.

October 29 (N-II:73)

1. *See April 26, n. 2. Sergeenko brought Tolstoy news of what had happened at Iasnaia Poliana after his departure. Countess Tolstoy learned of it only about eleven in the morning, from her daughter Aleksandra. She was unable to read the letter Tolstoy left for her, and instead ran out of the house, toward the pond. Aleksandra, Bulgakov, and other members of the household rushed after her. She slipped into the water, but Aleksandra Tolstoy and Bulgakov went after her and pulled her out and led her to the house. She later renewed attempts to*

take her life by various means, but they were all rather easily frustrated.

October 30 (N-I:263)

1. Vladimir Kozhevnikov, "The Relationship of Socialism to Religion in General and to Christianity in Particular," The Religious Philosophical Library. M. A. Novoselov had prepared this Library, which Tolstoy found at his sister Maria's.

2. Sergei's letter read: "October 29, 1910. Dear Papa, I am writing because Sasha says that it would be pleasant for you to know the opinions of us, your children. I think that Mamma is nervously ill and not responsible in many respects, that you had to part with her (maybe you should have done so long ago), however hard it may be for you both. I also think that even if something were to happen to Mamma, which I do not expect, you should not reproach yourself in any way. The situation was hopeless, and I think you chose a genuine way out. Forgive me for writing so frankly. Seriozha."

3. In the morning Tolstoy had gone with a peasant from Shamardino to rent an apartment. He arranged to move in on Sunday, October 31.

October 31 (N-I:264)

1. Tolstoy, Makovitski and Aleksandra were traveling when Tolstoy took suddenly ill. They got off the train at Astapovo, in Ryazan province. The station master, I. I. Ozolin, gave up a room for him.

November 3 (N-I:265)

1. At Tolstoy's request, Aleksandra Tolstoy telegraphed Chertkov to come, and he arrived on November 2. Tolstoy was overjoyed to see Chertkov, and was afraid that the Countess Tolstoy would find him.

2. Sergei Tolstoy arrived on the evening of November 2. Tolstoy was glad to see his oldest son. The other sons and Sofia Andreevna had come to Astapovo and were living in a railroad car; Tolstoy's children decided not to allow Sofia Andreevna to see her husband unless he asked for her, which he never did.

3. Dr. D. V. Nikitin; see June 7, n. 4.

4. Tatiana Sukhotina saw Tolstoy before his death. He kept asking her how her mother was; she avoided answering too specifically, so that he would not guess that she was close by. Chertkov wrote in his memoirs, "Throughout this conversation Leo Nikolaevich did not give any excuse by a single hint for thinking that he would like to see Sofia Andreevna."

5. Although Tolstoy hoped and believed that his whereabouts were a secret, the circumstances of his illness were well publicized, and reporters, public officials, and curious onlookers gathered at Astapovo. The diary entry for November 3 is the last thing that he wrote. He died on the morning of November 7. His body was brought back to Iasnaia Poliana and was buried without religious rites in the place he had selected.

Appendix

Tolstoy's cryptic "went riding with Goldenweizer, and wrote in the woods," is a reference to the signing of his testament which was kept secret from Sofia Andreevna. The text of this testament follows:

July 22, 1910   A Wood Near the Village of Grumont

In the year nineteen hundred and ten, on July 22nd, I the undersigned being of sound mind and in possession of all my faculties, make the following disposition in the event of my death: All my literary works, both those already written and those to be written between this time and my death, both fiction and non-fiction, published and unpublished, completed and not completed, dramatic and other works, translations, rewritings, diaries, private letters, rough sketches, *pensées* and notes, in a word, everything without exception written by me, up to the day of my death, wherever these works may be, in whosoever's keeping, whether in manuscript or published form, both the right to literary ownership of all my works without exception, the manuscripts themselves, and all the papers left after my death, I leave in the full possession of my daughter, Aleksandra Lvovna Tolstoy. Should my daughter, Aleksandra Lvovna Tolstoy, die before me I bequeath all the above to my other daughter Tatiana Lvovna Sukhotina.

Leo Nikolaevich Tolstoy.

Tolstoy's actual intention was to leave all his literary rights in the public domain. Since this was legally impossible, it was decided to make Aleksandra Lvovna sole legatee with the understanding that after her father's death she would renounce her rights, these rights to become public property in the custody of V. G. Chertkov. All this was set forth in a lengthy "Explanatory Note" drafted by Cherkov which Tolstoy wished to revise in some points of detail and signed on July 31.

Goldenweizer's *Diary* contains the following account of the signing of the will on July 22:

July 22 . . . When I arrived at Iasnaia, L.N. was very surprised that I hadn't brought the document. It turned out that he expected that I would bring the text, he would write somewhere in the wood and the witnesses would sign it later.

L.N. told me:

"I even prepared a little piece of cardboard [to put the papers on.]"

I told him that it could not be done without witnesses.

L.N. refused categorically to go to the Chertkovs'. Reluctantly, we decided to postpone it until a more favorable moment.

I went to greet Sophia Andreevna who was sitting in the garden at a table. She complained that she was feeling poorly and had a congested head and that in the morning they had applied leeches . . .

Off we went. . . .

L.N. said:

"The following plan occurred to me. You go ahead at a fast trot to Teliatinki and fetch them. I'll go through Zakaz and to Grumont and I will be waiting for you there by the bridge. Do you know these places?"

I said that I did and leaving L.N. to himself I hurried to Teliatinki. They were expecting us at the Chertkovs'. I hurriedly explained what was the matter. First they wanted to drive in a carriage but this was rejected as being too conspicuous. We decided to go on horseback. Sergeenko and Radynskii came along as witnesses. Vladimir Grigorievich decided that he'd better not come. He drafted a document explaining to the children the purpose of the official testament. He requested that this document be shown to L.N. for approval and that he should write on it to that effect.

We took along the text of the testament, the document, the piece of cardboard to put under the papers when writing, etc., and off we went. L.N. was waiting for us on a hill near the Grumont bridge. At first we didn't see him and began to worry, but as we rode up the hill we saw him in his white shirt, with his floating white beard, mounted on Delire. He had already been waiting for us for quite a while. We cut across the mown rye-field and entered Zaseka.

. . . I noticed, amidst a clump of trees, a very comfortable stump to sit on and we walked toward it. L.N. sat down on it and started copying the draft of his testament written on July 17th. For greater convenience, he asked me to dictate to him. When he was through, we checked it. L.N. had made a spelling mistake. He wanted to correct it but I advised against it in order to avoid marking the copy.

L.N. laughed and said:

"Let them say I can't spell."

We called Anotol Dionisovich Radynsky. L.N. told him that the document had been drafted in accordance with his wishes and written by him, and he signed in front of him, Radynsky. We also signed, I, Sergeenko and Radynsky.

L.N. said:

"These formalities are very painful."

Then he read the other document and said:

"All this (speaking of the first page and the beginning of the second) is very good but here I disagree with some passages."

Speaking of the passage saying that he wished all the manuscripts to be left to Chertkov to deal with according to his judgment whether they should be published or not, he said:

"We must add: 'On the same basis as he does it at present.' Otherwise the enemies of Vladimir Grigorievich will say that he got rid of all the others and got hold of everything."

Another point with which L.N. didn't agree was the clause (this he had told that winter to Aleksandra Lvovna) that everything written before 1881 (except "The Alphabet," "Popular Tales," and *The Iasnaia Poliana Journal*) should remain the possession, during her lifetime, of Sofia Andreevna.

L.N. said:

"What for? There's no need for that. Sasha knows herself what to do about it, there's no need to put it into words."

For the time being, L.N. decided not to sign these documents, especially since there was no hurry and he could give it further thought.

15. *Anton Chekhov*, ST. PETER'S DAY AND OTHER TALES. For the first time in English, here is a hilarious collection of early Chekhov stories and sketches. Resembling Dickens, Gogol and the Keystone Kops in their comic method, these stories will undoubtedly consolidate Chekhov's growing reputation as a major comic writer. Translated by Frances H. Jones. *A Putnam Capricorn Original.* 224 pp. $1.25 (Hardcover, $2.50).

16. *Thomas Nashe*, THE UNFORTUNATE TRAVELLER, OR JACK WILTON. Edited, with an Introduction, by John Berryman. Illustrated by Michael Ayrton. "The first novel in English" is the claim that has been made for this wonderful book. Published in 1594, it displays Nashe's madly inventive prose style, which has been compared to the style of Joyce's FINNEGANS WAKE, and Nashe's uncanny ability to create marvellously alive personalities. Of the first importance in the history of the novel. *A Putnam Capricorn Original.* 128 pp. $1.15 (Hardcover $2.50).

17. *Simone Weil*, WAITING FOR GOD. With an Introduction by Leslie Fiedler. T. S. Eliot said of it, "This book, by the late Simone Weil, is almost too important to be included in one's list of preferred reading for one year only." Andre Gide said, "It is clear that Mlle. Weil is the most truly spiritual writer of this century." 240 pp. $1.25.

18. *Robert M. Coates*, THE EATER OF DARKNESS, by the author of THE HOUR BEFORE WESTERLY. It is difficult to describe this superb novel adequately, but it can be said that it is written in an experimental style resembling that of the early Dos Passos and the style of the Nighttown scene in ULYSSES. It was originally published in Paris more than thirty years ago, and it has been called every-

thing from "a great comic adventure" to "the first surrealist novel in English." Completely revised for this edition by Mr. Coates, it contains an introduction by him giving in detail the circumstances of its composition and his intentions in writing it. *A Putnam Capricorn Original*. 128 pp. $.95.

19a, and 19b. *James Viscount Bryce*, THE AMERICAN COMMONWEALTH. Completely edited, abridged and introduced by Louis Hacker, Professor of Economics, Columbia University, and former Dean of the School of General Studies. A completely new edition of this great work on the American system of government. Always mentioned in the same breath with De Tocqueville's earlier work, Lord Bryce's superb study of the American commonwealth has been edited for Capricorn by a distinguished American scholar and historian for the present age. *A Putnam Capricorn Original*. 2 vols. $1.35 each (Hardcover, 1 vol. $5.00)

20. *George Moore*, CONFESSIONS OF A YOUNG MAN, A famous book by a most unusual man, this memoir concerns Moore's life in the Paris of the Nineties, when he lived a rich and crowded existence in his apartment in the *Rue de la Tours des Dames* (an unusually appropriate name), "with all its charming adjuncts, palms and pastels, my cat, my python, my friends, blonde hair and dark." It also details Moore's friendships with the Decadent and Symbolist writers, and with Manet, Degas and Renoir. This account sums up the artistic life of the Nineteenth Century, and was a prime influence on Ezra Pound, T. S. Eliot and James Joyce. 288 pp. $1.25.

OTHER CAPRICORN BOOKS

1. *John Dewey*, ART AS EXPERIENCE. 384 pp. $1.35.

2. *Rainer Maria Rilke*, NOTEBOOKS OF MALTE LAURIDS BRIGGE. 256 pp. $1.15.

3. *Alfred Adler*, WHAT LIFE SHOULD MEAN TO YOU. 320 pp. $1.25.

4. *Clive Bell*, ART. 192 pp. $1.25.

G. P. PUTNAM'S SONS

210 Madison Avenue • New York 16, N. Y.

PB 1137